Also by Ronald J. Drez

Voices of Courage
The Battle for Khe Sanh, Vietnam

Voices of Valor
D-Day, June 6, 1944

Twenty-Five Yards of War
The Extraordinary Courage of Ordinary Men in World War II

Remember D-Day
The Plan, The Invasion, Survivor Stories

Voices of D-Day
The Story of the Allied Invasion Told by Those Who Were There

The D-Day Companion
Leading Historians Explore History's Greatest Amphibious Assault

Heroes Fight Like Greeks

Ronald J. Drez

Ghost Road Press

Ghost Road Press
820 S. Monaco Parkway #288
Denver, Colorado 80224
www.ghostroadpress.com

Published and printed in the United States of America.

First Edition: October 2009

Designed by Evan Lee

Library of Congress Cataloging-in-Publication Data
Drez, Ronald J.
Heroes Fight Like Greeks / Ronald J. Drez

ISBN: 0-9816525-9-X   978-0-9816525-9-7
Library of Congress Control Number: 2001012345

*For Dennis Georges
and all who fought for Greece*

CONTENTS

FOREWORD

TECHNICALLY, ATHENS FELL to the German Army on April 27, 1941. But the hearts of freedom-loving Greek citizens didn't sink. Certainly Hitler had gained an upper hand in the Mediterranean Theatre, but he had vastly underestimated the staunch will of the Greek people. By 1942 there was a Greek People's Liberation Army (ELAS)—"Greece for the Greeks" being the prevailing heartland motto—whose members agitated bitterly for freedom. As documented here in *Heroes Fight Like Greeks*, the Greek Resistance guerillas, i.e. the overarching term for the myriad armed and unarmed individuals that challenged the German and Italian Occupation of Greece from 1941 to 1944, not only fought in hand-to-hand combat against Axis intruders but blew up railway bridges in acts of expert sabotage. Greek folk leaders like Aris Velouchiotis and Stefanos Sarafis recruited over 100,000 armed guerrillas to help liberate Greece from Nazi tyranny. These bloody skirmishes rank as some of the most harrowing World War II military actions in the Mediterranean. Yet, oddly, the historical record of the Greek Resistance heroes has been relatively slim and in some cases neglected.

Call it a historian's predilection, but I never tire of talking about the Second World War with good friends. Chief among them are Ron Drez (author) and John Georges (the inspiration), the collaborators on *Heroes Fight Like Greeks*. Both are New Orleanians who love French Quarter cuisine and can't get enough of the minutia associated with World War II turning points, from the Munich appeasement to the Nagasaki obliteration. Over the years I've talked with Drez and Georges about the Marine heroism of Iwo Jima, the U.S. Army 2nd Ranger Battalion at Pointe du Hoc, and the U.S. Navy at Midway. Perhaps like all history faddists, we seem to always be looking for another piece of the

World War II puzzle to jimmy into playing-board place. The idea of this book grew out of those New Orleans conversations. The Greek Resistance deserves a place in the Hall of Fame of World War II annals, and this study is the kickoff of a historical consciousness campaign.

Drez, a commissioned officer in the United States Marine Corps, was awarded two Bronze Stars during the Vietnam War. He also received the Vietnamese Cross of Gallantry with Silver Star for heroism in combat and the Presidential Unit Citation (if you're counting). Additionally, Drez has also written the best books in print on the Battle of Normandy. So he brings to World War II history an unparalleled knowledge about combat anguish that emanates directly from his own foxhole experiences. And *nobody* has ever personally collected more World War II oral histories than the indefatigable Ron Drez.

As for John Georges, he is a top-tier New Orleans business legend who has helped put the National World War II Museum on the map. Fluent in Greek, a dutiful father, and champion of all things Louisiana, Georges has studied up on the German invasion of Greece as if a Talmudic scholar. Full of passion, he knows the detailed history of the occupation of Athens and King George II's government in exile. He has been able to connect to Greek communities in America through his involvement in the Greek Orthodox Church, both locally as former president (New Orleans is the home of the first Greek Orthodox Church in the Americas) and internationally as an Archon, along with being a member of the order of St. Andrew, the protectors of the Ecumenical Patriarchate in Constantinople. A graduate of Tulane University with a degree in business management, he is currently CEO of Georges Enterprises, whose businesses include Imperial Trading Company, Dolphin Marine International, AMA Distributors and other holdings in food service, entertainment, real estate and construction businesses. But I have known Georges best over the years as the most enthusiastic and knowledgeable bookman pertaining to the Greek Resistance during World War II. Georges regularly travels to Greece on heritage tours to contemplate Greek grit and resilience from that bygone era.

An added impetus for John Georges to sponsor this book is

the story of his patriarchal father, Dennis A. Georges, a brave member of the Greek Resistance. Later, during the Greek Civil War of 1946-1949, Greek Communists apprehended the senior Georges. He was a P.O.W. But as democracy won out in Greece, Georges joined the Royal Greek Air Force, where he was promoted to the military intelligence communication division. While fighting in the Korean War with a United Nations division, Georges became a decorated hero. He saved American lives in a daring rescue mission. General Douglas MacArthur himself presented him with the Truman Citation. The senior Georges was now a dual patriot of both the U.S. and Greece. A walking encyclopedia on Greek philosophy, able to quote Plato and Aristotle on the fly, the senior Georges became the leader of the Greek community of New Orleans. I always found it touching that John wanted his self-deprecating father's heroic memory cherished for the ages.

One afternoon Georges asked me how best to honor in perpetuity the story of the Greek Resistance in World War II. As an author, the answer seemed quite obvious: commission a study on the Greek Resistance and start an oral history project. While I was too busy writing a biography of Theodore Roosevelt to spearhead the homage endeavor, I was smart enough to recommend Drez, who knew the Greek saga well. In fact, Drez used to regale me with wild-eyed accounts about how the Italians under Benito Mussolini had delivered an ultimatum to the Greeks, insisting they embrace the Italian Army as it crossed the Ionian Sea to occupy Greece. Drez had interviewed many Greek Resistance fighters. After touring the Greek villages Drez declared them among the gutsiest band of high-altitude guerrillas since Ethan Allen and the Green Mountain Boys.

What new generations of Americans oftentimes forget is that in 1940, Greece, under the indefatigable leader Ioannis Metaxas, was the only other ally fighting tooth-and-claw against the emerging Axis with Great Britain. Greece, in fact, repelled Italy when Mussolini attempted to bully his way into Greece from Albania. It was Metaxas who drew a line in the sand and said, "OXI!" (No!) Lots of commentators talk about Great Britain actually standing alone, but as Drez documents in this meticulously researched narrative, Greece was aligned with the Union Jack via a heroic Mediterranean defense against the Italian invasion. For the Free World of 1940, desperate for some upbeat news, the Greek backbone was a flashing cause for hope. Although it hasn't been properly captured in the old black-and-white newsreel footage, the U.S. and British governments' admiration for the Greek Army was immense. Much like the defenders of Wake Island in the Pacific, President Franklin D. Roosevelt, for example, regularly asked aides how Greece was holding up under the Axis onslaught. That was until April 1941 when bad news reached Washington D.C.: like Wake Island, the Greek government fell. But almost immediately a widespread Greek Resistance movement swelled from Athens to Crete. The "Greece for the Greeks" movement was unleashed in underground earnest. The sabotage of all things fascistic began.

As Drez makes abundantly clear in these information-packed pages, Greece *conquered* was not a country *tamed*. Few Greek citizens believed that the German proxy government headed by General Georgios Tsolakaglou was legitimate. From the get-go General Tsolakaglou lacked public legitimacy to govern metropolitan Athens. Many Greeks viewed him as a Judas Iscariot-like collaborationist. Tsolakaglou was scoffed at by millions of Greeks for his heavy-handed fascist leadership, further discredited because of his inability to halt the cession of large parts of Northeastern Greece to Bulgaria. With heads full of steam, Greek civilians revolted, angry over chronic inflation, horrific food shortages, and even starvation in rural villages. For the Allies, the Greeks became the model for active resistance. Both Britain and the U.S. invested clandestine assets to help the Greeks foil the Germans. For while the Nazis occupied Athens and other large Greek cities, Hitler never seized a hold of the Greek countryside. Greece, in fact, was the only occupied German territory where the army feared the fierce rural resistance. Greece had given the Allies their first victory over the Axis against Italy, and after April 1941 they became a real burr under the German saddle. The Nazi forces suffered deadly defeats at the hands of tough-willed resistance fighters. The Greek guerillas had to endure brutal winters in the mountains, often without proper clothing or food, to prevail. But prevail they did. Today, Greece is a gold-star member nation of both NATO and the European Union.

Most World War II historians rightfully devote long chapters to the risks taken by the British Army at Dunkirk. But, as Drez reminds us, scholars shouldn't lose sight of the fact that the British Army also dug-in its heels to liberate Greece from German-Italian tyranny. British Prime Minister Winston Churchill, in fact, risked everything to defend the Greek mainland and the Greek island of Crete. Under incredible duress, the German Army had to eventually withdraw from Greece, hightailing it as their fortunes started to dissolve. Meanwhile, the Greek freedom fighters continued to attack the Nazis by knife and gun until they evacuated the cradle of democracy. Lo and behold ... the democratic impulses of Greece won out!

Reading this book raises a profound question: Why has the Greek story been given such a short shrift in history? The answer: the Cold War. After the Second World War, Greece—in typical Greek tragedy fashion—engaged in its own Civil War. The country was torn by the polar opposite impulses of American-styled democracy and Soviet-styled Communism. For four years, from around 1944 to 1948, democratic-spirited Greeks fought against the threat of Communism with the same ferocity with which they had warred with the Axis. President Harry S. Truman came to the aid of Greece in his famous Truman Doctrine measures of 1948. With Truman's help Greece gave the U.S. its first real Cold War victory.

This book tells the incredible story of the Greeks' brave fight for liberty in the 1940s. Courage is the main course here. The massacre-driven Nazis had superior military equipment, but the Third Reich had neither human rights scruples nor rules-of-engagement ethics. They were brutes. They were murderers. They executed Greek Resistance fighters and innocent civilians on the spot. Many Greek villages thought to be harboring resistance fighters were burned to the ground, torched in true Gestapo fashion. This narrative is an essential remembrance to the fallen heroes of those days gone by. Additionally, thanks to John Georges's beneficence, Ghost Road Press will publish a future volume of oral histories in the coming years. Georges, always the philanthropist, likewise envisions having the National World War II Museum in New Orleans open a new Resistance Wing soon. You can be sure the Greeks won't be under-represented.

Douglas Brinkley
June 6, 2009
Houston, Texas

CHAPTER ONE
THE ROAD TO WAR

ON OCTOBER 12, 1940, Benito Mussolini paced his office in the massive Sala del Mappamondo in the fifteenth-century Palazzo Venezia in Rome. From his grand office he looked out past the great blue draperies to see the ruins of the ancient Coliseum in the distance: a panorama only made possible by his demolition of ancient churches and monuments that had previously blocked his view. He was a very angry man and paced the marble floors surrounded by the frescos of the Italian artist Mantegna. The painted walls in themes of triumphal arches were in stark contrast to The Duce's* temperament on this October day.

Mussolini was in no mood to feel triumphant. He had once again, for the countless time, been snubbed and out-maneuvered by his senior partner in the Pact of Steel, Germany's Adolph Hitler.

Ever since the May 22, 1939 signing of that historic pact promising trust and cooperation between the two countries and full mutual military support should either side go to war, the trust and cooperation had been one-sided: Hitler called the shots, and Mussolini made the concessions. Hitler's ideas were important, Mussolini's were patronized, minimized, and dismissed out of hand; The Führer* played from a position of strength, The Duce played from one of weakness. Even in the run up to the Pact of Steel, this German dominance was well perceived by his own Fascist Party members of the Grand Council. One even went

---

*Both terms translate to "leader."

so far as to deride him and shout out, "You are shining Germany's boots!"[1]

It just did not seem fair. He was the father of the fascist movement having come to power in 1922 when Hitler was still a fledgling rabble-rouser. Italy had been a country racked in turmoil, riots, strikes, and civil unrest, and ready for Mussolini's message for order and patriotism. Of course, those who were not quite ready for his message could expect violent convincing from the thugs of his *camicie nere*, the Blackshirts, so called because of their uniforms. By 1922, through persuasion or intimidation, Mussolini's fascists felt they had enough power to demand representation in the existing government. Predictably the ruling party denied their demands and Mussolini again turned to force.

On October 28, 1922, in a massive show of force, fascist supporters mobilized from various parts of Italy and marched on Rome. The King, Victor Emmanuel, and his army were not confident to resist them and so they did not, and these curious columns entered Rome unopposed. But Victor Emmanuel was not a stupid man and he decided that discretion was indeed the better part of valor, and seeing that Mussolini had the upper hand, invited the thirty-nine-year-old firebrand to form a new government and become the prime minister.

The triumphant Mussolini, who had not led the march on Rome and had stayed behind in Milan just in case something went wrong, accepted the king's invitation and began his reign as prime minister. He quickly transformed his prime-ministership into an absolute dictatorship. He won the support of the Italian working class through popular programs such as land reform, public works, and job creation. Steel production doubled and increased farming cut wheat imports by seventy-five percent.

But this former teacher and journalist always harbored visions of grandeur. He sought to revive the military glories of the old Roman Empire and was not hesitant to flex his military muscle. He praised conquest and warfare as necessities for a nation to be great and in 1935 invaded Abyssinia to avenge a humiliating defeat suffered by Italy in 1896. But the expected quick victory against this tiny country by his new Roman legions eluded him and was not to be. Instead, the Abyssinians held his invading army at bay and The Duce squirmed in humiliation. Finally, one year later, in 1936, only after resorting to overwhelming air power and the use of poison gas did he manage to bludgeon the Abyssinians into capitulation.

While this victory was hardly against a world power, it was a victory nonetheless and it spurred The Duce to flex his military muscle again: this time in the Spanish Civil War. Despite being one of twenty-seven countries to sign the League of Nations Non-Intervention Agreement, Mussolini intervened. He provided the Spanish Nationalists under General Francisco Franco with ninety aircraft and a cruiser. On November 28, 1936, he signed a secret treaty with Franco to provide military aid in return for bases in Spain should there be a war with France. The Duce was planning for the future. He would create the new Roman Empire and that included territorial claims to Corsica, Tunisia, Djibouti, Nice and Savoy.[2]

In the ninety days following the secret treaty with Spain, Italy sent Franco's Nationalists 130 more aircraft and 2,500 tons of bombs. They also chipped in 1,200 pieces of artillery and mortars, and over 12,000 machine guns. Topping that off was a gift of fifty small tanks and almost 4,000 motor vehicles.

But Mussolini's help to Franco was not limited to materiel alone. In December, three thousand Blackshirts were fighting in Spain and were part of the forces that overwhelmed Malaga. By February 1937, more than 30,000 Blackshirts along with 20,000 troops of the Italian Army were fighting with Generalissimo Franco.

A month later, on March 8, 1937, operating as an independent unit, 35,000 Italian soldiers followed 80 small tanks to attack the enemy stronghold at Guadalajara. But they were not able to break through. First the Spanish Red Army stopped the Italian armored thrust and then hurled it back with a significant loss of equipment and a humiliating 3,000 casualties.

The Civil War in Spain proved not to be the invasion of tiny Abyssinia and Mussolini's second military venture ended in failure. Spain blamed the failure of the Italian attack for the Spanish Army's defeat at Guadalajara. Franco added insult to injury and banned the Italian Army from operating as an independent unit in the future. But The Duce was undaunted and pressed his army on. Five months after Guadalajara, in August, the Nationalist Forces including the Italians were victorious at the Battle of Santander.

While final victory was still a long way off, and Santander was only one battle, Mussolini at last had a victory. He strutted and postured and hurled insults at his opponents who had opposed his military dabbling and his continued involvement in Spain. What did they know about greatness and leadership?

"I will make the Guadalajara defeatists pay,"[3] he fumed. But his moment of triumph was short-lived, and by December, the Reds had again successfully attacked and Mussolini faced the prospect of defeat, stalemate, and further scorn should his Spanish venture fail. His top general was not confident and was reluctant to be prodded into offensive action. General Berti groused about everything and gave the impression that he didn't believe in the Spanish mission. He blamed Generalissimo Franco for lack of unity, no drive, no decisive action, and was anxious to withdraw many Italian troops and leave a reduced force in battle positions.

The Duce was not happy and rejected Berti's assessment, and he ridiculed the general to his Foreign Minister and son-in-law, Count Galeazzo Ciano.

Ciano was in total agreement. Berti was a pessimist. "Lack of faith is the first step towards failure," he said. "Unilateral withdrawal by us would give strength and credence to those who say that Italy is exhausted and can no longer bear military efforts."[4]

Mussolini brushed aside Berti's advice and announced that his forces would remain until victory. But in the same breath, he cautioned Franco that time was of the essence and, "we cannot stay in a war that drags on forever."[5] But a month later there still had been no conclusive action and none in sight. The Duce prodded Franco. This time his letter was a two-edged sword. He reiterated Italy's commitment to Spain, but only "if Franco fights"[6] and threatened withdrawal, "if the Generalissimo continues to insist in a war of grueling delay."[7]

To show his determination to keep his side of the agreement, Mussolini intensified his bombing campaign on the Spanish coastal cities to break the Communist will to fight after a new Spanish offensive had sent the Reds reeling back. The Duce sensed victory and implored Franco to seize the opportunity to follow-up the breakthrough by employing the idle Italian divisions. "Either let them fight, or have them come home,"[8] he said in a huff.

Ciano voiced similar frustrations with Franco in his diary. "Franco must take full advantage of his success," he wrote. "Fortune is not an honest woman who dedicates her whole life to you. Fortune is a prostitute who offers herself fleetingly, and then moves on to others. If you don't know how to grab her by the hair, you lose her."[9]

But Franco was in no mood to grab Fortune's hair, and he ignored Mussolini's entreaties. He did not answer The Duce's cables and, consequently, Mussolini ordered the Italian air forces to disengage from all operations until the Italian infantry was deployed. Finally in March 1938, Franco attacked, and this time an Italian division was in his line and broke the Red front. It had been one year since the devastating defeat at Guadalajara, and victory was sweet.

Mussolini ordered the air forces to strike hard at the rear areas of the retreating Reds and brushed aside Franco's objections not to bomb the cities for fear of foreign complications. The Duce scoffed at such an idea. He was proud to be labeled as harsh, and was pleased that some thought him ruthless. Harsh action, he felt, would make Italy rise in the eyes of the Germans who "love total and ruthless war."[10]

By April, Franco's beefed-up line positioned itself to make a final drive to the sea to crush the Red forces. The Italian forces, led by the fiery General Gastone Gambara, fired the first shot in this new offensive. It was Gambara who had breathed life into the leaderless Italian Army and had enveloped and smashed the Red forces at Tortosa, and on July 13, led the final drive. Predictably, Italian General Berti saw defeat instead of victory in the offing and sent predictable lackluster reports to The Duce. But Gambara's cables were welcome relief, full of fire and confidence, and The Duce was impressed.

"Gambara is a general upon whom I have my eyes set," the beaming dictator proclaimed. "He is not one of those officers who enters the barracks mistaking the door ... to [be] a convent."[11]

The General's next message did nothing to disappoint The Duce. He reported that he was preparing to encircle Valencia, and although Red resistance was ferocious, and the line had bogged down, he was optimistic. Gambara reported that he planned to maneuver, not settle into stalemate or defeat. But despite his bold plan, the enthralled Duce realized that General Gambara was not in charge; Franco was, and it was Franco who was anemic in his reaction to the Red defense.

Mussolini was furious. "Make a note of it," he railed to Ciano, "today, August 29, I predict Franco's defeat. This man does not know how to make war. The Reds are fighters: Franco is not."[12]

Angrily, Mussolini made good his threat and ordered the withdrawal of the infantry unless the two Italian divisions were given two additional Spanish divisions to make the attack on Barcelona—under Italian command. But Franco was not moved to action, and shocked Mussolini by reluctantly accepting his demand to withdraw the Italian infantry. The ball was back in Mussolini's court and The Duce had to backtrack. To follow through on his threat would invite a Spanish defeat and world opinion would say that Italy had cut and run. He would be accused of abandoning Franco and the finger pointing would begin, while his enemies would cry that he was responsible for the overall failure. It would be Guadalajara revisited, only worse.

Mussolini modified his stance and announced to the world that he intended to march with his comrade until the end. But it was not blind loyalty that drove Mussolini to walk the final miles with Franco, it was money. Although he believed that Franco's inaction had lost the war and that he would be forced to search for a compromised victory, Mussolini was aware that Italy stood to lose four billion lire in credit, and The Duce was not willing to throw money down the drain.

So on October 24, Mussolini sacked the laconic Berti and

replaced him with the enthusiastic Gambara. Within a month, Gambara was knocking on Mussolini's door to announce a new offensive. The general felt that the entire Italian force in Spain could play a decisive role in a coming operation. This was music to The Duce's ears. It was not the windy, pessimistic reports from Berti.

Gambara had a willing audience as he laid out his plan and maps to the excited Mussolini. He asked for some replacements and three groups of artillery, all modest requests, and all instantly approved. The Duce asked if he needed more and the general said no, and with that was off to the front. During his short time in command, optimism had replaced pessimism, action had replaced inaction, and infighting had ended. Ciano reported, "The CTV (Italian Volunteers in Spain) is as right as it has ever been and relations with the air force have been conveniently cleared up."[13]

By Christmas 1938, Gambara's forces proceeded rapidly toward their objectives, outdistancing their Spanish counterparts. Mussolini appealed to the Germans to get Franco to move his troops. "There is the possibility of decisive victory, but the Spanish threaten to let it slip by again,"[14] wrote Count Ciano.

But Gambara forged ahead, skillfully maneuvering his army to outflank the Red forces and his daring raised the international community's eyebrows. France began to squirm, but Mussolini let it be known that if France interfered, Italy would fight France on Spanish soil.

By mid January Gambara was the ersatz leader of all the Spanish forces and rolled his army on. Rumors of French intervention flew from every quarter and a confident Mussolini was up to the challenge: "If Paris sends forces," he said, "we shall land 30 battalions at Valencia, even if this starts a world war."[15] The New Roman Empire was flexing its muscles.

But the rumors of French intervention turned out to be just that: rumors. Gambara rolled on, gobbling up heretofore contested Red territory, and Mussolini suddenly envisioned the exhausted Communist Army with its back to the sea and victory within his grasp.

On January 24, Gambara was in the suburbs of Barcelona

and two days later had overrun the capitol. Italy reveled in the news and Mussolini had indeed made the "Guadalajara defeatists pay." Only Madrid was left in Communist hands.

On January 26, 1939, Ciano wrote "Victory in Spain bears only one name, that of Mussolini, who conducted the campaign bravely, firmly, even at a time when many people who cheer him now were against him."

One day later, flushed with victory, Mussolini sought political vengeance. He demanded to see the Minister of Greece in the presence of the Italian Minister, Ciano. Reacting to a report that had been leaked in Bucharest that the Greek military attaché had made insulting remarks about the Italian army, The Duce felt it was time to take the Greek minister to the woodshed. The insulting remark had been made during the attaché's conversation with a Hungarian colleague and had been overheard by some whistle-blower.

When the hapless Greek minister arrived, The Duce fixed his stare on him and berated him in a one-sided conversation. When Mussolini had finished his harangue, he told the trembling minister that Greece had three days to fix this problem. If by that time Italy was not given complete satisfaction, "there would be serious complications."[16]

On the third day, the Greek minister was back, hat in hand, obviously with an answer that satisfied The Duce. Ciano was present and gloated at the results of the embarrassing meeting. He described it as an act of "abject submission," proving the "Greeks' fear of us."

On March 28, 1939, the Nationalist forces of Generalissimo Francisco Franco overwhelmed the Red forces in Madrid due in no small part to the previous offensive by Gambara. The war was over and the fascists celebrated one of their greatest victories. The Italian population spilled out into the streets of Rome especially in front of the Palazzo Venezia, where Mussolini stepped out onto the balcony to greet the cheering crowds. He folded his arms, thrust out his chest, and stuck out his chin and was overjoyed. Stepping into his study in the Sala del Mappamondo he pointed to his atlas opened to the map of Spain. He wore a triumphant smile as he tapped his finger on the page.

"It has been open in this way for almost three years," he said, "and that is enough. But I know already that I must open it to another page."[17]

The next page to which Mussolini referred was Albania which he annexed on April 12. His star never flew higher.

BUT THAT WAS THEN and this was October 12, 1940 and Hitler was now dominating the relationship just as he had dominated the armies of Europe. In a little over one year the German Army had overrun Poland, Norway, France, The Netherlands, Denmark, Luxembourg, and had almost encircled the escaping British Army at Dunkirk while capturing all its equipment and materiel. All of this done with Mussolini and Italy held at the end of a leash like a pet dog. It was the Germans who had dominated the headlines. The world saw the Germans march down the Champs Elysees; it was the swastika that the world saw flying from the top of the Arc de Triomphe, and it was German soldiers being photographed on top of the Eiffel Tower.

Mussolini could only look on. His army had been depleted by the long involvement with Franco, and his divisions were small, only two-thirds of a regular division. On paper he had seventy-three, but in reality only nineteen were at full strength. Italian artillery still sported guns captured from the Austrians in WWI and their tanks were like toys compared to modern armor. Their air force was formidable and their navy had two modern battleships with four more being outfitted, to go with nineteen cruisers, 132 destroyers and torpedo boats, and over one hundred submarines. But their naval Achilles Heel was fuel. They only had fuel enough to fight a one-year war.[18]

There was one German snub after another in the year after the Pact of Steel. But the final snub happened one week earlier on October 7. Without even the courtesy of an advanced notification to Mussolini, German troops entered and occupied heretofore neutral Romania. It was no surprise. King Victor Emmanuel had labeled the Germans correctly in 1939.

"As long as the Germans need us they will be courteous, and even slavish, but at the first opportunity they will reveal themselves as the great scoundrels they really are."[19]

Ciano also had experienced German deceit in the run up to the Polish invasion. "They have betrayed us and lied to us," he said. "Now they are dragging us into an adventure which we have not wanted and which might compromise the regime and the country as a whole. The Italian people will shudder in horror when they find out about the aggression against Poland."[20]

Still Mussolini could not resist the lure of power and spoils of victory should a war begin, and he did not want to be left out. Australian war correspondent and historian, Chester Wilmot, accurately described The Duce's dilemma.

"Mussolini found himself ousted from the driving seat in the Axis chariot." Hitler drove and Mussolini rode as the chariot careened down the road to an uncertain future. The faster it went, the more exhilarating and terrifying. The faster it went, the more it intrigued, excited and frightened The Duce, but although sorely tempted at times to get off, he simply could not.

He was, Wilmot said, "a bewildered footman ... tempted to leap off and risk lacerations when he feared it was heading for disaster." But with success on the horizon, Mussolini was a different person in the chariot, "clinging more firmly and leaning over to urge the driver on when prospects of quick and easy booty stretched ahead."[21]

He was now urging Hitler on but he had to tell The Führer he was not prepared to go to war with him just yet, but would do so if Germany could furnish all the materiel needed. When Hitler asked for a list of Italy's needs, Mussolini was forced to submit an embarrassing list that staggered the imagination and would have required 17,000 trains to deliver. Hitler feigned understanding and politely told The Duce that he planned, "annihilating Poland and beating France and England without help."[22]

So humiliated was Mussolini that he was reduced to posturing so as to look like an equal partner; neutrality to The Duce was a bitter pill. "Not being able to wage war, [Mussolini] makes all the necessary preparations so that in case of a peaceful solution he may be able to say that he would have waged it," said Ciano.

"This is war," lamented Mussolini, "but tomorrow we shall

declare to the General Council that we are not marching." [23]

It had been that way from the beginning. In September 1939, Germany had secretly sought a non-aggression pact with Russia. Italy was out of the loop.

"We already surmised that something was being hatched between Moscow and Berlin," complained Ciano. "As usual we are told nothing ... The Germans prepare to strike a blow without our knowledge—and from Vienna to Warsaw they have struck many." [24]

Mussolini and Hitler, Munich, 1940

Mussolini was reduced to reading the text of the Moscow agreement in the newspapers and he confided to his Foreign Minister that he was bitter about Hitler's rise to fame and that he, "would be greatly pleased if Hitler were slowed down." [25]

The Duce continued into a downward spiral of depression. The war would go on without him, and he would have to sit on the sidelines and be content with whatever crumbs Hitler would sweep toward him and he would have to proclaim his gratitude.

"The Italians, after having heard my warlike propaganda for eighteen years, cannot understand how I can become the herald for peace, now that Europe is in flames," he exploded."[26]

"For Mussolini, the idea of Hitler's waging war, and, worse still, winning it, is altogether unbearable,"[27] confided Ciano to his diary.

The best Mussolini could do was to write Hitler and offer his services to find a diplomatic solution to the all-consuming war, that is, if that's what Hitler wanted. If that was not the course of action that The Führer envisioned, then Italy would be prepared to enter the war, actively, at Hitler's side in October 1942! That was almost three years down the road. Again there was the patronizing pat on the head from Germany followed by a demand upon Italy's meager resources. Upon discovering that Italy was working its only nickel mine, the Germans asked for its production. Instead of refusing to part with his only source of the vital metal, especially considering his state of military unpreparedness, Mussolini offered to share the ore. Ciano was furious and dismayed to see The Duce grovel. "It is enlightening to see how these gentlemen act," he said, "as bullies and robbers. How long are we going to take this?"[28]

Even Ciano could not imagine the answer to his question. Simply put: Mussolini was going to "take it" as long as The Duce insisted on riding in the chariot with Adolph Hitler. If Ciano thought the nickel episode was bad, Germany's demand for Italian copper was worse. In February 1940, Mussolini was again determined to satisfy German demands despite the cost to his own country just to curry favor with The Führer. His advisors pleaded with him not to give goods to Germany that Italy itself lacked. But The Duce was unmoved and he intended to extract 3,500 tons of copper from the homes of the Italian people and strip sacred objects from the churches to meet the quota. Ciano objected.

"The churches do not need copper, but faith," Mussolini sarcastically answered, "and there is very little faith left."[29]

As time went on, Mussolini's frustration grew worse. "It is humiliating to remain with our hands folded while others write history," he fumed. "It matters little who wins. To make a people great it is necessary to send them to battle even if you have to kick them in the ass."

He railed on about the half-million Italian deserters he remembered in WWI, and present inaction of the Italian Navy which he felt should be deployed against the British and French forces. He stormed about and asked, "What's the use of building 600,000 tons of warship? Some yachts would be enough to take the young ladies for a joy ride."[30]

Despite all the shortages in the Italian military machine, The Duce could stand inaction no longer; and despite grave warnings from his military and civilian advisors, Mussolini chose to declare his active intervention with Germany on June 10, 1940. He defiantly stood on the balcony of the Palazzo Venezia and made his announcement to a less than enthusiastic gathering of the Italian population.

Then the unthinkable happened. On June 17, just as The Duce was hoping to unleash his military might, France capitulated and asked for an armistice. The war had been won. Hitler was again victorious and Italy had only stood on the sidelines. Again The Duce endured the embarrassment and humiliation of being left out. Ciano reported that Mussolini saw, "the hour of peace is growing near and sees that once again that unattainable dream of his life: glory on the field of battle is fading away."[31]

But before it faded, Mussolini was determined to make one more effort. On June 19, desperate for any military victory, even at the eleventh hour, he decided to attack the French in the Alps. The armistice was at hand and his advisors frowned and cautioned about the political consequences and appearances of kicking a man when he was down. The Duce was not impressed with appearances and was willing to risk anything to save face and meet Hitler with at least some sort of victory in his hand. But what if his attack failed and he did not win, or was hurled back? Could he bear to approach The Führer carrying the albatross of defeat around his neck?

Cooler heads prevailed and Mussolini decided to scale back and limit his attack to a small area near the Swiss border. But even this tiny operation drew objections from his generals who told him that they were not prepared to carry out this small attack despite having sat statically for nine months. Mussolini insisted and when the attack finally kicked off the following day, the

Italians barely moved and "halted in front of the first French fortification that put up some opposition."[32]

Achilles Starace, the General Secretary of the Fascist Party went to the front to inspect the Italian Army and returned with a dismal report. There had been, "a total lack of preparation of our army, an absolute lack of offensive capability, and the complete incompetence of the top officers," he reported. The tactics used were, "the same techniques that was employed more than twenty years ago."[33]

The Duce spun out of control with rage. He turned his attention to Greece. A report stated that English ships and planes were being given safe harbor and supplies in Greece. Mussolini threatened to take action against Greece, "if this music should continue," and Ciano reported that the Greek minister "tried weakly to deny it, but he left with his tail between his legs."[34]

Mussolini then wrote Hitler and offered the use of Italian land and air forces if, and when, the time came to attack Great Britain. Hitler ignored the request for several weeks and finally declined The Duce's offer. He politely explained that the refusal was based on logistical difficulties to supply two armies. No one could give a patronizing "No" to Mussolini like Hitler could.

On August 11, 1940, Mussolini again spoke about the possibility of military action against Greece. Was it desperation? It had been one year since Count Ciano had described Greece as "a country too poor for us to covet."[35] The Italian leadership scorned its small population of seven million and rudimentary agricultural society. But now, with no victory in sight, Greece seemed vulnerable and ripe for picking and maybe not too poor for Italy to covet. The Duce lusted for military action and victory. Again he was rebuffed and his hands were tied with a terse message from the Germans who wanted to avoid any Balkan crisis. When the Germans said, "No," Mussolini was helpless.

In early October Hitler and Mussolini met at the Brenner Pass at the border between Italy and Austria to discuss future plans and The Führer promised more importance in the Mediterranean area. The Duce was excited and upon his return to Rome on October 8, he ordered an initiative with Romania to request

Italian troops to be stationed in their country. Up to now only Germans had had a presence in Romania to ensure the free flow of oil from the Ploesti oil fields. Could this be the event that would trigger that first step of the new importance in the Mediterranean?

But even as Ciano prepared to send the request, German troops marched into Romania the previous day, trumping the Italians with nary an announcement to Mussolini. When he returned to Rome on October 12 The Duce learned that Berlin had announced that Romania had requested a German military mission to Bucharest and that the German Luftwaffe would be assigned the mission to defend the oil fields.

"Hitler places me in front of a *fait accompli*," The Duce fumed. He'd had enough. "This time I am going to pay him back in his own coin. He will find out from the papers that I have occupied Greece. In this way the equilibrium will be reestablished."

Ciano asked if his generals were in agreement, and Mussolini shot back, "I shall send in my resignation as an Italian if anyone objects to our fighting the Greeks."[36]

The usually conservative Ciano could see that Mussolini seemed to have his mind made up for a Greek military operation and this time Ciano agreed. "I believe that the military operation will be useful and easy,"[37] he said.

The date for the Greece operation was first set for October 26 and later postponed to October 28. Italian intelligence seemed to sense that the Greeks were favorable to the Italians since Greece had been under the dictatorship of General Ioannis Metaxas. Nothing could have been further from the truth. Since August 4, 1936 Metaxas had indeed ruled Greece with an iron hand but it was not a murderous hand. He, like Mussolini, was a fascist who started off as prime minister, then quickly dissolved parliament and stifled unrest and dissent. But his reasons for dissolving parliament were quite different from Hitler's or Mussolini's. He did not seek self-aggrandizement or territorial expansion; nor did he seek the glory of militarism or persecution and murder of undesirables or political enemies.

"Metaxas had no patience with Greek politicians," observed

British Ambassador Sir Michael Palairet, "and [he] exiled most of the more prominent ones to islands in the Aegean, where their most serious hardship was to be removed from the game of politics—the king of sport in Greece."[38]

In 1935 Greece had been on a road to self-destruction. There had been several attempted coups and the Communists and their strident agenda threatened the Greek way of life. Civil unrest and riots in the cities and countryside were the order of the day and undermined good order and discipline; and Parliament was so badly divided that it could not govern.

In practice Metaxas was nothing like The Duce and more like Francisco Franco in his opposition to the Communists. Metaxas was also a nationalist whose ambition was to restore order and to bring Greece to a social and political level of olden days and to increased Greek influence in the Balkans. That ran counter to Italy's expansionist schemes.

Unlike Mussolini and Hitler, Metaxas was not a dynamic person; he was incapable of delivering fiery speeches to arouse the population, and suffered from what some called an inferiority complex. He extolled the virtues of patriotism, order, religion and family values. He was small in stature and his official photograph gave him a look of former American President, Theodore Roosevelt, including thin wire-rimmed glasses. To the average Greek citizen he was a leader to be tolerated, and while few people sang his praises, a greater number disliked him, some intensely. His background had been in the army and he was a retired army general.

But he had been more than just a run-of-the-mill general. He was one of the top officers in the prestigious Potsdam Military Academy, the equivalent to the U.S. Military Academy at West Point. His fellow classmates nicknamed him "Little Molke" after the brilliant German General of WWI, for his exceptional ability to master strategic problems. Because of his short stature, he was known to wear high heels to elevate his height to his reputation.[39]

Someone described him as, "An enlightened despot who achieved national unity by introducing, into Greek society and the Greek polity, an element of discipline."[40]

"I discuss with everyone and allow ... every discussion and every opposition to me freely," Metaxas told his subordinates. "But when I make the decision, and in many a case I may take it contrary to your opinions, this decision will be definite and irreversible ... I do not permit to anyone ... any simmering opposition to my will manifested in any way.[41]

What Metaxas however did have was an enormous political problem. With the outbreak of WWII he immediately declared Greece to be neutral; it was his only reasonable choice. As a fascist he naturally leaned toward the Axis powers and their authoritarianism, but in reality the welfare of the Greek nation and its continued independence was not linked to the Axis, but to Great Britain and its powerful navy capable of dominating the waters of the eastern Mediterranean and guaranteeing Greek security, just as it had done in the past.

Metaxas conducted enormous trade with Germany. He liked Adolph Hitler, had no quarrel with the German people, and despised Mussolini, especially since the Italian Army was now camped on his northwestern border in Albania. On the other hand, Britain and France had pledged to maintain Greek and Romanian independence, and that trumped the Axis. German interest in Romanian oil and Romania's interior location, far from the sea, minimized the reality of the Anglo-Franco pledge to Romania, but Greece was another story. The strong Allied presence in the Mediterranean and Greece's seaside location convinced Metaxas that Greece would be valuable terrain in the event of war and that he had a reasonable expectation to count on the British pledge.

So in mid October 1940 Ioannis Metaxas girded for war. Despite his best efforts at neutrality, he had failed and the enemy was on his border and invasion was imminent.

The Italian invaders, despite having declared early on that they had no land-aggrandizing plans against Greece, now rehearsed the strategy and tactics of Contingency G, as the invasion plan was called. Mussolini was full of confidence and arrogance.

Earlier he boasted that his attack on Greece had been a long time in coming. "... since 1923 I have some accounts to settle, and the Greeks deceive themselves if they think that I have forgotten."[42]

Ioannis Metaxas

The Duce demanded a vigorous attack, including all-out air strikes, so that the first encounter would be a hammer stroke and "everything will go to pieces at the first clash."[43] The attack will be a total surprise. An ultimatum would be handed to the Greek government just prior to the attack with no chance of any warning to the Greek Army.

But under the surface of Mussolini's confidence were ripples of dissent. That dissent came from none other than Mussolini's top general, Marshal Badoglio and the three heads of his General Staff who all declared to Ciano that they were opposed to Contingency G. They warned that the attacking forces were too thin and it would be impossible for the navy to carry out the proposed amphibious landings because the water was too shallow. Worse yet, Badoglio could not see a quick victory and predicted that the war would spread and drag on straining Italy's delicate margin of resources. But Ciano scoffed and called him a pessimist.

Badoglio then informed Mussolini that if he was ordered to move against the Greeks, he would resign; but the die had been cast and Mussolini, in a fit of rage, let it be known that Badoglio's resignation would instantly be accepted if the Field Marshal should be foolish enough to tender it. The Duce informed Ciano that he would personally go to Greece, "to witness the incredible shame of Italians who are afraid of the Greeks."[44]

So as October approached November, Contingency G slipped into gear, Badoglio did not resign, and Italy's forty-one million people prepared to attack Greece's seven million. This would certainly be another Abyssinia.

Ciano wrote, "I began to draft the ultimatum which Grazzi[45] will hand to Metaxas at two o'clock in the morning of October 28. Naturally it is a document that allows no way out for Greece. Either she accepts occupation or she will be attacked."[46]

CHAPTER 2

PREPARATION AND PROVOCATION

IN 1940, THE IDEA OF WAR between Italy and Greece was anything but new. The two countries had fought against each other over several millennia, beginning with the war that had pitted the Roman ancestors of Troy against the Greeks and inspired Homer and Virgil to compose epics about that event. The Trojans found the Greeks to be tough adversaries and even when it appeared that the Trojans had gotten the upper hand, the Greek army had fight left in it. If the events at Troy and mythology are to be believed, the Greeks defeated the Trojans with superior intelligence, offensive action and especially surprise—the Trojan Horse. Virgil gave the Greeks the ultimate compliment as fierce fighters when he wrote, "Beware of Greeks, even when bearing gifts."[1]

But that ancient war was not the war to end all wars between Italy and Greece. In fact it was just the beginning. The Greeks fought the Romans under a variety of names: Spartans, Epirotes, Macedonians. They even fought each other, and the Turks, and the Bulgarians, and the Albanians, and everyone else who had designs on their territory and way of life. The Italians and the Greeks had occupied each other's land with impunity over the centuries as wars and politics dictated. To Mussolini another invasion of Greece was more like a rite of passage.

Nor was Contingency G launched in a vacuum. First there had been the Italian occupation of Albania, a country already under Italian guarantee and protection. An additional 1927 defensive treaty was to have lasted for twenty years, but the actual effect of that treaty allowed a slow Italian infiltration into, and control of, the financial, military, and political institutions of Albania.[2]

So pervasive was this control that ten years later, Count Ciano cunningly planned to upgrade Albania for possible future Italian use. After persuading Mussolini to inject 60 million lire into Albania construction projects, he explained, "One never knows what the future holds. We must be ready to grab opportunities when they arise."[3]

In 1939 an opportunity arose. Albania tried to renew the existing Alliance Treaty with Italy to secure its position as an independent state, but Italy wanted no part of such a restricting treaty. What Italy wanted was occupation of Albania for future operations. If there would be a war in the Balkans, the presence of an Italian Army already ashore would be infinitely easier than having to launch a seaborne invasion.

The takeover was short and swift, and followed a traditional Axis outline: First, a campaign of trumped-up incidences and disturbances in the country to be subjugated, usually instigated by thugs from the attacking country. In Italy's case, Count Ciano proudly described his thugs as a "small team of men ... enterprising and hotheaded ... in order to create the incidents which are to take place next Thursday evening, if the king, in the meantime, has not had the kindness to capitulate."[4]

After the "incidents," came the propaganda campaign to instill a fear of invasion in the population of the victim country, followed by the eventual ultimatum to allow Axis troops to occupy the offending country so as to quell the "disturbances," and restore "order." If the ultimatum was rejected, the invasion began.

By April 6, 1939, the Italians had followed that plan to a T, and it was time to deliver the ultimatum. King Zog and the Albanian Government rejected it and the Italians invaded. By April 9, they had overwhelmed the weakly resisting Albanians, occupied the country, and chased Zog out to Greece. In the short span of three days, the Italian Army, by bullying and intimidation, had acquired a base from which to launch future offensive operations in the Balkans, should that opportunity arise.

Ciano proclaimed haughtily, "Independent Albania is no more."[5]

There was only one problem with this expertly executed, intimidating take over of Albania: its unexpected consequence. Mussolini had even said, "no one will want to interfere with our dispute with Albania."[6]

But Mussolini was wrong.   England and France were greatly concerned with the bullying invasion and the threat to the Balkans, and the ever-rising menace of the Axis Powers to all of Europe. They demanded an explanation from the Italian government and Ciano scrambled for an explanation.

He announced to the world that this takeover was only temporary, and Italian troops would withdraw once order had been restored and everything was again secure. He even gave that same explanation to the Ambassador of the United States, who was asking his own questions.

But it was flimsy and no one was buying it. On April 13, both Great Britain and France issued guarantees for the independence and territorial integrity of Greece and Romania, and Greece began to prepare for the possible defense of its homeland.[7]

Map of Greece with Capitol at Athens (Attica)

Italy's 1940 campaign against Greece began with the old tried and true Axis formula that Mussolini had used against Albania, but with a new twist.

There had been the trumped-up military provocations, along with the usual vehement propaganda campaign and veiled threats; there had been the accusations of harboring British ships, and there were regular Italian flyovers of Greek land and air space by the powerful Italian Air Force. But in addition to the predictable intimidation, the Italians actually began shooting.

The shooting started on July 12, when three Italian bombers attacked and struck the ship *Orion*, an auxiliary ship of the Greek Navy on a resupply mission to the Gramvoussa Lighthouse on the western shore of Crete. The plane bombed and machine gunned the vessel, and then attacked the destroyer *Hydra* that had responded to the call for help.

Eighteen days later, on July 30, Italian planes dropped four bombs on destroyers *King George* and *Queen Olga*, and attacked two submarines with four bombs in the bay of Nafpaktos. The bombs missed and the Greek Navy gathered bomb fragments and matched them to the type of bombs used in the July 12 attack on *Orion*.

Two days later Italian aircraft again attacked, this time a patrol boat traveling between two islands, and the planes dropped six bombs. This prompted the Greek government to complain to Rome, but they received no reply. On August 7, Prime Minister Metaxas summoned the Italian Minister Grazzi for an explanation and understanding of Greek-Italian relations and was blithely told that Mussolini and Ciano were both amicably disposed to Greece.

Perhaps Metaxas's call was a signal for Italy to ratchet up the propaganda machine and begin the tale-telling, because on August 14 the Italian state-controlled newspapers began with accusations of Greece having anti-Italian feelings and not appreciating the Italian guarantee—whatever that was—and continually provoking the Axis Powers. Thinly veiled in those histrionics was the additional mention that Greece had not heeded the fates of Czechoslovakia, Poland, Norway, the Netherlands, Belgium and France.[8]

On August 15, 1940 off the island of Tinos,[9] a tiny island among the hundreds of islands off the Greek mainland, the pot boiled over. It was on the most sacred of Greek holy days.

The beautiful church of the Panagia Evangelistria, built in 1824 with gleaming white marble and its distinctive bell tower, dominated the seaside town of Tinos. The exquisitely constructed church was also the fitting repository of the most sacred icon in the Greek Orthodox faith to the Virgin Mary: a small figure of the Virgin, kneeling in prayer.

On this, the holiest of days, the locals and pilgrims from the far reaches of Greece celebrated the "Dormition of the Virgin Mary."[10] The procession, with those lucky enough to have been chosen to carry the sacred icon, found many of the faithful traveling the half-mile from the dock to the church on their knees, praying for curing miracles. The church's very name inspired hope: Our Lady of Good Tidings, and Megalohari referred to many miracles.

Spyros Melas stood on the mountainside overlooking the sea, in the dark of night, anticipating the holy day and the chance to see a beautiful sunrise. Finally the tip of the orange ball broke the horizon.

"I saw the all-white homes of our city, and began to recognize the silhouettes of the pilgrims who were walking slowly toward the hill to the church," he said. "I could see the golden light coming from the church, from the candles of those who had stayed there all night praying with their sick and the lame and the blind."[11]

As the dawn became more brilliant and a rosy light spread across the town, he looked to sea and observed the arrival of the Greek cruiser, *Elli*, swinging in a wide, graceful arc to drop anchor just outside the harbor's entrance. The ship was there as part of the celebration and some of its sailors had been chosen to carry the sacred icon in the procession.

"It was 0630," Melas said, "when a merry bugle's sound was heard. It was the command to begin the deployment of the flags. All at once the ship was covered with a triangle of its grand flag display. It was a happy time on *Elli*."

The three-hundred-foot cruiser was festooned with colored

flags on its port and starboard sides that seemed to rise to the sky on lines from its bow and stern to the top of its main mast.

"The decision had been made as to what sailors would be taking part in the honorary guard for the procession of the Holy Icon, and they had withdrawn in the stern quarter," Melas said.

Eight petty officers had been chosen to carry the Holy Icon taking turns, four at a time. But as the plans for the festivities proceeded, some observers noticed a small, unmarked airplane approaching from an easterly direction, flying at 3,800 feet. It was 0645.

"Within moments the gun crews are in their battle stations," reported Melas, as the ship's officers sounded the warning. "Gunnery Petty Officer Sigalas and the warrant officer in charge of the crew of the Skoda guns received the order from the bridge to train their gun on the airplane but to hold fire."

Elli had good firepower, especially anti aircraft capabilities. It sported three six-inch guns, two three-inch guns, and three 40mm guns. The gun crews fixed the small plane in their sights and tracked it on its westerly course.

"The plane makes two circles over the harbor of Tinos," said Melas.[12] "The crowd thinks that it is a Greek plane and raise their arms and wave to them in salutation."

But the plane made no hostile moves and continued on its way, slowly decreasing altitude until it disappeared in the western skies. An hour and fifty minutes later, at 0825, the gun crews were still on station as a precaution, and the deck was crowded with personnel who would participate in the honor guard and procession. The ship, bedecked with flags, was a beautiful sight and a colorful focal point of the pilgrims on shore.

Elli was also the focal point to Lieutenant Guiseppe Alcardi of the Italian Navy and skipper of the submarine *Delfino*, part of the 5th Submarine Group, on patrol from its island base at Leros. *Delfino* lurked below the surface of the Aegean at 60-foot periscope depth, three thousand yards from the gaily bedecked *Elli*. Alcardi observed the Greek cruiser for long minutes through the prisms of his periscope and pondered the verbal order he had been given. Cesare Maria De Vecchi, Italian Governor for the Aegean, had ordered him to attack and sink *Elli*,[13] and Alcardi fixed his periscope amidships on the cruiser.

In *Delfino's* forward torpedo room, sweating torpedo men had earlier heaved and hauled on the ropes and rigging that inched and slid four of the 3,700-pound weapons into the firing tubes. Once in, they closed the breech doors and locked them with a simple half turn of the handles to engage the interrupted screw threads. The gunnery officer in the conning tower signaled to open the outer doors of the torpedo tubes and the submarine was ready to attack.

The gunnery officer on *Delfino* had an easy task: determine the range to the stationary, anchored ship and fire the torpedoes. After a final sighting, Alcardi commanded, "down periscope," and gave the order to fire. In quick succession, compressed air propelled the four Italian torpedoes from their tubes and activated their twin propellers. The sleek weapons sliced through the several thousand meters of the blue Aegean and approached the cruiser in a fan pattern, leaving their telltale, bubbling wake on the surface.

On board, Lt. (j.g.) Kyriazopoulos prepared to disembark for the procession having just promised the eight petty officers who would carry the Icon that he would light a candle for them at the church. But at the gangway, the lookouts aloft shouted and he stopped in his path to look seaward.

"On-coming TORPEDO from Starboard!" the lookout screamed, having seen the terrifying wake approaching at fifty miles per hour. But it was too late. The twenty-three-foot torpedo slammed into the side of the cruiser and detonated its six-hundred-pound warhead.[14] The ship convulsed under the explosion and men fell to the deck.

Spyros Melas watched in horror and reported: "The torpedo that hit *Elli* exploded exactly below one of its boilers, the one that had been maintained active. Due to the proximity of the explosion to the boiler-room, the active boiler exploded and its supply of oil caught fire."[15]

The flag-bedecked ship was dead in the water, ablaze, and began to list. The crew worked frantically to regain power to try to beach the stricken ship, but the fires were out of control, sweeping the deck in great sheets, and Captain Hatzopoulos gave the order to abandon ship. At 0945, *Elli* began to sink, and in just thirty minutes plunged to the bottom, its grand flag display still flying. Eight men were dead and twenty-six wounded.[16]

The other three torpedoes had missed their mark, but one slammed into the wharf sending a geyser of water, mud and debris flying hundreds of feet in the air. Fragments of that torpedo, with identifiable Italian markings were later recovered, but Metaxas decided to try and salvage neutrality from this blatant act of war and reported that the nationality of the attacking submarine was not known.

Nor was the August attack on *Elli* the last hostile action against the Greek Navy. Two destroyers, *King George* and *Queen Olga*, sailed the following morning from the Port of Salamis, a large island just off the mainland near Athens, to provide an escort for the vessels that would transport the anxious pilgrims from Tinos.

Captain Gregory Mezeviris was aboard *King George.* His ship's immediate sailing the previous day had been postponed "to allow time for the belligerents to be informed of this movement and avoid ... a new misunderstanding," he said.

"We spotted an airplane, with no nationality identification signs, flying at 2,000 meters altitude, flying toward *King George.* I ordered the artillery officer of the ship, the anti-aircraft shooters to closely watch the aircraft and the guns to get ready to fire."

While the crewmembers had their eyes riveted to the sky, they saw tiny black specks fall to the earth. Eight small bombs impacted several hundred meters from the destroyer.

"Immediately we started fire against the plane," said Captain Mezeviris, "and the ship was ordered to zigzag at full speed to avoid the enemy fire. Two more eight-bomb loads fell, the last a few tenths of meters from the ship. Unfortunately the rough seas made even more difficult our machine gun shooting, and the plane was not hit, but disappeared in the horizon flying at high altitude."[17]

In Rome, Ciano received the message that a Greek vessel had been sunk by an unknown submarine and realized that this could trigger a nasty reaction. He knew nothing about the attack, but had his own opinions.

"I consider the intemperance of De Vecchi at the bottom of it," he said accusingly. And Mussolini also looked surprised and ignorant of the whole matter. "The Duce ... wishes to settle this incident peacefully. I suggest sending a note to Greece."[18]

The Italian government rejected all accusations even though none came from Metaxas. Much later, when they were confronted with the torpedo fragments they were reduced to suggesting that the British might have attacked since they had, at one time, bought Italian torpedoes from the Fiume factory.[19]

Two months later, Hitler's Romanian venture had pushed The Duce to the brink of frustration and prompted him to declare that he would "pay him in his own coin." With that, Mussolini unleashed Contingency G on Greece.

THE MAINLAND OF GREECE is divided into three general areas or regions: Thrace and Macedonia in the north, Epirus, Thessaly, and Central Greece in the center, and the Peloponnese, a peninsula in the south barely connected to the mainland by the four-mile wide Isthmus of Corinth. The rest of Greece consists of 2,000 islands of which only two hundred are inhabited. Almost eighty percent of the land mass is mountains, the largest being the Pindus, an extension of the Alps. This massive cordillera averaging 8,700 feet runs down the center of the mainland and is called the spine of Greece. It uniquely barricades the region of Epirus from Macedonia and Thessaly. So mountainous and hostile is Greece's landscape, a local myth grew around its formation. When God created the world he distributed all the available soil through a sieve. He then tossed the remaining stones from the sieve over His shoulder, and there was Greece.

Mussolini's Contingency G was an ambitious master plan to occupy the whole of this mountainous, forbidding country in three phases. The first would be to attack from Albania in the northwest into Epirus and the Ioanian Islands. After this initial success, reinforcements would kick off the second phase, the conquest of Macedonia on the other side of the massive Pindus. Mussolini hoped that Bulgaria would join in on the attack and pin down Greek forces in Thrace and eastern Macedonia and lead to quick victory. After these campaigns, the rest of Greece would somehow be occupied.

The initial Epirus attack would be along that ninety-mile front and carried out by Italy's XXV Ciamuria Corps. The XXVI Corizza Corps would position itself in the Macedonian sector and maintain a defensive posture until the development of the Epirus attack. Placing a large mountain range between two sections of the army was not good tactics, but the mountainous terrain allowed no other choice.

The Greeks anticipated a two-front war with the Italians in the northwest and the Bulgarians in the east, and developed their plan called IB, named for the two potential enemies. The Epirus defense would begin at the border with Albania and be a defense in depth with fall back positions should the line become untenable. The Greek VIII Infantry Division was in Epirus, fully mobilized, and on the other side of the massive Pindus, facing the Italian deployment, was a larger, corps-size force: The Army Section of Western Macedonia. In the west, the defense against Bulgaria would be a stalwartly constructed defensive line.

How could the Greek Army have been so alert and totally mobilized on such short notice? The credit goes to the Greek leader and dictator Ioannis Metaxas. Despite doing back flips in the name of neutrality, including hiding the damning torpedo evidence from the sinking of *Elli*, Metaxas prepared Greece to defend itself. Under his able Commander-in-Chief, Alexander Papagos, the army developed an up-to-date military communications network, and since its small air force could never stop the numbers of the large Italian air force, they beefed up their anti-aircraft defenses. But most importantly the army began training its reservists.

In an effort to give neither the Italians nor the Germans an excuse to attack, Metaxas mobilized discreetly. Training reservists without attracting attention would not be easy, so he and Papagos instituted a seemingly meaningless number system to call-up of reserves. Newspapers and radios announced call-ups with these insignificant, random numbers, and no one could detect the nature or numbers of troops involved, not even the soldiers themselves.[20]

The call-ups were cleverly staggered. Beginning in May the reserve class of 1935 was called for a 45-day retraining course; weeks later it was 1920 and 1930; and then 1934. At the end of the training periods, the men were discharged, fit and ready with no evidence of a military build-up. On August 16, the day after the sinking of *Elli*, the classes of 1919 and 1934 were called, but at the end of that training, they remained under arms as did all those subsequently called.[21]

Nor had Metaxas been idle in defensive matters prior to the Italian threat. Bulgaria was Greece's most likely enemy in 1936 and he decided to build a series of fortifications along the Greek-Bulgarian border. In the four years of construction, the Metaxas Line covered 155km (96 miles) and consisted of twenty-two strongpoints, the largest being the Roupel Fortress. The defensive line followed along ridgelines approximately 1,000 feet high and contained observations posts for communications and artillery, mortar positions, machine gun nests and rifle positions, all connected by a series of tunnels. It was a formidable position to resist frontal attack. An attacking army first had to attack uphill just to reach the fortified defensive line.

But despite Metaxas's attempt at secret mobilization, his preparations did not go totally unnoticed. The Italian government had made no attempt to gain intelligence on the state of Greek preparedness, but the Foreign Minister to Greece, Emmanuel Grazzi, had his ear to the ground and he sent a disquieting report to The Duce and Ciano.

He told them that the bulk of the 250,000-man Greek Army was mostly deployed on its borders, but more importantly, the Greek population, under Metaxas, had rallied behind him. Grazzi reported that Metaxas seemed to have, "adopted the attitude of defending Greek territorial integrity and neutrality to the limit. Never has Prime Minister Metaxas had such total unanimity behind him."[22]

Mussolini and Ciano dismissed those unpleasant warnings out of hand, perhaps because they so desperately wanted to attack and envisioned Contingency G as a huge success to redeem Italy's tarnished image, and they coveted it, "jealously, as if they feared someone might rob them of it."[23]

That eager anticipation might have been responsible for overlooking the weather. Nowhere is there evidence that anyone in command, during the planning phase, took note that although Greece is mostly dry and sunny, its rainy season begins on the first of November and in Epirus it gets very cold with lots of snow.

Mussolini had preferred to listen to the analysis provided by the Albanian Minister, Francesco Jacomoni, whose observations were more in keeping with those of The Duce's if not outright pandering.

"The Greek population as a whole does not seem inclined to fight," he said. It would be a token resistance to save face with the world and show that they had, "tried to resist the aggression of the authoritarian states." He concluded: "the government is hated by many. The king is neither esteemed nor loved."[24]

But Jacomoni's assessment missed the point. Love and esteem, especially for Metaxas, was not the subject. The defense of Greece was, and, like him or not, the Greek population had rallied to Metaxas's call. Even those who disliked him intensely, including those he had exiled to the far reaches of the Greek islands, returned for the inevitable struggle.

"I loathe the Metaxas regime," said one. "I think the man is a bastard—but by Christ, he's a good soldier."[25]

Among all the flaws of Contingency G, none was worse than the physical size of the army committed to make the invasion. It was now limited to six attacking divisions and one in reserve at the insistence of Lieutenant General Visconti Prasca who would command the whole operation. The senior general and head of the General Staff, Marshal Pietro Badoglio thought the force much too small to tackle the conquest of Greece, and had pushed for twenty divisions and threatened resignation because of the bad plan. But the impatient Mussolini silenced him, and he let Badoglio know through the grapevine that he would gladly accept the general's resignation.

But why would any commanding general turn down twenty divisions for an attack in hostile terrain against an entrenched enemy, especially since the attacking force carried only five days supply of small arms ammunition, fuel was limited, and a protracted campaign would doom the venture? Success was only to be found in a short, decisive campaign. Had not Mussolini made that clear in an October 25 letter? "Attack with the greatest determination and violence. The success of the operation depends above all on speed."[26]

The answer lay in the fact that Prasca was very much like Mussolini in his own addiction to the principal of self-aggrandizement and vainglorious pursuits. Hidden in the rules of the bureaucratic Italian Army was a formula for rising to the top rank of full general. If an officer commanded two corps, six divisions in combat, he was considered to have commanded a full army, and thereby eligible for the lofty rank. If a larger force were to be committed to this operation, it might call for a more senior general and Prasca would be left out, and bypassed.[27]

Thus General Prasca dutifully reported to The Duce that, "The geography of the Epirus is such as to make it difficult for Greek re-enforcements to reach it. This operation, which should lead to the liquidation of all the Greek forces, has been worked out in every detail and is as far as is humanly possible, free of any possible error."[28]

But in reality, it was hardly free from any possible error. The military and political situation was now quite different from the time when Contingency G had first been drafted, and a number of "errors" were brought up at an October 15 high command meeting with Mussolini at the Palazzo Venezia. Everyone who should have been there was: Count Ciano; General Mario Roatta, the military attaché; General Francesco Jacomoni, the Minister to Albania; Lt. Gen. Visconti Prasca, Commanding General; General Ubaldo Soddu, the Vice Minister of War; and Marshal Badoglio, chief of the General Staff.[29]

Mussolini had the bit in his teeth and his eyes set on the total occupation of Greece. He stood to speak first. "This is an action I have meditated on for many months, before our entry into the war, and even before the outbreak of the war itself," he said.[30]

When he finished his proclamation, General Jacomoni was the first to broach the subject of difficulties as he saw them: The Greeks might get aid from Great Britain since they had committed to protect Greece. But the words were hardly out of his mouth when Mussolini interrupted and announced that there would be no aid from Great Britain. Jacomoni bowed in verbal defeat but suggested that they should consider the possibility that if Italy were able to occupy only part of Greece then, would that not leave air bases for the British to occupy and bring them into striking distance of Albania, southern Italy and other Italian targets? The Duce moved onto another subject. Other objections were similarly brushed aside.

General Roatta realized that objections, "would not have served to avert the war Mussolini wanted."[31] The meeting ended.

It was odd that Mussolini had not invited a representative of the navy to the meeting, but that very afternoon a naval officer caught up to Roatta and questioned the logic of the whole operation. He just didn't understand it.

Wasn't speed imperative, and wasn't the army going to try and occupy the whole of Greece with an attack that would advance, "slowly, by land and on foot?" the naval officer asked. Where was the speed? And just as soon as the Italian forces attacked and entered Greece, wouldn't Great Britain react and send forces, "which we are attacking Greece in order to avoid?" And wouldn't Greek bases put the Royal Air Force dangerously close to the fleet at Taranto?[32] It sure didn't make sense to him.

CONTINGENCY G CALLED for six divisions of 75,000 men, supported by a first class air force, to step onto the battleground in the shadow of Mount Pindus to confront 35,000 Greek defenders fighting for their homeland. The Italian divisions would be mostly on foot with the cavalry on horseback, and mules, oxen, and other beasts would haul the wagons and artillery on the few, primitive roads in the area. In addition to an Italian division being two-thirds the size of a normal division, there was another drawback. Each division had only twenty-four vehicles.

Prasca's plan was to emulate the German pincer movements that had rolled over the armies of Europe. His left wing would seize a key pass in the Pindus Mountains to cut off Greek retreat while the right pincer seized the key harbor and town of Prevesa, securing his supply base and denying it to the enemy. The main thrust would attack up the middle to engage and smash the Greek forces dug in on their first line of defense along the Kalamas River and a key bridge around Kalpaki. If, as he expected, the Greek defenders collapsed, then he would decide whether to push on toward Athens without waiting for reinforcements.

While the general met with The Duce in Rome to discuss his grand plan, the beautiful autumn sunlight streamed through the windows of the Palazzo Venezia in contrast to the weather along the Albanian-Greek border, where there was no sunlight. In fact, Major Fatuzzo, the commanding officer of the Aquila Battalion, wrote to his diary his own perception of the weather in his corner of the world.

On October 27, as he sat shivering along the Albanian-Greek border, and wrote, "The war starts tomorrow. The rain is frenetic and incessant. Water gets into the tents; it's hard to sleep."[33]

Not until October 26, when the weather had changed dramatically in the Epirus Region, did anyone seem to have considered the weather. Hours of unrelenting rain sent a deluge of water cascading from the mountains to the valleys below and small creeks and streams soon became roaring torrents of white water. Several Italian generals wanted to postpone the start of the invasion until better conditions, but there was no guarantee of improving weather in those mountains until the rainy season, and winter, was over.

General Visconti Prasca did not need another reason to delay. He was anxious for the start of the invasion and he knew The Duce was straining at the leash so he brushed the generals' objections aside with the nonsensical statement that the weather affected all combatants. The Greeks would also have to endure the elements.

That self-serving proclamation completely ignored reality. The Greek defenders were dug-in, in prepared positions, awaiting the Italian attack. They would not be slipping and sliding and maneuvering along primitive roads and animal tracks trying to negotiate the quagmire of sucking mud. The Greek mortars and artillery had long since been zeroed-in on the obvious axis of the Italian approach, and, because of the terrible weather, any possibility of Italian maneuver was gone, and the approach route would be absolutely confined to the roads.

The Greeks did not have a threatening air force that could be grounded by bad weather. They hardly had an air force at all. But the Italians did, and that air force had an important role to play and was scheduled for extensive use against the dug-in Greek defenders in support of the advancing Italian infantry. Italian supply columns would have to negotiate the very same paths through the mud behind the infantry while the Greek supplies and materiel were already staged or scattered near their defensive positions.

Winter had come to the Pindus Mountains with its winds and rain and snow that pounded the encamped soldiers. There was no winter clothing, and reduced visibility was no friend of the Italian infantry counting on air support.

As if things couldn't get worse, a planned, advanced, clandestine infiltration through the Greek lines by Albanian saboteurs to disrupt communications, create confusion, and incite rebellion, had run amuck. This shadowy operation had been the brainchild of the cocky and boastful Francesco Jacomoni who had predicted that, "in Albania the attack on Greece is awaited keenly and enthusiastically."[34] But it seemed that after Jacomoni had paid the saboteurs' fees, he was left holding the bag as the saboteurs took the money, became shadowy figures and vanished into the winter's gloom without confusing, disrupting or inciting anything.

King Boris III of Bulgaria proved to be no help either. Mussolini had tried to get him to conduct a simultaneous attack on the Metaxas Line to tie up Greek forces in the east, and the king finally answered sending a late-arriving, sealed message for The Duce. It was for his eyes only.

The sealed message was bad news for Mussolini. King Boris had opted out, politely. While not saying outright that he had been influenced by Germany's desire to avoid a conflict in Greece, or that he feared an attack by the Turks, Greece's ally, it was obvious that Boris III wanted to do a little fence sitting. But he was adamant in his appreciation of the weather and the winter. He would confide to Hitler several weeks later that "weather and road conditions in the Greek-Bulgarian border region would not allow the commitment of major forces before the beginning of March."[35]

Boris's note was not long, and it detailed the difficulties Bulgaria was having supplying and equipping its army and bringing it up to a state of readiness, but the key line was that Bulgaria would, "refrain from armed action." The Duce called him, "gutless."[36]

On October 26, less than forty-eight hours before invasion, the Italian air force precipitated yet another provoking incident, to what end is only a guess.[37] While flying over Greek territory, Italian planes dropped three bombs, indiscriminately, sixty miles to the southeast of Athens. The government quickly censored all reports of the incident in the interest of neutrality, and Metaxas sought to calm his advisors by explaining that this was most likely a forerunner to some Italian political demand.

He could not see this as a prelude to war. Metaxas's military mind concluded that only a fool would attack with the onset of winter in the Pindus region and with the limited troops that Greek intelligence had detected on the border. In fact, he thought that the chances of invasion now were more remote than when the weather had been favorable.

That same evening marked the kickoff of the Greek theatrical season in Athens. The inaugural opera at The National Theatre of Greece was Puccini's *Madam Butterfly*. Puccini's son was to be there and it was fitting that the Italian Embassy should host a party to reciprocate and proclaim the friendship between Greece and Italy. All the high-ranking government and social figures would attend and embassy staff had spent long hours preparing for the gala event and had decorated the reception hall in the finest traditions of diplomatic protocols. Each table's centerpiece had flowers and flags of the two nations prominently displayed, and the chefs had prepared a spectacular cake with decorative icing and the words: "Long Live Greece." Metaxas had certainly been right. This was no time for war.

But after the opera, and as the gala progressed into the night, the reception room was not calm and cordial with the sound of clinking glasses, laughter, and the hum of casual conversation.

People seemed to come and go with nervous regularity and there was a lot of whispering, eager ears and nervous expressions. No one got around to cutting the cake.[38]

The Teletype machines in the message center had caused this nervousness when they sprang to life as the guests continued to gather for the reception. They clicked and clacked noisily, spitting out long ribbons of punched yellow paper, and their keys flicked up and down printing out a long, cyphered text from Rome. The text was simply line after line of groups of five-digit numbers, and secretaries began to feverishly work to decypher and decode the gibberish into readable Italian. Finally, at 0500, they presented Ambassador Grazzi with the twelve-paragraph document.

It began with a nonsensical accusation that Greece had not followed a "good neighbor" policy that was incumbent upon it as a declared neutral and had allowed Great Britain to use its territorial waters and its ports to be used by the British fleet. It also accused Greece of provoking incidents against Albania, particularly terrorism against the people of Ciamuria. It claimed that Greek neutrality had been, "tending continuously toward a mere shadow."

"It is obvious," the message read, "that the Greek Government has been transforming Greek territory ... into a base for war operations against Italy ... which the Italian Government has every intention of avoiding."

Grazzi read on through Count Ciano's concocted, wordy note that "allows no way out for Greece."

"The Italian Government, has reached the decision to ask the Greek Government as a guarantee of Greek neutrality, and a guarantee of Italian security, permission to occupy with her armed forces, several strategic points in Greece for the duration of the present conflict with Great Britain. The Italian Government asks the Greek Government not oppose this occupation and not to obstruct the free passage of the troops carrying it out."

Then came the threat: "Wherever the Italian troops may meet resistance, this resistance will be broken by armed force, and the Greek Government would have the responsibility for the resulting consequence.[39]

Ambassador Grazzi stuffed it into his case and left the now empty reception hall. He had twenty-three hours before his meeting with Ioannis Metaxas.

At 0230, Grazzi's military attaché pulled the limousine in front of the waiting ambassador for the fifteen-minute drive to the Greek leader's upscale villa. The guard recognized the visitors and rang the bell at the front gate twice to summon him, but there was no answer. After ten minutes, and a phone call to the residence, a light flicked on and Metaxas himself opened the door clad in a dressing gown, recognized Ambassador Grazzi, and invited him in.[40]

The two men moved to a small room on the ground floor and Grazzi, using the French diplomatic language, told Metaxas that the Italian government had ordered him to present him with this message. He extended the note to the Greek leader who read it slowly, shaking his head as he read.

His first question was what were the "strategic positions" to be seized? Grazzi looked sheepishly and admitted that he did not know but informed Metaxas that Italian troops were massed on the Albanian border, and, unless he made an immediate decision, would attack at 0600. To that, Metaxas replied that he was ready to discuss the whole matter, but Grazzi informed him that there was no time for discussion; he needed an immediate answer.[41]

"I could not set my own house in order—much less surrender my country—in three hours," Metaxas bluntly told the Italian Minister. "The answer is no."[42]

Grazzi was astonished by the answer and since he personally liked the Greek leader, he told him that he would not report that the ultimatum had been rejected but would wait until the 0600 deadline.

The military attaché drove Grazzi back to the Italian legation where he waited by the telephone for the call he hoped would come, but the phone remained silent.[43]

Ioannis Metaxas wrote in his diary: "I shall place the problem of Greek dignity over and above everything else. I shall not bow my head to the Italians."[44]

He then was on the phone, talking to the king, issuing orders for contingency plans that had long been in place, talking to the British ambassador, and calling his cabinet to an immediate meeting.

At 0600 Athens awoke to the wail of sirens and the incessant ringing of church bells. First a few citizens and then a massive crowd poured into the streets shouting, War! War![45] They were not living up to the Italian expectations of Greek lethargy with no stomach for confrontation. The assessment presented to Mussolini on Greek spirit by his advisors on October 15 was completely wrong.

Jacomoni had called the Greek population, "profoundly depressed." Ciano had said that there was a sharp divide between the "plutocratic" ruling class and the common people. Those on the low rung of Greek existence were "indifferent to all events, including ... our invasion."[46]

These cheering and singing Greeks were none of the sort. They were aroused and raced through the streets embracing friends and strangers alike.

The shops did not open that day, and the crowd grew larger. The people began to raise their thumbs in unity, and then the chant broke out: "We will throw them into the sea," and "we will eat them alive."

The insults followed as the Greek citizens reflected upon Italy's dismal military record. They reflected on the Italian provocations, and their own pent-up emotions, and the terrible sinking of *Elli*, and they laughed at the thought of the "macaroni eaters" as fierce soldiers.[47]

Far to the northwest, along the Albanian border, in the rain and snow, Prasca's army crossed the border into Greece. Contingency G began.

CHAPTER 3

INVASION

THE JUBILATION IN ATHENS knew no bounds. Metaxas declared a general mobilization and the Larisis train station was a hub of activity. It seemed that everyone had gathered there, including soldiers already boarding for the trip to the Albanian front.

Chrysoula Korotzi was one young girl who had heard the sounds of the sirens wailing across Athens that Monday morning while she and her brother jumped around their bedroom engaged in pillow fight.

"Everyone was really happy, it was like a fair. Everyone went down to Larisis Station, and they were singing ... and they were driving down in cars, too."

There was a popular Greek female vocalist named Sophie Vembo and she would later be dubbed "the victory singer," but in the enthusiasm of the times, the Greek population quickly modified the words to her songs to fit their patriotic spirit.

"It was Vembo that sang all those songs," said Korotzi. "Her first song had been written for another reason, but they wrote new lyrics about the war:

'With a smile on their lips our boys go to war,
And the Italians run as they give them what for!'

"They had the songs like:

'Mussolini, you old fart, we're gonna tear you all apart.
Your Italians are so tough,
But it's obviously just a bluff,
We're gonna push you all the way back to Rome.'

"No one was left out of this war. The nation was as one, and it was the enthusiasm our soldiers—those brave lads—left with."[1]

Vasilis Rosas worked with the navy at the Salamina Yard. At the sound of the sirens he too prepared to leave his house for the dock.

"The calmness displayed by the Greek people at that time was phenomenal." Rosas said. "I packed a few woolen vests into a little case and set off for work, indifferent to whether we would be bombarded or not.

"On the way to the navy yard I came across something no one could have expected: there were sailors dancing, and singing through megaphones at the top of their voices on the warship *Averof*, which was lying on its side in a dry dock. This wasn't war. It was a fair!

"We were attacked for the first time by Italian warplanes, which dropped their bombs, but hit absolutely nothing. All they managed to do was to kill thousands of fish, and even before the aeroplanes had withdrawn, everyone set out in whatever boats we had to grab the fish which had come to the surface in the foam."[2]

This first day of war had Greek radios playing the national anthem, nonstop, and, when the time came, all of Athens stopped to listen to the official statement from the government. It was short.

"Italy has declared war. The Italian Ambassador having awakened the Prime Minister at 3:00 a.m. this morning, delivered an infamous ultimatum. The Prime Minister rejected it. Hostilities began at 5:30 a.m. The frontier troops are defending our freedom."[3]

That was all, and the carnival atmosphere continued with a new fervor. Citizens demonstrated with Greek and British flags adding color to the throngs of humanity, and some even waved American flags. The people were chanting "OXI, OXI,"[4] and reacting to the general mobilization notices to sign up in the army.

When Italian planes appeared overhead, no one thought of retreating to shelters; the aroused citizens shook their fists to the sky and chanted even louder, "Mussolini you old fart, we're going to tear you all apart."

Tragically the first casualties of this new war would actually come from an aerial attack when an Italian mission bombed the port of Patras, one hundred miles west of Athens. The bombing run killed over a hundred Greeks who conceivably had not yet heard the news of war.[5]

Ptolemaios Kaliafas was a 19-year-old medical student in his second year when war was declared. He wasn't even a Greek citizen but was terribly moved by the outpouring of Greek patriotism and enthusiasm. The wail of the sirens did not frighten or depress him.

"It was the morning of October 28 and we were waiting to go into our anatomy lecture when the sirens started," he said. "We figured out what was going on right away and started shouting that it was war."

Kaliafas and his fellow medical students got into an excited conversation that Greece would stand up to the Axis and defeat them.

"Germany and Italy were superpowers back then," he said. "There wasn't a single European army to stand up to them. The English and the French had been swept aside in fifteen days! And yet when the Italians declared war on us, we rose up and took to the streets.

"Where did this confidence come from? Find me a single person who didn't believe that we'd beat the Italians. In fact, we felt relief that we could get back for the bombing of the [cruiser] *Elli*."[6]

The *Elli* incident stuck in the craw of all Greek citizens. The attack had been a shameful episode of bullying at its worst: Italy was a superpower, with its bloated little leader, picking on a country one-sixth its size in a sneak attack on a holy day. It had been an international outrage, and a just cause for war against the Italians. But it had been swept aside and under the rug by the Metaxas government in the name of neutrality. Now that repressed outrage found release in the streets of Athens. Many Greeks relished the opportunity to shout that it was about time, and they weren't going to take it anymore—that they should have been at war with Italy since August 15.

"The only question," asked Kaliafas, as he took to the streets with his student friends, "was when exactly we were going to drive the Italians into the sea?

"I volunteered on the very first day of the war. And since I was a mountaineer, and a member of the mountaineering club, I was put into the Alpine Regiment. There were no specialist alpine troops or special alpine units, but they gave us a bit of training and the First Company of the First Battalion was formed."[7]

Elftherios Sklavos did not have to enlist. In fact, his enlistment was up. He had been called up for military service in 1938 for a two-year hitch, and his final day was Thursday October 24. He was looking forward to a new civilian career.

"The captain said to me, 'Sklavos, come in on Monday to get your discharge papers. Hand over whatever you have—your weapons, your sword, your helmet—whatever—but you can stay in uniform.'"

But on Monday, Sklavos too heard all the bells ringing and the sirens wailing and the people shouting, 'War,' as he set about to get his discharge.

"I jumped out of bed and got over to the captain at regimental headquarters, and he said, 'You're here. You took your time. What took you so long?'"

Sklavos explained that he had come as soon as he could and the captain looked at him warily and asked him the obvious question, "So, you've come for your discharge papers?"

The young soldier nodded that he had and added, "That's what you told me to do, isn't it?"

"Well," answered the captain, "this is no time for discharges, there's a war on!"

So the bewildered Sklavos discussed with the captain the next step. Sklavos filled two trucks with weapons and equipment to outfit the reservists being activated, and delivered them to the embarkation point. He then ran a personal errand for the captain before returning for further orders, but when he arrived back at regimental headquarters, his captain and his outfit were gone. In their place were new reservists, unpacking and moving into the barracks.

"They're on their way to Piraeus to get on the boat," said the new colonel, and with that Sklavos took off in hot pursuit.

"I set off for Piraeus," Sklavos said, "and just as I got into the harbor I saw the boat, and it was leaving, and I shouted. 'Captain! Captain! It's Sklavos'... and a boatman said, 'What are you shouting about?' And I said 'That's my regiment. Do me a favor and take me over.' 'Go home, you idiot', said the boatman, 'That lot is going to war.'"

So Elftherios Sklavos returned to the barracks and his new colonel kept him as a messenger since he possessed a rare bicycle. After twenty days the predictable happened.

"I'd go here and there for him, I was really useful," the young soldier said. "And the colonel called for me one day, 'Come over here, Sklavos. Did you know you were a deserter?' "Then they put me in the guardhouse."[8]

In Athens, Premier Metaxas received a flood of telegrams from the leaders of the free world. The first came from King George VI of England: "Italy has found her threats useless against your calm courage," he said. Prime Minister Mackenzie King of Canada added: "The cradle of the noblest civilization that mankind has known, when the country to which we owe whatever is fine and beautiful in life is being attacked, the place of all true men is at its side." Turkey chipped in with: "Long live Greece," and India was prophetic: "The future of the Balkans depends on the fate of Greece."[9]

IOANNIS METAXAS CALLED a meeting of the owners and publishers of the Athens newspapers. Despite the power of government censorship, he wanted to explain his reasons for entering war against Italy and wanted their support.

"I need not only your pens, I need you hearts," he began. "I want you to know all about our national encounter." He told them that in 1936 he had been determined to oppose German and Italian aggression should that happen, and to make sure that Greece would be on the side of the Allies of WWI.

"Do not ever think the decision to say 'NO' to the Italian ultimatum was taken on the spur of the moment. Do not ever imagine we entered the war unexpectedly, or we did not spare every possible effort to avoid it,"[10] Metaxas continued. He reminded them of the events of April when the Italian Army occupied Albania. He had remained calm and avoided military conflict when most countries would have reacted, and refused to be provoked into Italian schemes. In August the sneak attack and sinking of *Elli*, could have driven Greece over the brink, but even that outrage did not trump his efforts to remain neutral.

"From the first moment that the crime was committed by Italy, we did not permit to be made known that we possessed material evidence about the nationality of the offender."[11] All this in the name of sparing Greece the horror of war.

He revealed that advisors to Adolph Hitler had encouraged him to avoid any action that Mussolini might label provocation. Hitler had warmly invited Metaxas to join the "New Order," and Greece would be handsomely rewarded economically. Of course there would be a small "price to pay." When Metaxas asked what that small price might be, he was told that he must cede certain Greek territory to Italy and Bulgaria.

"In order to avoid War," Metaxas explained, "we had to willingly become slaves and to pay the price, by giving Greece's right and left arms to be amputated respectively by Bulgaria and Italy ... It would have condemned Greece to a willful enslavement, together with an amputation of national lands."[12]

He asked the newsmen to not lose courage, and to support the policy against the attackers. He wanted them to first convince themselves on the importance of this national mission and then be the national voice to keep the flame of patriotism alive in the population.

"Greece is firmly decided to defend her territories," he somberly told the newsmen, "even if she has to fall."[13]

ONE HUNDRED AND FIFTY-FIVE miles to the northeast, along the Albanian border and facing the Italian Army division massed west of the Pindus Mountains, was the town of Florina. Six-year-old Konstantin Georgountzos had left home early that morning of October 28 and walked to his grammar school where he had started the first grade the previous month.

"As we entered the class the teacher informed us that our country was at war with Italy and the school is closed and we should return to our homes." The young boy returned home and informed his mother of the situation.

"My mother with her four children, me being the oldest, planned to leave the place and started packing. My father had a rather high position on the local town hierarchy. I remember he was often seated next to the general who commanded the local garrison of that section of the border and to the governor of West Macedonia. My father had to stay where he was posted and help with the war effort of the country."[14]

Florina, unlike Epirus west of the Pindus Mountains, had a tiny rail line that connected to the main line to Athens. His father, who could accompany them to the main line, helped the young Konstantin, his mother and three siblings aboard for the two-hour ride.

Konstantin vividly recalled the panic and the terrible train ride. "Delays, stops, reports of hostile airplanes bombing cities and railroad lines were frequent," he said, "and the few hours trip to the junction was unending."

It was night when they finally arrived and the station was a madhouse.

"A child was lost there and could not be located in the dark without lights, and in the night with so many people traveling, the trains full of soldiers going to the border area and others returning, and mostly families with their children. After hours of waiting, a train finally arrived, and my father left, and it took us for the rest of the journey to Athens."[15]

At the other end of Greece, in eastern Macedonia, in the city of Drama, another young boy, nine-year-old Dimitri Tsaras also reported to school on October 28. Drama was only twenty miles from the Bulgarian border to the north, and the Tsaras family was not new to war. Dimitri's father had been an officer in the Greek Army in 1912 during the Balkan War. He was captured by the Bulgarians, endured a horrible imprisonment, inhumane treatment and torture, and was one of just a few who returned from that captivity alive.[16]

As early as 1935 there had been war in young Dimitri's life. It was at the time that Greece was being torn apart by internal strife leading up to the takeover of the Metaxas Regime and he was only four years old.

"It was during that period of time that planes came and bombed Drama," said Tsaras. "My father was in hiding and my uncle grabbed me and took me to the basement under the house. Hearing the bombs falling, I was screaming and I wanted my father."

Five years later, there was again war.

"When we went to school on the twenty-eighth of October, we lined up as we used to and they announced that all classes were cancelled because we were attacked by Italy, so there would be no school. Of course, we celebrated."

When he returned his father called a family meeting of his mother and three children of whom Dimitri was the youngest.

"He said he didn't think Italy would be much of a problem, but there was no way that Germany would not help Italy, and in doing so he felt that the Bulgarians were going to come in.

"His first priority for us was to move out and leave our home." They would move south to the town of Stilida, just east of the great rail center of Lamia.

"The plan was to move there where we would be away from the Bulgarians. My father wanted nothing to do with them," said Tsaras. "We packed as many things as we could carry, and went by train, and at Thessaloniki we had the first exposure to an air alarm. People came from the station and opened the doors and asked us to follow them to shelters."

When the alarm was over, the train proceeded south to Larissa.

"Larissa was a major railroad intersection similar to Chicago in terms of railroads," said Tsaras. "Any trains going to the front in western Greece had to go through Larissa. We were put on a side line and informed that we would be there for several hours because of troop movements.

"Sometime after midnight the sirens sounded. The railroad people opened the doors and said, 'you better get out. There's a plane coming. Go!' but nobody told us where to go."

His father told them they needed to get away from the station since it was such a good military target and there was a full moon which would help the bombers, so they ran into a field.

"We walked and walked in mud up to our knees," said Tsaras, "and we got down on the ground and the bombs fell, and my brother and I were counting how many. My father called to us and said 'if we go, we'll all go together.'"

But the bombs did not hit the station.

"The Italians were not well known for their accuracy, and they missed the railroad station. They missed the military airport but hit the hospital. Where we were laying on the ground, we had come across barbed wire, and when we looked up, on the other side of the barbed wire was the military airport."[17]

The Tsaras family continued on to their destination. All around them was frantic activity as the country girded for war.

"There was a spirit of unity," said Tsaras. "It was like a dream especially for a nine-year-old. This is when I started becoming aware and started to realize what was happening and what could happen. There was great interest in listening to the news."[18]

THE VIII DIVISION of the Epirus Army was under the command of General Haralambos Katsimitros. Dug-in at Epirus, west of the Pindus Mountains and west of the town of Florina, it was prepared to defend against the expected Italian attack.[19] On October 30, Katsimitros issued his General Order Nr 30904 to his division to be promulgated to all officers and enlisted:

"We fight against a cunning and coward enemy, who suddenly attacked us without a pretext in order to subjugate us. We fight for our houses, our families and our freedom.

"Officers and enlisted men, keep your positions steadily and decisively looking forward, since in a short time we are going to counter-attack in order to throw out the enemy from our native soil that gets infected by their presence.

The day that the coward foe will be thrown to the sea reaches. Keep strongly your positions and this is going to take place soon."[20]

The Italian battle plan called for a three-pronged attack. On the extreme right, 5,000 men with thirty-two guns in the Littoral Group would push southward, seize the vital port of Prevesa, and then wheel to the left to attack Arta and expose the flank of the city of Ioannina, the capitol city of the Epirus Region. In the center, the entire Ciamuria Corps, with 25,000 men, sixty-six guns, and ninety light tanks would advance on Kalpaki en route to seize Ioannina. On the extreme left, in the shadow of the Pindus Mountains, the Julia Alpini Division, with 11,000 men and twenty guns, would drive for the key mountain pass at Metsovo[21] (Map p. 67). This three-pronged attack was to be the knockout blow to the Greek Army in the Epirus Region. The Italian Army would have captured the capital, seized the key passes through the mountains, and laid open the road to Thessaly, Athens and victory.

On October 28, at 0500, the outposts of the Greek VIII Division made contact with the vanguard of the Italian Ciamuria Corps, advancing on the center axis. It was a full hour before the expiration of the ultimatum handed to Prime Minister Metaxas by the Italian minister. Five columns advanced against Katsimitros's line west of the Pindus Mountains in the driving rain. Italian artillery boomed across the mountain range in the Western Macedonian area, but not in support of these advancing columns. The bad weather had also denied close air support to the infantry, and the Italian planes went on to bomb other targets and the ports at Salamis, Skaramangas, Piraeus and Patras.[22]

The screening elements of the Greek VIII Division skillfully engaged the advancing Italian columns with an elastic defense, forcing the Italian vanguard to deploy into a battle formation. As soon as that force had deployed, the Greek soldiers gradually disengaged and fell back to new defensive lines, to occupy new prepared positions, and, as the rain fell, peered over their rifle sights to again await the arrival of the Italian columns.

The defending Greeks knew the countryside like the backs of their hands. They also knew each other, having been recruited from the same areas, and for the past nineteen months, since 1939, had guarded the Albanian border to defend against just such an attack.[23]

Meanwhile the Italian soldiers, having probed to their front and found the enemy had vanished, reformed to continue their advance. But they moved only a short distance along the sloppy road before Greek sniper fire dropped the first few men at the next turn. Again the Italians deployed and again the Greek defenders disappeared in the rain. The Greek outposts perfectly executed this tactic to delay—exactly what an outpost was supposed to do.

The Italian offensive doctrine called for the attack to be "recklessly pursued." The theory was that any obstacles and resistance could be overcome by utilizing initiative, audacity and personal courage to get the attack moving again. That boldness and audacity was called *élan*, and the French had appealed to the élan of their soldiers, a generation earlier, to overcome all obstacles in WWI. That élan led the French forces to launch frontal assaults of flesh and bone against German quick-fire machine guns. The folly of that tactic was visible on the killing field between the trenches strewn with corpses and shattered bodies.

In 1940, Italian tactics had changed little. The Greek forces would quickly learn that the Italian attacks were indeed ferocious, and the Italian soldier was indeed filled with élan, but they also learned that the fury of those attacks was short-lived. When Italian small-unit leadership failed, the attack usually ran out of gas in a half hour. If the defenders could absorb the ferocity of the attack for that time, they had a good chance to prevail.

At the company level (130 men) the Italian maneuver force consisted of three platoons with two squads, each squad with twenty men and a light machine gun. The lead platoon advanced in the attack in two columns with the machine guns at the point. When the Greeks opened fire, the machine gunners immediately returned suppressing fires while the two maneuver columns deployed left and right to envelop the flanks.

But the envelopment was never a wide encircling maneuver. Instead it sought to find the enemy's flanks on a narrow front, usually within fifty yards, and this was a deadly flaw. If the Greek defensive line extended past fifty yards, the entire defensive force could easily engage the platoon's attack without worrying about its flanks. Against quick-fire machine guns and mortars this maneuver was futile.

Italian General Claudio Trezzani spoke of his small unit leaders, and their élan as opposed to their leadership.

"As long as it's a question of risking one's skin, they are admirable," he said. "When, instead, they have to open their eyes, think, decide in cold blood, they are hopeless. In terms of reconnaissance, movement to contact, preparatory fire, coordinated movement, and so on, they are practically illiterate."[24]

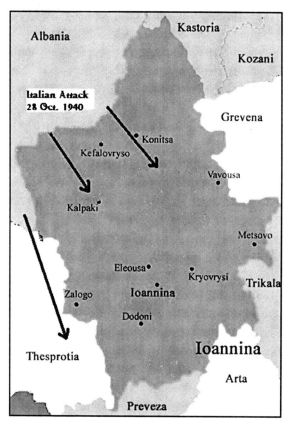

So the Italian Army was virtually limited to the frontal assault, and the frontal assault called for overwhelming numbers against the defenders; and in the mountains of Greece, the Italians could hardly maneuver much less bring overwhelming numbers against the defenders. In the Epirus attack, the Italians fielded twenty-two infantry battalions against fifteen Greek infantry battalions, and even though the Italians possessed an overwhelming superiority in artillery[25] and air, they just didn't have enough boots on the ground, and the boots that were on the ground were not skilled in providing or coordinating those supporting arms. Whatever advantage Italy's ninety small tanks might have provided in that mountainous terrain was lost when the torrential rains converted the roads into a track-deep, sucking quagmire.

But all these weaknesses in the Italian Army should not have mattered. The three-pronged attack should have been in name only. The Italians never expected Metaxas to say "OXI." The advance of the columns to Athens should have been more of a parade without confronting defending Greeks. Lt. Quarantino Marco expected his advance to be just that—a ride through the countryside.

"We had no idea war was coming," he said. On the dawn of October 28, we were packed into a sector opposite Florina. Our colonel assured us ... that Metaxas had told Ciano that the Italian army had received permission to cross Greece and Yugoslavia. He said that Greece and Yugoslavia had joined the Axis and that Greece would never oppose our might."[26]

The Greeks had skillfully built their defensive fortifications all along the obvious routes of the Italian approach, and had occupied those positions in the Epirus sector with a simple but effective plan of action. The government had mobilized the Epirus population and set them to the task of defending the region. They made maximum use of the natural obstacles of rivers, streams, and mountains, especially in the areas where the roads elevated toward mountain passes.

One such area was at the village of Kalpaki where a narrow pass split the massive Pindus Mountains. General Katsimitros knew that pass would be critical to the Italian plan, and predicted Kalpaki to be the first objective of the attacking Italians on their march to seize the Capital of Epirus at Ioannina.

To attack Ioannina the Italians would have to capture the pass first, and because it was uphill and narrow, the pass was a perfect spot to defend. The Ciamuria Corps was poised to bring two divisions with artillery and air support against the Kalpaki defenders whose numbers were only a third. But because of the weather and the pesky, collapsing outposts, it had taken the corps twenty-four hours to cover the fifteen miles from the border to their attack position in front of Kalpaki.

On the other fronts, the Italians advanced with little opposition. On their right flank, the only adversary confronting the Littoral Group was the torrential rain that whipped into the soldiers faces masking even their view of the Adriatic Sea. The weather had cancelled a proposed operation to capture the island of Corfu just off the coast, so the group pressed on to the south and then turned to the east and managed to secure a small bridgehead over the Kalamas River even though the Greeks had destroyed the bridges.

Once across the river, the Littoral Group would be in a position to severely threaten Ioannina and Katsimitros's headquarters. But the Kalamas and its streams continued to rise and became raging, white-water torrents that swept away everything in its path. The advance ground to a halt[27] after almost thirty-seven miles.

Kalamas River before the storm

ON THE ITALIAN LEFT flank the 11,000-man Julia Division with its twenty guns attacked across the Albanian border and moved to penetrate into the Pindus Mountains and envelop the Greek right flank. Facing this powerful division was the small, 2,000-man Greek Pindus Detachment under the command of Colonel Konstantinos Davakis who was responsible for that forbidding mountain area between Epirus and Macedonia. His small unit leaders were eager, but lacked rank and experience. Four of his eight companies were led by second lieutenants and inexperienced reserve captains, and less than ten percent of his non-commissioned officers were regulars. The Pindus Detachment also lacked arms, clothing and ammunition but still launched an initial counterattack against the invading Italians. It failed and they were unable to halt its advance, but they began the tactic of giving ground grudgingly.[28]

Julia Division fanned out on a broad, twelve-mile front and pushed five powerful columns and several smaller ones into the steep mountains.[29] The area had no roads, only animal paths and tracks, and the main attack came in the center of the thinly spread Greek line. After the first day, the Pindus Detachment had fallen back but was holding. Davakis began to receive reinforcements that had arrived onto the battlefield and fed them into the most needed areas. He also sent out an urgent order to collect any type of apparatus that could be used as transportation from all of the Pindus villages and to assemble these devices and animals in one central village. From there ammunition and other supplies could be moved to his defending forces. Elderly men, women, and children ignored the constant rain, snow and freezing cold to assist the army as porters, drivers and handlers.[30]

The Italians continued their attack on October 29 and 30, and gradually dislodged the stubborn defenders after fierce fighting in the most hostile of weather conditions. In some areas the withdrawal was not orderly and panicked soldiers fled to the rear. The right of the Greek line had held, but the Italians had broken in the center and Julia Division pushed on for a deeper penetration hoping to eventually wheel to the right to begin its approach to its outflanked objective, Metsovo.

But the Italians had also made a serious tactical error in

their successful advance. The error didn't look serious at the time. General Mario Girotti, Julia Division's commander, had counted on the imposing 8,000-foot peaks of the Pindus to be his effective flank security against Greek forces to the west as he advanced toward Metsovo. He had not been alone in that thinking. No less than the Chief of the Italian General Staff, Marshal Pietro Badoglio, had called the imposing range an "insuperable mountain barrier"[31] that covered the Italian left. For whatever reason, Girotti chose to not occupy or outpost key peaks as he pushed forward. Who could blame him? One look at those terrible mountain peaks of the Pindus was enough to confirm them as a formidable obstacle.

But the rugged mountain peaks of the Alps had also been formidable obstacles in 219 B. C. during the Second Punic War. Certainly Hannibal and his fifty-thousand Carthaginians and forty elephants could not cross. Generals Girotti and Badoglio would have agreed with the commanding Roman general at the time that the Carthaginian Army could just not do that.

Julia's threatening advance had not gone unnoticed by the Greek high command. General Alexander Papagos, the Greek supreme commander, frantically stripped forces from the Macedonian Front and poured them across the mountain into the Pindus battlefield. He also ordered Greek forces from everywhere in the country to begin marching toward the battlefield.[32]

Greek Army with band and artillery

But ordering soldiers to Epirus and actually getting them there were two different things. The distances to the extreme northwestern region of the country were enormous and the terrain rugged, if not impossible. Greece's mountains ran on a north-south axis and the existing poor roads generally followed the valleys along that same axis. There were no railroads to the battle area. That meant the Greek soldiers, from their remote locations, responding to the order to move to Epirus, were mostly on foot, carrying heavy packs, and crossing mountain belts. Their faithful companions along these primitive tracks were long lines of horses and mules loaded with heavier arms and materiel.

An American war correspondent also moving toward the front, passed these curious columns of Greek soldiers and their animals making the grueling trek. "They were swinging northward ... and had been traveling like this for several days," he said. "The soldiers shouted and waved at us. They were bright-eyed, wiry built men. They looked strong, even if most of their uniforms were rumpled and messy and seemed about two sizes too big ... 'Poor devils,' we said. 'What chance have they got against the Italian Army? Maybe the Fascists' mechanized divisions are a third of the way to Athens already.' But these little Greeks ... didn't seem at all worried."[33]

Greek column

But the Fascists' mechanized divisions were not a third of the way to Athens as the reporter feared. In fact they were hardly across the Albanian border, and were, in fact, bogged down in Epirus.

On the right, the swollen Kalamas River and a defending Greek line had stopped the attack of the Littoral Corps. In the center, the Ciamuria Corps, with its mechanized force, was stalled in front of the town of Kalpaki, unable to advance because of a belt of fiercely held defensive positions, pulverizing Greek artillery and impossible roads. The Greek artillery was particularly devastating. Most of the guns were first-class French pieces as opposed to the Italian artillery that consisted of refurbished, Austrian cannons from WWI. The Greeks easily outgunned the Italian horse-drawn and mule-packed artillery. They were far superior to the guns of the light tanks of the Centauro Division in both range and caliber.[34] Furthermore, the Greek gunners had pre-registered their artillery concentrations on the very ground that the Italians now sought to occupy.

To make matters worse for the Italians, the Greek IX Division in Western Macedonia, across the Pindus, had advanced their battle line toward Albania in a threatening move to freeze Italian reserves that might otherwise be sent to assist in Epirus. The marching reserves from the far reaches of Greece began to arrive on the battlefield in a steady stream. They were immediately deployed to Epirus to confront the bold advance of Julia Division on its trek toward Metsovo.[35]

On the left, the Italians had been successful and had quickened their pace, and were on a mad dash for Metsovo and the key pass through the mountains. Once in control of that town and the pass, they would have effectively cut off the escape routes to the east and would have bagged the Greek Army in Epirus.[36]

On November 3, the division occupied the town of Vavousa, twenty miles south of the Albanian border,[37] where they anchored their communications and supply center. Having swept aside all resistance, the Italians were now prepared to attack toward Metsovo, the linchpin of the whole offensive. Metsovo's fall would be catastrophic.

The Italians would possess the vital pass leading to Athens.

They would have driven a huge salient, or bulge, into the Greek defensive line effectively outflanking the forces at Ioannina, and the VIII Division on the Epirus Front would be cut off from the adjacent forces of the IX Division in Western Macedonia. The Epirus Front would be encircled and would collapse and the entire Greek defensive line would be doomed.

The outnumbered Pindus Detachment had not been able to stop Julia. It had fought heroically during those first days of attack and had absorbed the full weight of the division's onslaught. They had been outnumbered five to one, and could only slow the Italian advance. They had been driven back six miles in the terrible rain, snow, and freezing cold, and Julia Division still rolled on. They were on the verge of collapse when the Greek I Division arrived in the battle area.

The I Division assumed control and absorbed the exhausted Pindus warriors into its numbers and immediately set about to reestablish the battle line. On November 1, the division attacked the exposed left flank of the extended Italian Army that had failed to secure the rugged peaks. First Lt. Alexandros Diakos led his company in one of the attacks and was killed in the desperate struggle. He became the first of many Greek officers to die defending the homeland.[38] On the next day, the heroic leader of the gallant Pindus Detachment, Colonel Konstantinos Davakis fell, gravely wounded, and was evacuated.

The Greek High Command rushed cavalry and artillery to block the passes leading out of the Pindus Mountains toward Metsovo, hoping to contain the onslaught, but Julia Division continued undaunted in its headlong rush, still not heeding its flanks and either ignoring, or unaware of the I Division and it counterattack on its flank and rear. As the Italians were consolidating their occupation of Vavousa, they had actually been cut off from the trailing section of their army.[39]

Newly arrived Greek cavalry and 155mm artillery sealed the passes coming from the mountains toward Metsovo. The surrounded Italians began to attack in all directions seeking to break out. An Italian regiment rushed to the front to secure a pass for the entrapped division to escape to the rear and back into Albania. On the nights of November 6 and 7, Julia Division was in full retreat. The retreating columns were pounded from the high ground and attacked by cavalry from the rear.[40]

The forces stripped from the Macedonian sector struggled to cross the giant mountain range to reinforce the units confronting Julia. The roads were bad and covered with snow, the animals broke down, and some units lost their way. On the night of November 10-11, an elite Greek Evzone Mountain Regiment also made a forced march to cross the mountains, and they were met and assisted by the civilians in the mountains, especially the women.

The Women of Pindus shouldered great loads, dragging and hauling ammunition, guns, materiel, and supplies up the steep slopes and rocks of the forbidding mountain. When animals broke down, they stripped the loads from the dead or exhausted beasts and carried them on their own backs or in teams. They knew the mountains well and guided the Greek forces along the best routes. Many took up shovels to keep the tracks and roads open from the falling snow. They disassembled weapons into smaller pieces to be able to transport them, and, with the Greek forces, hauled the Army's equipment to the crest and over to the other side.[41]

Women of Pindus

"Red faced Greeks marched toward the invaders with fixed bayonets," a combat journalist described. "Near them trudged their women, erect, with food and even ammunition balanced on their heads; and their mules, diamond-hitched with heavy loads."[42]

By November 13, the Greek Army had occupied the main crossings from Albania along the entire Pindus section. The mountain area had been completely recaptured thereby securing the fragile link between Epirus and western Macedonia.

The price that General Girotti had paid for his mistake of not securing his flanks was the barrage of deadly machine gun fire and exploding mortar projectiles that rained down on him from above. The Italians had no answer to threaten the Greeks on the high ground. The infantry then swept down and broke the Italian line. The Julia Division virtually disintegrated. Bombarded from every height, their lines had first cracked and then broke, and they retreated, abandoning weapons and materiel.[43]

The Greek Army in the Pindus had suffered heavy casualties, but they had inflicted great losses on the Julia Division. The division had been shattered with five hundred casualties and 1,200 prisoners. The loss of arms and equipment was enormous.

The staggering defeat of the Julia Division in the rugged Greek mountains caught the eye of the news reporters around the world.

"Today we read about the Greek women," wrote the St. Louis Post-Dispatch, "their faces wrapped in shawls, clearing the mountain passes with big snow shovels, so the Greek infantry can pursue the Italians. Again, when every man was needed for fighting, Greek women have brought supplies and ammunition up the mountain sides—80-pound packs on their backs up 3,000-foot peaks.[44]

When the Evzones had crossed the Pindus and reached Epirus, they occupied some of the high ground that Girotti unwittingly bypassed.

The Greeks had "fought with elemental fierceness. The lair was threatened. They captured heights by making draft animals out of themselves. Even the women dragged cannon behind them. There was no thought ... for personal safety."[45]

In their victory, the Greek Army also learned an old military axiom and would embrace it anew as their tactic against the Italian invaders. This axiom was the oldest of military principles: Seize the high ground.

AT 0900 ON NOVEMBER 2, the Italian air forces launched a massive aerial campaign against the Greek forces entrenched at Kalpaki in the center of the invasion area. The previous day, 169 Italian warplanes had bombed targets at Metsovo and Piraeus, and the naval base at Salamis and the Isthmus of Corinth. Now they turned their attention on Kalpaki.

Wave after wave of planes dropped their deadly loads on the Greek positions, especially the Grambala Hill that dominated the battlefield. The attack went on for hours, forcing the Greeks to huddle in the bottom of their positions as the bombs shook the earth. Finally it was over, and at 1500 the Italian infantry attacked with their tanks leading the way. For a change the driving rain was not an Italian enemy—the sun had returned on November 1 and shone brightly.

At the onset of the attack, the Italian infantry successfully scaled and occupied the strategic, 4000-foot high, Grambala Hill situated to the right of Kalpaki. The Greek forces had failed to occupy that vital high ground, and now were in danger of being outflanked and their entire defensive line turned. The Italian commander pleaded for additional troops to deliver the hammer stroke to the Greek line, but none were available, and the success of the great Italian offensive hung in the balance.

The Greeks reacted with lightning quickness. Recognizing that his forces could be cut off from Ioannina and Metsovo, General Katsimitros ordered an infantry battalion, armed with only rifles and bayonets, to march through the night and attack the Italians entrenched on the top of Grambala. As dawn broke, the Greek battalion was in position. In a desperate fight on the morning of November 3, with flashing steel and rifles swung as clubs, the Greeks pushed the Italians off the hill and restored the battle line.[46]

But the Italians were undaunted. At four in the afternoon,

the Centauro Division with its eighty tanks attacked the Greek defensive line and the Kalpaki hills. Now on firmer ground, the tank treads found traction and the light vehicles surged ahead. The tank barriers stalled some, but others broke through, firing on the Greeks to their front.

High in the surrounding hills, Greek artillerymen spun their hand wheels and elevated and traversed their barrels to engage this deadly, mechanized threat. Soon a rain of steel projectiles plunged down onto the Italian armor, breaking the back of the attack and stopping the assault in its tracks. Tanks burned, ammunition in the fires exploded and turrets flew into the air. Italian tankers perished inside their steel coffins. Many tanks that were not hit withdrew in great confusion.

But the Italian infantry was still not done. They mounted yet another successful afternoon attack, driving Greek forces off two key hills adjacent to the city. During the night of November 4, the Greek defenders could hear the sounds of the surviving tanks maneuvering for yet another thrust. The Greek infantry silently withdrew from their front-line positions in the dark, and fell back to adjacent positions to avoid the full fury of the armored assault.

At 1000 it came in a combined armored-infantry assault. It struck the vacated Greek lines with little effect. Still, sixty tanks pressed forward to cross the river in front of the city. A few bogged down in a swampy area, but others pressed forward and were engaged by the full force of the defending Greeks desperate to stop their advance. A second attack on November 6 was also repulsed, and on November 7 the Italian Air Force returned to punish the Greeks with an even greater vengeance. At 1030, the last planes had completed their bombing runs, and the infantry attack began anew. Even the Italian cavalry charged out and swooped down with flashing swords on the embattled Greek positions, but horses and riders withered in the explosions of the deadly artillery fire.[47]

Still the Italians attacked, and again seized the north face of critical Hill Grambala. Again the Greeks furiously counterattacked and dislodged them. The Italians pounded the Greek defenders with constant artillery, air, and tank fire for five grueling days, but could not dislodge the determined defenders. They bombed neighboring Metsovo, Ioannina, and the bridges connecting the road network to disrupt the Greek supply line, but still the Greek VIII Division held.[48]

On November 8, the Italian attack in the center was spent. The Greek soldiers observed them digging defensive positions and moved forward to reoccupy the positions abandoned prior to the tank attack.

The battlefield was strewn with the misery of war. A combat reporter described the scene: "Dead Romans. High in Metsovo Pass, embracing the mud, a young Italian lay with his head and chest crumpled by machine gun fire. No Italian had charged farther than [he] into Greece. Spread-eagled behind him lay more dead ... all around them in the mud were footprints—Greek footprints."[49]

THERE WAS NO JOY in Rome. Eight days into Contingency G, and word from the front was not good. Mussolini had been briefed that the Greek resistance was "greater than anticipated."[50] On November 4, while the desperate struggle in front of Kalpaki raged, and Julia Division's fate near Metsovo hung in the balance, The Duce called an emergency meeting at Palazzo Venezia, and reluctantly admitted that Marshall Badoglio had been right: it would indeed take twenty divisions to defeat Greece. General Roatta sensed an opening and immediately seized upon the opportunity to plead with Mussolini that he quit micromanaging, and let the service staffs do their jobs.

The Duce had already decided that heads had to roll and announced that he would relieve General Visconti Prasca and replace him with General Ubaldo Soddu, the vice minister of war. He also announced that the Italian force in Greece would be increased to a new twenty-division Army Group. But that would take time, and by best estimates the Italian Army could not be brought up to that strength for at least two and a half months. Badoglio thought it would be more like four.

In the meantime, something would have to be done to deal with the armed and dangerous Greek Army. Count Ciano reluctantly noted, "it is a fact that on the eighth day of the operations the initiative is in their hands." However he had not despaired, and added, "I don't think that we have come to the point where we must bandage our heads, although many are beginning to do so."[51]

But Ciano also did not know the reality of the situation. His diary reflected the extent of his ignorance, and the misleading, melodramatic military reports that senior Italian generals were sending to Rome to cover the extent of their own ineffectiveness and Italian failure.

"Our soldiers did miracles," he wrote. "Entire Greek Divisions were stopped by the resistance put up by platoons of custom guards, and the Greeks did not pass until the defenders died to the last man."[52]

This type of storytelling was not limited to just the generals who felt the heat of failure. Politicians also sought to distance themselves from previous statements and to put a good face on the bad situation. The foreign minister to Greece, Emmanuele Grazzi, who had delivered the ultimatum to Ioannis Metaxas, felt he had to tell his own stories.

He reported that conditions in Greece were dire, and "their resistance was made of soap bubbles." He also degraded Metaxas and minimized his heroic stance, omitting the part about Metaxas telling him "No!" Grazzi concocted his own yarn. "Metaxas, who receives our ultimatum in his night shirt and dressing gown, was ready to yield," he lied. "He became unyielding only after having talked to the King, and after the intervention of the English minister."[53]

On November 10, the Palazzo Venezia was the scene of a spirited meeting between Mussolini and his service chiefs. Months of rationalization and wishful thinking had seduced Mussolini to launch Contingency G, and now Contingency G was no longer on a path to Athens. The army was dug-in on the defensive, trying to hold off the fanatically, attacking Greek forces. The Duce began the meeting by pointing the finger of blame toward General Visconti Prasca and Albanian Minister Jacomoni, whose patronizingly unrealistic and optimistic opinions he had only been too eager to embrace a few weeks earlier. Certainly they were to blame because the plan "had not gone as one might have thought."[54]

But The Duce was confident. In his opinion the Greek spirit was "already exhausted or in the process of being exhausted." He was also confident that the offensive would be able to be resumed in a month and proclaimed December 5 to be the date. But couched in his optimistic proclamations was the dread that lurked in his heart. He did not want his army to be humiliated for "not having been able to break through the Greek defensive system."[55]

He ordered an extensive bombing program to further punish the Greek population and break down their will to resist. "All urban centers of over 10,000 population must be destroyed and razed to the ground." He would not be able to stand it if "the conviction that we are incapable of defeating the Greeks should be spread abroad in the world." The Duce had spoken.

Now it was Marshal Badoglio's turn. He took the floor and paced deliberately. Had he not told everyone that they needed twenty divisions to engage the Greek Army, and hadn't everyone scoffed at his assertions? He let the words sink in. And had not Mussolini spoken down to him and accused him of extreme pessimism?

He crafted his words to distance himself from the shaky military situation on the Greek Front. The Duce sat and listened. Badoglio recited the facts as recorded in the Supreme Command's diary. Everyone knew the chronology, but Badoglio could not resist such an opportunity to address the docile Mussolini himself. It was a time for vindication and rhetoric. He continued.

Was it not The Duce who had called the October 14 meeting concerning the size of the invasion force, he asked, fixing Mussolini in his stare. "And did I not declare that twenty divisions were necessary. And didn't we meet again the next day in this very same room, and at that time, YOU took the decision to attack ... We attempted to do everything that could be done in that space of time in the best way possible."

But Badoglio was still not through and Mussolini still sat, listening. The field marshal might never again have this opportunity to be high-minded, to vindicate himself, to cast the blame for failure on others.

"I have made these remarks," he continued, "that neither the *Commando Supremo* nor the *Regio Esercito*[56] staff had anything to do with this affair, which was carried out in a manner that totally contradicts our whole system, which is founded on the principle of first preparing oneself well, and then taking risks."[57] He was through. Badoglio had washed his hands.

CHAPTER 4
INTO ALBANIA

THE SIZE OF THE GREEK ARMY continued to swell as the walking reserves entered the Epirus and Macedonian Regions. Forces previously entrenched around the Metaxas Line to the east, along the Bulgarian border, were now redeployed to the west, a move made possible since Bulgaria's King Boris had opted out of Mussolini's joint venture. With the Italians digging defensive positions in Epirus, General Papagos had little to worry about an offensive that would threaten his flanks, and took that opportunity to commit those idle forces to increase pressure on the enemy.

And increase pressure they did. They infiltrated into the rear of the strung out Julia Division, to deliver deadly, morale-breaking attacks on the exhausted Italian Army.[1] Little by little and day by day, the numbers of the Greek Army swelled to first equal, and then surpass those of the Italian Army.

In Rome, Palazzo Venezia remained blissfully ignorant. Count Ciano was relieved. The situation did not seem as bleak as some first reports indicated. The dispatches from the front painted a better picture. He concluded, "the Greeks have only a thin military line and, having broken it, we shall move on with ease."[2] He obviously knew nothing of the soldier ant march of the Greeks, inexorably moving to the battlefield from the far reaches of the country, and the Greek Army's ever increasing numbers; and he certainly knew nothing about the Women of Pindus and their heroic, Herculean efforts.

The military failures in Greece had been distracting to the Italian High Command. Mussolini agonized each day over the fate of the operation that would elevate his stature in the eyes of Adolph Hitler. Perhaps because of this agony, or because he was tired or distracted, The Duce and his naval advisors made another serious military mistake.

After he had decided to invade Greece, he was certainly aware that Great Britain would honor its guarantee to land troops and send elements of the Royal Air Force to support Greek operations. It was Mussolini himself who had stressed speed in the Greek invasion and had told Ciano, "If we allow the Greeks too much time to think and breathe, the English will come."[3]

When the Royal Air Force occupied Greek airfields in support of the Greek Army, especially to the northwest, parts of the Italian Peninsula suddenly came within range of British aircraft. The port of Taranto, just across the Adriatic on the southern tip of Italy, could become one of those lucrative targets. The great Italian fleet, strongest in the world, with its six battleships, was anchored there as a constant threat to the weaker British fleet. But the great fleet seldom sortied out to expose itself or seek out the British fleet. Instead it chose to remain available as a fleet in readiness.

Marshal Badoglio recognized this new threat to Taranto by the Royal Air Force, and had advised, after the start of hostilities, that the fleet should be moved as soon as possible since it would no longer be safe in its snug harbor. It would be necessary to move at night to avoid British aerial detection and attack, and would require a full moon since the Italian fleet had no radar.[4]

But by November 11 the fleet had not moved and still remained in port despite several days of favorable conditions with either a full moon or near full moon. But neither had the British forces deployed enough aircraft to the northwestern reaches of Greece to be able to pose such a threat, and Taranto itself bristled with its own air defenses.

Twenty-one batteries of 100mm guns and two hundred light anti-aircraft guns protected the anchorage against air attack; the ships themselves brandished their own guns. Additionally, over four thousand meters of netting hung from floats and extended down into the water to a depth of twenty-six feet to protect against torpedo attack. And although a recent storm had destroyed sixty barrage balloons, twenty-seven still flew above the harbor with their attached, wing-shearing cables to protect against low flying aircraft.[5] Moving the fleet seemed to be a low priority.

On the evening of November 11, 170 miles southeast of Taranto Harbor, the Royal Navy initiated a daring plan called Operation Judgment. The 28,000-ton British fleet aircraft carrier *Illustrious* turned its bow into the wind and prepared to conduct launch operations for its attack aircraft lined up on deck with propellers whirling and deck crews scrambling into position.

With a whip of his colored flag, the flight deck officer launched the first aircraft. Royal Naval Aviator Lt.Cdr. K. Williamson powered his 690-horsepower aircraft down the 670-foot wind-swept flight deck and lifted off into the night. He was the leader of the first wave of twelve *Swordfish* aircraft armed with torpedoes, flares and bombs bound for the Italian fleet at anchor at Taranto. The eleven other aircraft of his wave quickly launched after him and disappeared into the night. A second wave of nine aircraft, led by Lt.Cdr. J. W. Hale followed the first force.

These *Swordfish* aircraft, built by the Fairey Aviation Company in 1935, seemed at best more suited to World War I, and should have rightly been flown by the likes of Germany's Red Baron or America's Eddie Rickenbacker.* They seemed ancient in the modern age of sleek, single-wing fighter aircraft and were the butt of many jokes. Their own pilots called them "string bags." At worst the double-wing aircraft was compared with American barnstormers and crop dusters.

The *Swordfish* was just thirty-six feet long, had fixed landing gear and sported biplane wings spanning forty-five feet. They looked anything but menacing. The pilot and two-man crew were not in closed cockpits, but sat in cramped, narrow seats exposed to the weather and buffeted by the wind.

Its biplane design led critics to claim that it was born "obsolete." *Time* magazine was more to the point, describing the *Swordfish* as, "ancient-looking, single-engine contraptions with enough wire between their wings to rig a hen yard."[6]

---

* German and American WWI aces.

But despite the planes lack of respect, it had some redeeming qualities. It could take a beating and keep on flying, and, most importantly, it could carry an impressive load of ordinance. The 5,200-pound aircraft could lift almost a third of its weight in bombs and mines.

For Operation Judgment, eleven of the twenty-one *Swordfish* carried an enormous 1,600-pound, 18-inch diameter torpedo, suspended on their centerlines.[7] The twenty-one foot torpedo looked almost too big for the thirty-six foot biplane, like a small eagle struggling to fly with a large fish clutched in its talons.

The other ten planes carried a mixture of flares and bombs and the entire strike force flew in the darkness toward the anchored Italian fleet. At a speed of 120 miles per hour, the flight was more than an hour to the target. Each plane was minus the third crewman, and in his place an extra fuel tank increased the aircraft's range.

Williamson knew that the Italians had no radar and hoped for an undetected approach. He was surprised to see tracer bullets cut through the darkness. An errant plane had brought the Italian antiaircraft crews and weapons to life.

"There suddenly appeared ahead the most magnificent firework display I had ever seen," he said. "The whole area was full of red and blue bullets. They appeared to approach very slowly until they were just short of the aircraft, then suddenly accelerated and whistled past."[8]

At 2215 the attack began. Lts. L. J. Kiggell and C. B. Lamb released eighteen flares over the harbor to illuminate the Italian ships. At 2314, Williamson wheeled into action and brought his aircraft down just off the water and flew straight to the attack. He avoided the barrage balloons and launched his torpedo. No sooner than it hit the water and began its course, antiaircraft fire from a nearby ship stitched Williamson's plane and he crashed into the sea. But his torpedo squeezed between two destroyers and streaked on its course to detonate against the hull of the battleship *RN Cavour*, ripping a large hole in the bulkhead near the keel.*

Following the second *Swordfish* strike that missed its target, Lt. N. M. Kemp maneuvered his aircraft to attack the battleships. He launched his torpedo at *RN Littorio* and then pulled hard out of his glide path to gain altitude. The torpedo ran true and struck the ship on her bow sending an orange ball into the night. One minute later, the stricken *Littorio* again convulsed. This time from a torpedo launched by Lt. H. A. Swayne who delivered his weapon against the battleship's stern. The rest of the planes in the first wave launched their torpedo and bombs with less dramatic results. At 2320, just six minutes after Williamson launched the first torpedo, the attack from the first wave was over and the eleven surviving *Swordfish* were flying back to *Illustrious*.

At 2350, the second wave's illumination planes arrived over Taranto, dropping their eight flares. The torpedo planes were right on their tails and Lt. C. S. Lea delivered the first attack. He cut his engine, silently swooped down to glide height and releases his torpedo before powering up and ascending back into the sky. The torpedo cut through the water and found its mark, smashing into the bow of *RN Duilio* with a thunderous explosion. The ship shook from bow to stern. A minute later, flight leader Lt.Cdr. Hale and Lt. Torrens each glided their *Swordfish* on an attack line. They each released their torpedoes, and one of them struck the battleship *Littorio* for the third time.[9]

---

*Williamson and Lt. N.J. Scarlett were captured.

The rest of the second wave conducted torpedo and bombing attacks with negligible results, and in those attacks, a second *Swordfish* was shot down.* Just after midnight, Operation Judgment was over. Taranto Harbor was a shambles. Three of Italy's six battleships had been struck and disabled by five British torpedoes. The very next day, the Italian Navy moved the fleet to the north toward Naples, closing the barn door after the horse was gone. The fleet, in the span of one night, had ceased to be a viable threat to the British Navy in the Mediterranean.

In Rome, Ciano wrote: "A black day. The British have attacked the Italian Fleet at anchor in Taranto without warning and have sunk the dreadnoughts *Cavour* and seriously damaged the battleships *Littorio* and *Duilio*. These ships will stay out of the action for many months.[10]

If the Italian High Command thought that the news could not get worse than the disaster at Taranto, they were wrong. On November 14, two days after Operation Judgment had thrown a crippling punch to the gut of the Italian Navy, General Papagos tried for the knockout and ordered a general offensive along the entire Macedonian front in Greece.

Up until then, the action had been to the west of the Pindus Mountains, in Epirus, with the Greek VIII Division defending against the Italian onslaught. Now Papagos beefed up the IX Division on the Macedonian Front, and added the I and XV Divisions to form B Corps.[11] This new corps attacked in freezing weather to drive the Italian defenders from their positions and off the key mountaintops and sent them flying back toward Albania.

The collapse of the Julia Division on the Italian left had exposed the Italian flank, and the entire line was forced to retreat or face being cut off and encircled. Italian reinforcements, rushing to the front, were thrown into the fray with little organization or formations. Men without supporting arms tried to plug the gaps and stop the Greek juggernaut but were rolled under the deadly artillery barrages.

---

*Lts. G.W. Bayley and H.J. Slaughter were killed in action.

The Italian 11th Army, on the coast, which in the early days of November had made such progress, was also hurled back in disarray,[12] now with the entire strength of the newly formed A Corps. The VIII Division had been joined by Divisions II and III. The entire Italian front teetered precariously on the brink of collapse—and then it did. General Soddu could hardly have expected that his first duty as the new commander of the Italian Army would be to preside over its retreat, but that's exactly what he did. On November 18, as the army's units were already falling back and individual soldiers fled to the rear to escape the Greek advance, Soddu gave commanders the discretion to withdraw.

He wrote, "From this moment, resistance on present positions has the purpose of permitting the evacuation of equipment and artillery."[13] From Rome, Field Marshal Badoglio agreed with Soddu's retreat. "It is a question of hanging on," he said, "then we shall prevail."[14]

But prevailing was an option not in the mind of those who were not inclined to "hang on." In Rome, as The Italian High Command received the disheartening reports from the battle front, they were quick to recall the early boastings of General Visconti Prasca and his ill-fated proclamation before he launched Contingency G that the plan was perfect and "free of any possible error." His words now made him an easy target for the inevitable finger pointing.

Ciano wrote, "As a matter of fact, the organization of our forces was altogether defective," and Mussolini would later lament, "Every man must make one fatal error in his life, and I made mine when I believed General Visconti Prasca."[15]

But it was none other than Count De Vecchi, the governor of the Aegean, who was most anxious to distance himself and to escape from the reality of the Greek debacle. In the run-up to invasion, he was most vocal in encouraging and prodding Mussolini to attack Greece, and it was he who had been the architect of the *Elli* attack to goad Greece into war. Now he wanted out.

"He is thinking seriously of offering his resignation," Ciano mocked. "He realizes the time has arrived for the rats to scuttle, [and] wants to be the first to land."[16]

By November 21 the Italian Army was no longer in Greece. The Greek Army had driven it back to its starting points in Albania and even further beyond. As if the Greek infantry was not enough for the Italians to deal with, newly arrived aircraft of the British Royal Air Force joined the outnumbered planes of the Greek Air Force to strafe and pummel the retreating Italian columns. All that remained of the Italian Army in Greece was their dead soldiers, 5,000 captured prisoners, lost equipment and abandoned weapons.

The list of lost equipment and arms was impressive, enough to outfit two Greek divisions. Eighty cannons and fifty-five anti-aircraft guns topped the list. The Italians also contributed twenty tanks, 250 trucks and other rolling stock, and 1,500 motorcycles and bicycles to the cache. To add insult to injury, the Greeks mounted the Italian tanks and used them to chase the Italians in hot pursuit.[17]

The collapse of the Italian line and the pell-mell retreat in the freezing winter weather was dismal. The soldiers were desperate with little leadership, little food and little support.

Captain Fernando Campione, with the Italian Siena Division, described the dreadful conditions:

"Some soldiers are dragging themselves along limping," he wrote. "Others have put their knapsack, rifle, cartridge pouch on a mason's pushcart ... They are marching heavily, slowly." He reported over two thousand casualties—killed, sick, wounded, missing—from the division.

"The sight of our retreating troops is sadder than ever, because of the painful sight of long columns of tired, tattered soldiers slowly dragging themselves along ... More than ninety mules are lying along the road, either singly or in groups of two or three at various intervals; they collapsed from exhaustion and were abandoned on the spot with all their load."[18]

BY MID NOVEMBER, the Greek Army in the Albanian Theatre of Operations had grown to approximately 232,000 men with 556 guns and 100,000 pack animals.[19] That army, with the addition of 70,000 Greek soldiers deployed along the north and east frontiers, created a huge logistical and resupply problem.

The immediate solution in the Albanian Theatre was to move all forces to the west of the Pindus Mountains. The threat of an Italian attack in western Macedonia was now nil, and by moving those forces across the Pindus to Epirus, resupply using the small carriage road from Ioannina to Koritsa would be less of a headache.[20]

By November 22, the Greeks had driven the Italian Army out of Koritsa, the third largest town in Albania, despite a frantic defense by 72,000 men in six Italian divisions. Nothing could stop the Greek onslaught.[21] To the south, the Italian 11th Army, having been routed from their defensive positions in Greece and forced back to the Albanian border, now fell back further.

Still the Greek reserves swarmed to the battlefield. One of the new arrivals was Elftherios Sklavos, still trapped in the Greek Army because of that administrative snafu that had failed to discharge him in the days prior to the start of hostilities. He had chased his old unit to its embarkation port, trying to catch up, only to see his friends sail away as he yelled at them and his captain from the shore. In the days that followed, the unlucky Sklavos became the victim of a second administrative error that classified him as a deserter when he was reported missing as his unit landed in Epirus without him. Finally, at the guardhouse, things were sorted out, and now he was bound for the Albanian Front.

"Some officers showed up at the guardhouse, herded us up, took us all to Larisis Train Station, and put us straight onto the train on Platform #1," said Sklavos. "We arrived in Koritsa. The Italians had just left ... they'd just cleared out and we went into some abandoned houses and found cologne, guitars—all sorts of stuff—nice woolen blankets ... they'd just abandoned them and ran. And we made ourselves very comfortable."[22]

But Sklavos and his friends did not stay comfortable for very long. The next they were on the march, in hot pursuit of the remnants of the Italian 9th Division. The march continued, nonstop, and the soldiers murmured among themselves, asking if anyone knew where they were going. No one seemed to have an answer. On all sides of the marching column the scenery was the same: snow and mountains.

"We got to a mountain ... snow everywhere, fog, night falling," said the young soldier. "Then someone said, 'We've got orders to stay here and set off in the morning.' And where are we going to stay? I asked." And the answer was, "Here! Here, in the snow!"[23]

In the morning the mountains echoed the Greek bugles sounding reveille to raise the shivering soldiers from their cold sleeping places. Sklavos struggled to rise but sank waist-deep in the snow. There was no breakfast. There was no food. There was just the Greek column on the march again.

"We march on and on and on, all day and all night, and all the next day," Sklavos said. "They kept retreating, and retreating, and retreating ... and we kept walking, walking, walking. We must have walked for six or seven days, nonstop ... no food, no water, no nothing. We'd just put a little snow in our billy cans, heat it up over some newspapers we had until it melted, and we'd drink a little water."[24]

The relentlessness and speed of the marching Greek column was its own worst enemy, not the retreating Italians. The food for Sklavos and his hungry comrades was far to the rear, on the backs of a dozen mules, struggling under their great loads, trying to catch the army, but falling further behind each day.

"The animals had nothing to eat, they started dying," said Sklavos. "[The driver] put their loads on the other animals ... as much as they could carry ... but they too kept on dying till there were none left."[25]

The animal driver finally found himself alone, and filled a sack with five loaves, cigarettes, brandy, olives, wine, raisins, and whatever else he could find and carry, and continued his own march on foot. On the seventh day, he finally caught up.

THE GREEK ARMY would not let the Italian forces breathe. As soon as one attack was finished, and the exhausted Italian soldiers dug into a new position, General Papagos initiated another advance on a different section of the wide front. On November 27, B Corps, which had begun its drive in Macedonia, again attacked in the northeast toward the town of Pogradec. Twenty-four hours later, the furiously attacking Greeks had again driven the Italian forces from the hilltops and pierced their defensive line. With Greek soldiers again threatening to encircle, the Italian left flank fell back to straighten the line. On November 30, Pogradec was in Greek hands, but the hard-fought victory had cost Greece 3,000 of its soldiers.[26]

Still the army pressed on. In quick succession, between December 3 and 8, the Greeks defeated the Italians in fiercely contested combat at Premeti, the port and naval base at Santi Quaranta, and the Italian 9th Army base at Argyrokastro. The attack at Argyrokastro was unleashed on the newly arrived, elite defenders, ironically called The Battalion of Death. Greek artillery delivered its rolling barrages against their positions throughout the night, and shortly before dawn, the dreaded infantry attacked. The silently moving Greeks used no rifle fire to give away their locations but advanced only with grenades and bayonets to take the city.

By November 22 they took the town of Chimara, even deeper into Albanian territory,[27] and the vital port of Valona came within striking distance. But the desperately defending Italians, mindful that the port was their lifeline, finally stopped the Greek advance.

"The Italian positions fell one after another," said one Greek historian. "Starting with Koritsa, the church bells, announcing the successive victories, never ceased tolling; Pogradec, Premeti, Santi Quaranta, Argyrokastro, Chimara ..."[28]

But these remarkable battlefield successes masked the terrible ordeal and fighting conditions the Greek Army had endured to continue their unrelenting attack. The winter weather was the worst in memory, food was almost nonexistent, and still they pressed on.

"It was Christmas Eve," said Private Vasilis Katsikis who was dug-in along the Greek defensive line. "The supply line had been severed completely. There was nothing at all—just hunger and nothing else. Seeing as it was Christmas, our captain gave us each a small piece of bread. A piece of bread and a piece of halvah*—the same size as communion bread; and a tin of salmon with a little fish in it. And those were the only supplies we had for fifteen days, along with two loaves [of bartered bread]. That was it.

"Hunger, poverty, and we were barefoot. Lots of soldiers felt so cold they put water in their helmets and warmed it up and then put their feet in it to warm them up, and that's how they got frostbite. Anyone with a bit more sense realized what a disastrous thing this was to do; and, instead, walked up and down, backwards and forwards at night. And some of the soldiers in the trenches would do the same thing—up and down—so the blood circulated so they wouldn't freeze."[29]

The scope of the Italian defeat was captured for the world in the dispatch of a battlefield correspondent writing for *Time* magazine:

"Snow sifted last week through the mountain peaks and troughs of perpendicular little Albania. It laid a white blanket over thousands of stiff dead Italian soldiers on bleak slopes and in forested ravines ... where Italian commanders strove to make a stand against the relentless, amazing Greeks."[30]

Nor was the small and outnumbered Greek Navy idle during this time. Unlike the powerful Italian Navy that had chosen to remain holed up in the confines of Taranto Harbor, the Hellenic submarine force sallied forth to strike its own blows.

On December 22, the submarine *Papanikoles*, under the command of Lt.Cdr. Miltiades Iatrides, sank the Italian oil tanker *Antonietta* in the Adriatic Sea and captured the entire Italian crew. Iatrides' attack was the stuff of legend. He had not engaged the Italian tanker with either his deck gun or his torpedoes. Instead he powered his submarine forward and rammed into the side of the oil tanker, sending it to the bottom. Two days later he struck again. This time, *Papanikoles* slipped two torpedoes into the 3,900-ton troop ship *Firenze* and sank it near the straits of Otranto.

Not to be outdone, on December 29, Lt.Cdr. N. Hatzikonstantes, commanding the submarine *Proteus* torpedoed

---

* A gritty, crisp Balkan confection.

and sank the Italian transport ship, *Sardinia*. But then disaster. An alert Italian patrol boat spotted *Proteus*'s periscope and rammed the Greek submarine, sending it with all hands to the bottom. Just two days later the Greek submarine force struck again, and ended the critical year of 1940 on a high note when *Katsones*, commanded by Lt.Cdr. Athanasios Spanides, torpedoed and sank a second Italian oil tanker, *Quinto*.[31]

But the navy was not done. The daring Greek destroyers started the new year where the submarines had ended the old. On January 5 , 1941, five destroyers, *Vasilissa Olga*, *Vasileus Georgios*, *Spetsai*, *Psara* and *Kountouriotis* crossed the Otranto Straits, touted to be controlled by the Italian fleet, and took up firing positions off the Port of Valona. With their five-inch guns, they shelled the beleaguered Italian Army, its defensive positions, and its vital supply center and stockpiles. They strafed the shoreline with their 37mm anti-aircraft guns, and when the day's work was finished, the destroyers returned to base unscathed.[32]

While the world celebrated the Greek victories against the Italians both on land and sea in 1940 and 1941, little was written to record and detail the unrelenting Greek attack on the Italian Army; and much of what was written was flawed. The Greek plan had been to avoid war, maintain neutrality, and prepare to defend the homeland as a last resort. But once Italy invaded Greece, the Greek Army, ably led by General Papagos and former general and Premier Ioannis Metaxas, positioned itself to first stop the onslaught and then shift to the offensive as soon as possible to repel the invaders.

After that the army conducted a sustained offensive in spite of shortages of men and materiel. The Italians keenly felt the pressure of that offensive both on the battlefield and in Rome.

Italian battlefield commanders, steadily bombarded and forced to fall back, were anxious to not be humiliated. As such, they foolishly sent concocted reports to mask the severity of the battlefield situation. In the winter of 1940, Ubaldo Soddu, also succumbed to this tendency. He reported from Albania, as his army was being driven out of Koritsa, that there was an "orderly retreat without pressure from the enemy." But four days later Ciano found out differently.

"Bad news from Albania," Ciano wrote. "Greek pressure continues, but above all our resistance is weakening. If the Greeks had enough strength to pierce our lines we might yet have a lot of trouble."[33]

On November 30, Mussolini spiraled down in despair in the face of the undaunted Greek attack. He reported to the Council of Ministers on the current state of military affairs. He did not miss the chance, however, to exempt himself from all responsibility. He patted himself on the back for having handled the "political" decisions, and announced that they had been "handled perfectly." The military situation was an entirely different story. Of course, he had nothing to do with that. It failed because of General Badoglio.

Ignoring the fact that Badoglio's objections to Contingency G had been long and strident, and known to all in the High Command, The Duce unabashedly proclaimed that "Badoglio was not only in agreement, but was even over-enthusiastic." He added, "The situation is serious, It might even become tragic."[34]

Four days later, Albania was worse. Ciano reported, "the 11th Army must now make that withdrawal from Argirocastro and Port Edda (Santi Quaranta,) which we had hoped to avoid."[35]

The Greek Army systematically punished and defeated one of the heretofore undefeatable Axis powers. This Greek success had been made possible by the successful execution of their Plan IB. That plan had called for an initial defense all along the Greek border, from Epirus near Albania to Thrace opposite Bulgaria, and then an aggressive and unrelenting offense in Epirus when the opportunity was right. It did not call for digging trenches and simply waiting for an enemy attack.

But some early, contemporary reporters, for reasons known only to them, ignored these facts and wrote accounts that can best be described as bizarre. A *New York Times* correspondent, A. C. Sedgwick, wrote: "Greece's heroic struggle against Italy was carried on more despite the Metaxas Fascist regime than because of it ..."[36] He made no attempt to explain his observation.

Perhaps Sedgwick felt compelled to disparage any Fascist regime in the name of rightful propaganda since German and

Italian Fascism were indeed murderous, enslaving ideologies that endangered the free world and had plunged it into war. But if that was his motivation, and the Metaxas regime was indeed inept as he claimed, the *New York Times* correspondent, should have relished the opportunity to detail why Metaxas's dictatorship was ineffective, and just how this successful Greek offensive was unfolding, as if by magic, on its own. But he did not, and his flawed dispatch did an injustice to the adroitness of the Greek leadership, weakened his own credentials, and distorted the truth. And for what purpose?

It was, in fact, Ioannis Metaxas who was the master of the offensive, and was the driving force behind the Greek successes. It was he who had displayed the coolness and courage to resist being prodded into war. It was Metaxas who had recognized military talent and had appointed the right man, General Papagos, to command the Army. His tactical Plan IB was a winning one, supported by Papagos, and the old general and the new general conferred every day for hours to plot their next moves,. They worked hand in glove.

It was also Metaxas who, while having the same power as Mussolini and Hitler to subjugate and censor the press, did not. Instead he brought the journalists in, made his papers public, and asked for their honest support and reporting during the coming crisis. How Sedgwick could report that all this happened "despite the Metaxas Regime" is unclear.

That type of flawed research and reporting, however, was not limited to just the irresponsibility of some war correspondents of the press and wire services. The Greek Army's brilliantly executed offensive got short-shrifted by one of its own generals because of a shoddily written piece, purporting to be a critical history of the Greek War.

Former Lieutenant General Demetrios Katheniotes was the chief author of this official military study. He had been assisted by a group of like-minded former Republican* officers. He bluntly criticized the strategy and tactics of those in charge. Certainly he might have had grounds to be critical on any number of

---

* Referring to Army officers opposing the return of Monarchy in 1935.

matters involving Greece's conduct of the war, but strategy and tactics should not have been on his list.

He accused the Greek Command of being addicted to the French strategy of the "defense." In a display of high-minded nonsense, the "Katheniotes Report" accused the Greek High Command, Metaxas and Papagos, of being addicted to the French mindset of the defense, and had "closed its eyes to the possibilities of offense."[37] He offered as his proof of this "defensive addiction" a document that fell far short of raising anyone's eyebrows and was certainly no smoking gun.

It was an innocuous order from the High Command to the commanding general of the VIII Division who had the daunting task to first engage the invading Italians. It read: "The difficult position of the Division is recognized. Given the numerical superiority of the enemy the government of course does not expect victories from the Division. It does expect the Division, however, to save the honor of Greek Arms ..."[38]

Translated by most anyone, particularly any military officers that had experienced combat, this would mean: We know you're outnumbered; do the best you can; give ground grudgingly and good luck.

If this selected scrap of paper was his proof of the Greek Army's addiction to the French principle of the defense, it fell woefully short. One could actually conclude that Katheniotes, had he been in charge, would not have defended in front at Kalpaki and Metsovo, but would have encouraged his numerically "inferior" Greeks of the VIII Division to abandon their fighting positions, charge out into the open, and assault the numerically "superior" Italians in a vainglorious, foolhardy, suicidal attack.

But fortunately Katheniotes was not in charge, and the VIII Division, operating under the orders and support of General Papagos and the High Command stopped the Italians cold with a steel curtain of superior Greek artillery and a rock-solid defensive line. After the Italian attack had been staggered by the artillery blows, the VIII Division shifted to the offense and defeated the invaders on the fields in front of Kalpaki.

And was it not the I Division in the Pindus Mountains that attacked the flank and rear of the 11,000-man Julia Division while on its mad dash to "victory?" And had not that division cut the Italian's division in two, and hurled it back, and kept it on the run all the way back to Albania? How the Greek Army got from thirty miles inside its own territory to forty miles inside Albanian territory by employing defensive tactics to defeat the Italian Army was a phenomenon that General Katheniotes failed to explain.

If the general and his fellow authors had difficulty distinguishing offensive action from defensive tactics, the Italians could have set them straight. On December 4, Ciano wrote, "We have lost Pogradec and the Greeks have broken through our lines."[39]

An Italian major wrote, "The Greeks are pursuing us by day and night. Half of my men are killed or taken prisoner. There is no hope whatever. We will be driven into the sea."[40] That type of desperation was not caused by staring across some no-man's land at a dormant Greek force entrenched in a defensive posture.

Perhaps it is worthy to note that Katheniotes' writings might have been influenced by a terrible bias. He was one of hundreds of Republican senior officers who had been "purged" from the army in the early 1930s. These officers supposedly offered their services at some time as this present Italian crisis rose, but Metaxas said "No," and the King concurred, and with good reason. Those officers had been part of the group that had dethroned the King's father a generation earlier.[41]

Maybe professional jealousy played a significant part in the far-fetched Katheniotes Report. Professional jealousy has always been the elixir of bias, especially in the military. Count Ciano said it best describing his own generals: "Jealousies among generals are worse than among women."[42]

It had been General Papagos, whose picture had graced the cover of *Time* magazine,[43] and who had been the toast of the free world, not General Katheniotes and his fellow "purged" assistant authors. It had been General Papagos who had been called a "military marvel," and praised for developing the tactics "to attack the Italians from behind and above."[44] It was Papagos and his men, not Katheniotes, who Prime Minister Winston

Churchill had forever lionized with the words, "Hence we will not say that Greeks fight like heroes, but that heroes fight like Greeks."[45] While Papagos was fighting the Italians in the frozen north of Epirus and Macedonia, and later basking in his well-deserved glory, Katheniotes and his rejected fellow Republican officers "had nothing to do but spend their days in the coffee houses of Athens."[46]

The consensus of the world and the well-documented actions of Papagos, Metaxas and the Greek High Command did not fit Katheniotes' description of a Greek leadership that was "blind to the possibilities of the offense." Whatever the reason for this nonsensical assertion and the tone of his report, Katheniotes' conclusions were off the mark and smacked of an attempt to grasp at straws, disparage the excellent Greek offensive and its coordinated leadership, and proclaim facts that simply were not so.

The government eventually suppressed the flawed report, and its supporters cried "foul," preferring to ignore the author's obvious and documented bias and jealousy. Those supporters claimed that the Katheniotes report had been suppressed because it had been unsparingly critical of the High Command.[47] They offered no evidence for that claim.

Sixty years after publication, it is fair to say that final judgment of the report's value as a serious official work can be found in the knowledge that the Katheniotes Report has been consigned to obscurity. But its flawed research and contrived proclamations probably contributed to decades of little serious scholarship and great misunderstanding of the Greeks and their participation in the victory of WWII.

IN THE OPENING DAYS of 1941, Great Britain's Prime Minister, Winston Churchill, turned his eyes to Greece. It was the first time he had been able to breathe a sigh of relief since the Spring of 1940 when the German onslaught overran Eastern Europe and almost bagged the British Army at Dunkirk. He had watched with grave concern as the German juggernaut gathered invasion craft on the northern shores of France, threatening a seaborne cross-channel attack to conquer the United Kingdom. In mid July, 1940, Adolph Hitler rattled his saber again. "Since Britain shows no sign of understanding, I have decided to prepare a landing operation against that country ..."[48]

By September the British people braced for an invasion that seemed possible at any time. British General Headquarters had signaled a grim, one-word code to its military commands. That single word was *Cromwell,* and its brevity masked the enormity of its warning message: "Probable invasion within twenty-four hours."[49]

On August 13, 1940, Germany unleashed the Day of the Eagle, the operational name for the air offensive meant to bring Britain to its knees, defeat the Royal Air Force, and make possible the seaborne invasion. The aerial fights in the skies above the fields of southern England in the summer of 1940 became a fight of desperation and survival for both sides. Losses of aircraft and crews were frightful. The Germans had the bigger force, but they fought at the end of a long flight and over hostile territory, and their losses were much greater than British losses.

On September 7 the German attacks became more desperate and shifted from military targets to the populous cities. Three-hundred German bombers launched what became to be known as The London Blitz.[50] The German Luftwaffe rained down a deluge of bombs on multiple targets in the south and conducted an unrelenting air campaign against London and its citizenry. All-consuming fires swirled in great storms throughout the beleaguered city every night, lighting the skies of Southern England for miles. Churchill's cabinet was forced to move underground during the rain of destruction, and the Home Front prepared to meet the invaders on the beaches.

But in the end, the Luftwaffe's attacked failed to defeat the Royal Air Force and, without control of the air, the cross-channel attack was impossible. On October 12, Hitler called off Operation Sealion and postponed the cross-channel invasion until the following spring. By October 31, the German raiders no longer flew their devastating bombing runs over London and the citizenry came up from underground.

Britain had stood virtually alone. They had not only resisted the maximum effort by the German Wehrmacht, they had actually defeated her vaunted air force. But they remained an island in a hostile sea of enemies.

By January 6, 1941, Churchill was well aware that he no longer stood alone. The startling success of the Greek Army over Fascist Italy had held the world on the edge of its seat in the same manner as the Battle of Britain had the free world holding its breath. The world had turned its eyes to the battlegrounds of Epirus, Macedonia and Albania like the moth drawn to the flame; and although many enthusiasts had to open their maps to find out just where all of this was, there was no shortage of jubilant press releases and comic renderings of an embarrassed Mussolini.

So in January, Churchill issued his new directives for the conduct of the war. First order of business was the quick defeat and dispatch of the Italian forces fighting in northeast Africa and threatening Cairo. But second in the order of importance was the Balkans and supporting the Greeks in their war against Italy and the anticipated war against Germany. Churchill felt that was a certainty if for no other reason than to save the Axis's face.

The German Army was already in Romania; their very occupation and military presence had been the event that had so infuriated Mussolini and led him to invade Greece. Churchill also realized the possible advantages to having a Balkan Front. The Greeks had Italian forces tied up in their now desperate, defensive positions in Albania. Those forces could not be deployed to face the British Army in Egypt. So Greece was in every sense of the word a fighting ally.

Then there was the matter of the British government's guarantee to Greece, given in 1939 when the Italians annexed Albania. It would be an international embarrassment to now abandon Greece and renege on its word. Britain would suffer a devastating propaganda blow and present an enormous victory for the Axis. Potential allies, sitting on the fence, would be pushed off. There was no doubt that Britain would soon be drawn into the Balkan conflict.

"It is quite clear to me," said Churchill, "that supporting Greece must have priority after the western flank of Egypt has been made secure."[51]

In October, shortly after the Italian attack, Britain sent four squadrons of aircraft to support the Greeks, and now the prime minister moved to send more. On January 9, three days after his new assessment for the direction of the war, Churchill put teeth into his commitment.

"We shall have to consider the dispatch of four or five more squadrons of the Royal Air Force to Greece," he said, "and possibly the diversion of part of the 2nd British Armoured Division."[52]

But that was hardly a popular decision to the British generals who were fighting the Italians in the desert with critical shortages of men and materiel. Especially annoyed with Churchill's decision was the British top general, Archibald P. Wavell. He bristled at the thought of having his Middle East forces stripped to be sent to Greece. He minimized the threat posed by the German concentrations in Romania and on the Yugoslavia and Bulgarian borders and signaled* his opinions to the Chief of the Imperial General Staff.

"Our appreciation here is that German concentration is move in war of nerves designed with object of helping Italy in upsetting Greek nerves." He then added, "Nothing we can do from here is likely to be in time to stop German advance if really intended. It will lead to most dangerous dispersion of force and is playing enemy's game." [53]

When Churchill read the signal he was furious. He was in no mood to have his orders mitigated, nor to argue with his general who disagreed with the severity of the German threat to the military situation in the Balkans. He signaled back to Wavell, in no uncertain terms, that the general's understandings were "far astray from the facts,"[54] and that the German concentration was not merely a "move in war of nerves," nor a "bluff to cause dispersion of forces."

He then had the final word. "We expect and require prompt and active compliance with our decisions ..."[55] Churchill would honor Britain's guarantee to Greece.

---

* A signal is a radio or wireless transmission. Like a telegram, it cuts out as many words as necessary, especially articles, since it is sent in cypher by Morse code.

CHAPTER 5

BETWEEN THE APSOS AND THE AOOS:

THE BALKAN FRONT

ON JANUARY 13, THE CHASTENED General Wavell flew to Athens to confer with Greece's King George II. Churchill had bluntly told Wavell, "Your joint visit to Athens will enable you to contrive the best method of giving effect to [my] decisions. It should not be delayed."[1]

King George II immediately impressed Wavell. The British general thought the King, "stout hearted and sensible." He was equally impressed by Ioannis Metaxas, serving as both premier and general, and thought that General Papagos, the commander in chief, seemed more to be Metaxas's chief of staff.[2]

The men spoke at length concerning the German threat, and Metaxas thought that the danger of immediate invasion was remote, but, he cautioned, in six weeks it could be imminent. He thought a force of twelve divisions would be needed to repel the German invasion, and advised Wavell that his country could provide three. The British would have to provide the rest.

Prior to the meeting with Wavell, Metaxas had presumed that his ally could furnish a force capable of mounting a full-fledged expedition to engage and eventually stall, if not defeat, a German attack. He did not expect, nor did he ask for, any assistance from Great Britain to deal with the Italians in Albania. He would drive them into the sea or back to Rome by himself.

Wavell was in a tough position. He was there to find out how Britain could help Greece and had to begin by telling Metaxas that Great Britain could not make up that gap in men and arms.

Britain could provide only specialists and mechanized units at the present time.

The Greeks sat across the table and said nothing and Wavell continued. Having told Metaxas what the British Army could not do, he turned to tell them what he could do. He offered to immediately send a company of light tanks and a regiment of artillery for the Albanian Front.[3]

But Metaxas could only frown. What they most needed was planes, anti-aircraft weapons, transportation—both mules and rolling stock—and anti-tank guns, in anticipation of the possible German onslaught.

They also desperately needed clothing. The soldiers of the Greek Army were clothed in tatters. While captured Italian clothing and materiel had helped, it didn't begin to make up all the shortages.

When Metaxas realized that twelve divisions were not possible, he pondered whether a small British contingent would be worse than no assistance at all. Would not a small British force embolden the Germans to attack and defeat the British on Greek soil? And then, would not Hitler be able to falsely proclaim that it was the British occupation that had compelled him to intervene in Greece? Would that not provide Hitler with an easy international alibi to justify his invasion? These were tough questions, but their answers were self-evident, and caused Ioannis Metaxas to refuse the small forces that Britain offered.[4]

The meeting between Wavell, King George II, Metaxas, and Papagos ended on January 17. But during that time the German menace loomed larger with increased air attacks on the British Navy. The carrier *Illustrious*, the hero of Taranto, was severely damaged. Over two hundred of her crew were killed and wounded in a Luftwaffe attack launched from Italian airfields in Sicily.

IN ROME, MUSSOLINI'S frustrations reached new heights. He had changed generals again, and in December had issued a draconian order to his men fighting in the frozen mountains and snowfields of Albania. He ordered them to die at their positions.

"More than an order from me," The Duce said in explanation, "it is an order from our country.[5]

Mussolini could see his dream of world importance slipping away. He once confided to his official biographer, "I am obsessed by this wild desire, it consumes my whole being: I want to make a mark on my era with my will, like a lion with its claw!" And with his fingernails he scratched a chair back from end to end.[6]

The only impression he was making on the world was captured in the hundreds of political cartoons portraying him as a bumbling, bragging, not-to-be-believed fool.

So in an effort to save his war with Greece and to salvage some semblance of respectability, he fired General Soddu and, true to form, replaced him with the "monumentally unpopular" General Ugo Cavallero, formally the army chief of staff and "consummate Mussolini sycophant."[7]

The Greek pressure against the Port of Valona, the vital Italian lifeline, had been ever increasing, and Soddu was not good at handling Greek pressure. He was in over his head. He had the annoying trait of daily meteoric mood swings.

"One day everything is rosy," complained Ciano, "and another everything is black." But the straw that broke Mussolini's back was not the peaks and valleys of mood swings, but the unnerving revelation that his top general, whose army was fighting for its very life, and for Italian prestige in frozen Albania, was in his tent at night composing film music.[8] That was too much for The Duce to take and Soddu had to go.

Mussolini also took action he had sworn never to do. He initiated contact with Hitler to discuss German assistance. He asked for German military intervention to attack Thrace, the easternmost region in Greece, via an approach through Bulgaria.

This had to be the ultimate humiliation. This was an attitude far removed from The Duce's confidence and arrogance in 1939 when he sought an equal footing, and equal recognition with his German partner. At that time he had boasted, "in case of war with France we shall fight alone, without asking Germany for a single man ..."[9]

Even more recently, as his army was being driven out of Epirus, and back into Albania, Mussolini continued to strike an arrogant pose and echoed a 1940 version of his 1939 refrain.

"With absolute certainty I tell you we will break Greece's back. Whether in two months or twelve months, it little matters ... Whatever happens, I will never turn back."[10]

His spokesman, Giovanni Ansaldo, punctuated Mussolini's proclamation with his own statement. "We must win the war in the Mediterranean with our own army, quite alone."[11]

But underneath his façade, arms folded and chin jutting out, Mussolini was swallowing a bitter pill. Earlier, in December, as the Greek Army overwhelmed the Italians at Pogradec, he had privately telephoned Ciano and broached the unmentionable subject of German assistance.

"This is grotesque and absurd, but it is a fact," Mussolini lamented. "We have to ask for a truce through Hitler."

Ciano was aghast. This ran against all that Fascist Italy stood for or hoped to accomplish. This could not be happening. This would mean the end. Was it not possible to regroup, form a new defensive line, and resist with fresh forces? Might it just be that the commanders are bad, and the men need to be led, and are ready to fight?

"What is important now is to resist, and to stick in Albania," Ciano advised. "Time will bring victory."

But it was humiliation that also motivated Ciano's advice. He had said, "I would rather put a bullet through my head than telephone [the Germans]."[12]

SO THE ITALIAN ARMY began 1941 with a new commanding general who exuded optimism and "who does not believe in the possibility of defeat in Albania."[13] Cavallero's first action as commander of the forces in Albania was not a bold dashing plan for victory, but a theatrical performance in front of Mussolini, with bowing and heel-clicking—the temptation to patronize was just too great. On December 31, he went before The Duce, as some humble, fawning servant, and asked for "permission" to conduct a large offensive action against the Greek forces.

It was melodramatic and more at stage strutting. "It is like asking the hare to run," scoffed Ciano. "No one more than The Duce gnaws his lips on account of this interminable [defense]."[14] He would later call Cavallero "that perfect clown, who would even go so far as to bow to the public lavatories if this would be helpful to him ..."[15]

A week later, Cavallero signaled Rome that his attack would come soon; perhaps within days. But by January 11, he still had not attacked. Instead, the Greek Army attacked him and captured the key town of Clisura. Again there was retreat, more lost equipment, more Italian prisoners. In Rome, Ciano tried to put on a good face.

"[It] means nothing. [Clisura] is a mass of huts in more or less dilapidated condition, but it is a name, and British-Greek propaganda is already sounding the trumpets of the press and radio. It also proves that the wall of resistance, that famous wall which we have been expecting for seventy days, has still not been formed."[16]

Five days later Ciano was more concerned. "On the Clisura front another Greek attack takes place. Let's hope that our troops can hold."[17]

But the Italians did not hold. On January 18, the Greek forces destroyed yet another elite, recently arrived, Italian division. This time it was the *Lupi di Toscano,** that, like the elite Battalion of Death, was greeted with Greek artillery, grenades and bayonets. Rome could only counter by issuing a communiqué calling the bayonet a "barbaric and inhuman" weapon.[18]

Then on January 21, the unstoppable Greeks launched yet another furious attack, this time in the Trebessina Mountains that dominated the approaches to the Italian Army and its port at Vrona. They seized the two key mountaintop positions, Hills 731 and 717, and established a commanding view of the entire ground that the Italian Army would have to cross if they intended to attack the Greek Army.[19]

Mussolini spiraled down. He had received nothing but a steady stream of bad news, and still there was no offensive from Cavallero. In a fit of rage, he blurted out, "If anybody had predicted, on October 15, what actually happened later, I would have had him shot."[20]

With Italian commanding generals passing through a revolving door in Albania, the question begging to be asked by many Italians was: where is the great hero of the Spanish War, General Gastone Gambara? Was it not he who had taken a dispirited Italian Army on the brink of defeat in Spain and transformed it into victors? Was it not the gallant Gambara whose offensive tactics had brought a smile to Mussolini's face, and did he not relentlessly attack and pursue his adversaries?

---

* Wolves of Tuscany.

Wasn't he the obvious choice for command since he knew Albania like the back of his hand? Where was Gambara in Italy's hour of need?

Well, he was on the battlefield, but not in command of the Italian Army. He commanded the Italian VIII Corps, with absolutely no chance of being elevated to *Commando Supremo*. The reason that he was not considered for the high command was a fitting tribute to Italian military bumbling and incompetence.

Ciano was dismayed that Gambara had been bypassed. "I have not succeeded in getting him a command in Albania," lamented the foreign minister," although he lived there for four years. The Italian General Staff does not like him. He is not one of them, and has committed the unpardonable sin of advancing by leaps and bounds in his career ... linked to the names of our victories in Spain."[21]

The Italian General Staff had spoken. They had decreed that General Gambara was not a member of their elite club, and that there was no room for him at the top in Albania.

Perhaps if Mussolini could have witnessed some of the battlefield performances of the Italian Army he might have found room for Gambara. In the snows and mountains of Albania there was little battlefield leadership and so the Italian soldiers had little motivation to fight. The Greeks were just the opposite.

Elftherios Sklavos's unit, attacking on the western flank in the same miserable weather in Albania as the Italians, was also short of weapons. They were short of food and ammunition but not short of fighting spirit. The Italian defenders cringed when they heard the Greek battle cry, "Aera,"* as the Greeks continued to advance, and many times, because of that haunting cry, they withdrew rather than fight.

"We didn't have any weapons in the beginning," Sklavos said, "and we'd shout "Aeeeraaa!!" all the time. The Italian hand grenades were red and your cigarettes fit inside them nicely, so we used to disarm them and make them into cigarette cases. Even if they only had cigarettes inside, if we held them [menacingly], and shouted, as soon as the Italians saw the

---

* The Wind.

grenade, they recognized it and, whoof! it would be up with their hands, and "Buono Greco, buono Greco" and "Una faccia, una ratsa." •

AT THE VERY same time as British and Greek leaders met at the king's Tatoi Palace in Athens to discuss their future courses of action, a similar Italian-German meeting commenced on January 18 in Berchtesgaden. It was set for three days to discuss the critical situation of the Italian Army in Albania, and what Germany planned to do about it.

In the course of that conference, General Alfredo Guzzoni, the Italian Assistant Secretary of War, met with German Field Marshal Wilhelm Keitel, commander of the German Army. Count Ciano was embarrassed by the inferior appearance of Guzzoni compared to the straight, erect, impeccably uniformed German field marshal. It was another case of inferiority.

"It is humiliating to present such a small man with such a big paunch and with dyed hair to the Germans,"[22] said Ciano.

But Guzzoni's appearance wasn't the only source of humiliation. Keitel informed Guzzoni that Germany had prepared Operation Alpenveilchen to send a full mountain corps of three divisions to Albania, since it seemed unlikely that the Italian Army would be of any assistance when Germany launched its attack on Greece. With the German corps in the center of the line, and the Italians on either flank, the Germans would conduct the attack and break the Greek line.

The Italians had previously asked Germany not to send troops to the Albanian Front, and Guzzoni again presented the request in an obvious attempt to save face. If breaking the Greek line had been the primary focus, then the Italians should have welcomed any help to finally defeat the damnable Greeks and bring an end to the misery of the army in Albania. But breaking the Greek line was the Italian focus only if the Italian Army could break it alone. Whether Keitel acquiesced to Guzzoni's wishes or

---

• "One face, one race," alludes to a common Italian-Greek ancestry.

realized that the German corps could be better deployed elsewhere is unknown, but Alpenveilchen was scrapped before the conference ended.[23]

On the last day of the conference, Hitler assembled all the principles of the two national governments for a final session to announce details of his plan for Operation Marita, the invasion of Greece.

First, Germany would attack Greece. It was absolutely critical that the British not be allowed to secure Greek airfields and ports as forward bases for future possible attacks against the Axis. Second, Hitler announced that Germany would guarantee that neither the Soviet Union nor Turkey would attack Bulgaria. Bulgaria was a key for German troop movement and sat on Greece's critical eastern frontier.

Lastly was the subject of Romania. It was the German occupation of Romania, and Mussolini's jealousies concerning that occupation, that had originated the entire mess at hand. It was ironically fitting that in the end nothing had changed from Hitler's original 1940 stance. After months of war between Italy and Greece, after thousands of deaths, after Italian defeats, after British involvement and now German counterinvolvement, Hitler concluded that Romanian territory, and its vital oil fields would be absolutely protected and safeguarded by German forces and German forces alone.

He cautioned that all preparations for Operation Marita must be done secretly lest the assembly areas become subject to attack or interference and the overall plan exposed to the world. The initiation of the attack would be for the German Army to cross the Danube, just as it had begun the war by crossing the Polish border. Once that river crossing started it would no longer be possible to continue to disguise Germany's intention, and therefore Greece must be attacked as soon as possible after the river crossing.[24]

In Greece, several days after General Wavell's entourage had departed the strategic meeting in Athens on January 19, Ioannis Metaxas became desperately sick. It was his second hospitalization in six months. In the spring of 1940 he had hemorrhaged internally, and the doctors speculated his bleeding was due to arteriosclerosis. Now, a German medical specialist from Belgrade was rushed to his bedside as well as the chief surgeon of the British Mediterranean Fleet.

It had been just two weeks earlier, on January 7, on his seventieth Nameday,* that Metaxas had been hailed as a great Greek hero for his brilliant plan and defense of the homeland against the attacking Italians. Even reluctant adversaries joined in his praise. His army now had the Italians bottled in a tight pocket with their backs literally to the wall of the Adriatic Sea in Albania.

Metaxas had modestly told his gathered audience that the praise belonged to the people of Greece, "All this is not my doing," he said, "but that of the Greek people, who always stood up true to their tradition, so long as they were united and disciplined, rather than slavish, blind political followers; ... all my efforts from the start—when I assumed power—were directed at recovering these virtues, so that the nation would be psychologically ready for the 28th of October."[25]

But now Metaxas was gravely ill and his health continued to deteriorate. A Greek destroyer moved at flank speed to the island of Tinos to retrieve the most sacred icon of the Virgin Mary, and its miraculous healing power, from the church of the Panagia Evangelistria. Twenty-five years earlier it had also been brought to the bedside of King Constantine.[26]

But as the days slipped by, so did the prime minister. Blood transfusions, oxygen, and the Holy Icon could not save him. He slipped away at 0530 at his home on January 29, 1941, and was pronounced dead a half hour later. It was septicemia resulting from a streptococcus infection that was ruled to be the official killer.[27]

Some eulogies were critical and, at the same time, eloquent. "He ruthlessly abrogated all civil liberties and constitutional guarantees, created a secret police and Nazified youth organizations," wrote *Time* magazine. "But unlike Axis dictators, he fomented no wars, rarely made speeches, indulged in no

---

*Few Greeks celebrate their birthday. They celebrate the date of death of the Saint for whom they are named.

pageantry, maintained no sycophants to shout his praises ... He was a hardheaded, hardworking, unpretentious administrator in shell-rimmed spectacles who rested his claim to authority on the fact that he got things done."[28]

King George II said, "John Metaxas ... has left our midst to take his place in the chorus of illustrious figures of Greek history." The new Premier Alexander Koryzis added in eulogy, "You have opened the road to victory. We shall march along, inflexible and determined. We shall reach the end."[29]

The question now was could Premier Koryzis, the former Governor of the National Bank of Greece, team with Commander in Chief Alexander Papagos, to carry out General Metaxas's detailed military plans without him.

The Greek nation buried "Little John" Metaxas, the self proclaimed premier for life, in a tomb just below the Acropolis. In life he had said, "So long as I am prime minster I do not give away an inch of Greek territory."[30] He had kept his word. For better or worse, Greece would have to go on without him.

Koryzis' first impressions on the British were not impressive. He was not Ioannis Metaxas. His words did not convey the confidence and optimism of the late premier. In fact, he told the British Army's representative that, to him the situation seemed "desperate.' He went on to recite a laundry list of negatives: bad weather—the worst winter in memory—little transportation, diminishing materiel and armaments. Koryzis gave the gloomy report that, in eight weeks, the weapon that the Italians feared the most, the Greek artillery, would be out of ammunition.

This prompted Wavell to announce the availability of an armored brigade group and two brigades of the New Zealand Division. He would follow that with another armored group, and two Australian brigades, and then the whole Australian Division, all depending on shipping availability.[31]

The British went into action with Churchill forcefully in the lead. He wanted a maximum effort and he signaled Wavell in February. "We should try to get in a position ... to transfer to Greece the fighting portion of the army that has hitherto defended Egypt."[32]

It was an opportunity that involved great risk, but great risk was required to reap a great reward. Churchill knew this would be no picnic. His plan called for sending at least four divisions, one of them armored, and as much of the Royal Air Force that Greek airfields could handle. He put the shipment of ammunition on top priority.

His plan went far beyond a token effort to help a fighting friend. Because of the Greek military successes against the Italian Army, Churchill held out hope for the possibility of actually forming a Balkan Front. Just a month earlier this idea would have been unthinkable. But the military situation had changed greatly since October 1940, and the dark days of the Battle of Britain, possible invasion and the London Blitz. Britain had then truly stood alone, but the Greek Army had made this idea of a Balkan Front a possibility.

Now, if Yugoslavia and Turkey could somehow be persuaded to join the cause with Greece, Churchill calculated that the front could very well pit the strength of fifty divisions against any German attack.

He knew it was a long shot. He had no illusions of an easy success much less a guarantee against failure, but it was worth the effort, and the beginning of that long-shot mission was, "the sending of speedy succour to Greece against an attack by Germany."[33]

He then signaled Wavell on the possibility of failure.

"In the event of it proving impossible to reach any good agreement with the Greeks and work out a practical military plan," he said, "then we must try to save as much from the wreck as possible."[34]

Churchill's use of the word "wreck" spoke well of his understanding of the long odds of success. Wavell signed on to Churchill's plan, but frankly assessed the difficulties as he saw them.

"The Greek plans for the defence against Germany were sketchy, but ... they have been considering them since, Greek and Turkish hesitations and Yugoslav timidity have made our task very difficult," he told Churchill.

He knew the difficulties of the enormous task before him, and his first enemy would not be the German Army but the inadequate ports and shipping to rapidly move men and materiel to Greece. "Our arrival," he said, "is bound to be somewhat piecemeal."[35]

THE PACE OF THE WAR suddenly quickened. Bulgaria could no longer disguise its loyalties or continue its charade as a neutral, disinterested party. On March 1, Bulgaria agreed to honor the Axis Tripartite Pact, signaling Germany to begin its march to cross the Danube.

The next day, the massive German 12th Army, consisting of five infantry corps, four armored divisions, and the entire 8th Airborne Corps began the crossing.[36] On March 3, Mussolini arrived in Albania to inspect his Army and to witness an expected Italian offensive entitled the *Operazione Primavera*[•]. The following day the first British convoy set sail from Alexandria, Egypt with men and materiel bound for Greece.

Eight British warships provided security for the vital convoy to ensure, as Winston Churchill phrased it, "the sending of speedy succour to Greece."[37] That convoy landed at the Port of Piraeus on March 7 and discharged the 57,000 British soldiers of four divisions.

On March 8, as the combatants approached the point of no return, Georgios Vlachos, a Greek news reporter, published an open letter to Adolph Hitler in the newspaper *Kathimerini*. Vlachos cut through all the rhetoric, alibis, half-truths and false statements of the Axis leaders that had led to the threatening German invasion. His nineteen-paragraph letter detailed irrefutably the schemes and lies and treachery of both Italy and Germany for all the world to see.

"Excellency," he began, "as you are aware, Greece wanted to stay out of the current war ... Even if one does not take into account Greece's direct statements, nor the documents that it published, nor the many speeches and documents certifying its intention to stay out of the war, one should pay heed to the following: That when the Greeks found the fragments of the

---

[•] Operation Springtime.

torpedo that sank the light cruiser *Elli* in the port of Tinos (on August 15, 1940) and they confirmed that it was Italian, they hid the fact."

He continued, "You remained a spectator of this battle, and we were told that you said: 'This issue does not concern me. It is an Italian problem. I will not intervene unless English soldiers disembark in Thessaloniki in large numbers ...'"

"So, the operation against Greece was not deemed necessary for the Axis at the start. But is it now? Why? So that there may not be a new front against Germany in the Balkans? But that is nonsense ... Is it so the Italians can be rescued in Albania? Will not the Italians be seen by the whole world as being defeated totally ... Let the Italians leave Albania of their own accord. Let them tell everyone that they beat us, that they got tired of chasing us around, that they have had their fill of glory and are now leaving. We will help them."

Then Vlachos gave the answer to the excuse that Hitler was sure to present to the world to justify his attack.

"But you may ask, Excellency ... What about the English? We did not bring the English to Greece, the Italians did ... You will try to invade Greece ... We do not believe that [your] heavily armed state of 85 million people [Germans] fighting to create 'a new world order' will attack one small nation fighting for its freedom against an empire of 45 million [Italians.]

"If called upon, the army of Greece, whatever it is that remains free, will stand in Thrace the way it stood in Epirus. It will fight in Thrace as it did in Epirus. It will fight hard. It will die. This land that taught the world to live will now teach it how to die."[38]

ON MARCH 3, after dark, at the Skaramangas Shipyards near Athens, two Greek destroyers tried to land along a dock made treacherous by a brisk, prevailing northwest wind that blew them uncontrollably into a hard landing. The first ship, *King George*, made it with some difficulty, but the second, *Queen Olga*, hit hard, damaging her hull. There was no time to think of repairs. There would be time for that after the mission.

The gangways went down and the ship's crew stood by. Captain Gregory Mezeviris stood on the deck of *King George* and was in overall command. He had given only verbal orders to the two ships' captains and had committed nothing to paper.

Suddenly, through the gate to the shipyard, Greek fire engines approached the dock. There were no red lights or blaring sirens, and there were no escort vehicles clearing their path. The only escorts were not firemen at all, but the senior officers of the Bank of Greece and bank security agents, all in plain clothes. The workers riding the trucks set about to unload the heavy cases of "coins" that had been transported from the bank to be sent to the branch bank in Heraklion in Crete.

"To avoid alarming people, it was paramount to keep absolute secrecy," said Mezeviris. "To the workers that loaded the cases, it was said that they contained coins, [and] sailors, supervised by naval officers brought the cases aboard the destroyers. Among the preventive measures taken in expectation of the German attack was the transport to Crete of the gold of the Bank of Greece."

Mezeviris also ordered security for the cargo by the sailors under supervision by the ships' executive officers.

"The destroyers sailed at nightfall at thirty knots, in order to arrive at Souda Bay and unload ... during the night. Several hours before sunrise the cases had safely been placed inside the dock warehouse."[39]

After some difficulty finding someone to sign for the cargo, and worried that an enemy air strike might hit in just the wrong spot, Mezeviris convinced the commander of the gendarmerie to take possession and deposited the bars in the bank the following day. He then ordered the destroyers back to sea so they would not attract an air attack.[40]

BRITISH AND GREEK negotiations continued with much confusion on the exact line to be held in the event of a German attack. By early March, the Greeks had still not relocated troops from the east, from Macedonia and Thrace to the Aliakmon Line. While this move seemed to the British to be absolutely necessary, they were not in Papagos's shoes. He feared panic among the population in the east caused by a sudden withdrawal of the army, and he was terrified that the twenty-day move would endanger the army to being caught in the open should the Germans attack.

Nor had any troops been relocated from Albania. While it might have been militarily defensible to take the Greek soldiers out of the Albanian Line, Papagos was aware that those very soldiers had endured every hardship, had wintered in the mountains with little food and clothing, and had bled and died to drive into Albania. The shattered morale of his army to pull them out and cede victory to the Italians was more than anyone could bear.

General Wavell thought the Greeks had not lived up to the January agreements, but despite his disappointment conceded, "It was admittedly a hard decision from the Greek political point of view to abandon Western Macedonia and Thrace without a fight, and it may be that when the point came, the decision proved too hard to take."[41]

While the Greek sentiment was understandable, both sides had readily agreed that the strongest position from which to resist was Aliakmon. To not defend there was to invite defeat. To that end, a second understanding was taken. Three Greek divisions would remain in Macedonia holding the original line, but they would concentrate three other divisions and an additional seven battalions to put teeth in the Aliakmon Line. The British Expeditionary Force would proceed also to Aliakmon and British General Maitland Wilson under the supreme command of General Papagos would command the troops in the line. To the British, this final agreement was as contentious as the "haggling of an oriental bazaar."[42] A telegram to Churchill laid it on the line.

"The hard fact remains that our forces ... will be engaged in an operation more hazardous than it seemed a week ago."[43]

Churchill was mindful of the deteriorating situation but first in his mind was the British commitment. "We must ... liberate the Greeks from feeling bound to reject German ultimatum. If on their own they resolve to fight, we must ... share that ordeal."[44]

Field Marshal and Prime Minister of South Africa, Jan Smuts, summed up the dilemma. "The gravest risks confront us whatever we do ... The Greeks have done better than anyone could have expected. The public opinion of the world is strongly on their side. If we do not stand by them, we shall be held up to public ignominy."[45]

Smuts was absolutely correct on world opinion being in Greece's corner and equally aware that Britain was also in the spotlight. Already *Time* magazine was editorializing and drawing Britain ever closer to Greece:

"The presence of German armored units in the area was news. They were doubtless in the Mediterranean area to operate against Greece. If so, the Greeks' two remaining hopes were that the German tanks would prove no more efficient in hilly country than Italian tanks, and that, to the extent that Dictator Hitler had come to succour Dictator Mussolini, George of Britain would help George of Greece."[46]

Smuts concluded his thoughts. "I think that London must realize that a first-class front is being built up here. I very much doubt whether now the Germans intend to invade England. Isn't it better to fight them in the Balkans?"[47]

ON MARCH 9, General Cavallero launched his long-awaited Italian offensive, in the presence of The Duce, in the hopes for some sort of Italian success before the Germans occupied center stage. The clock was ticking.

During the winter, Cavallero had received ten new divisions, and now deployed them to attack. Facing this new force, the Greek Army could muster only thirteen divisions to defend, but those divisions were dug in solidly on the eight-mile ridgeline formed by the western slopes of the Trebessina Mountains and the smaller Bregou-Rapit. The entire line was skillfully placed perpendicular to the Apsos River to the north and the Aoos River to the south, precluding any Italian flanking attack without first executing a river crossing.

Bisecting this formidable Greek line was a narrow gorge, the Proi Madh Riff, with steep, near-vertical walls constricting the Desnitsa River and rising to the height of the Greek line far above. Maneuver there was not possible unless the narrow mouth of the gorge could be forced. The Italians would have to attack frontally.

The objective of this massive Italian attack was aimed toward Clisura and the strategic pass through the mountains back into Greece, and a long-awaited breakout. But between the Italian Army and Clisura were the Greeks, and in the center of their line, to the north of Proi Madh were the distinctive Hills 731 and 717 of Bregou-Rapit. The first battle of the Balkan Front was at hand.

CHAPTER 6

OPERAZIONE PRIMAVERA

AT 0600 ON MARCH 9, 1941, General Gastone Gambara stood observing the distant, imposing peaks of the Trebessina Mountains and Bregou-Rapit as his infantry waited for the order to attack. Although Gambara was not the Supreme Commander, he was the commanding general of an Italian Army Corps and he would hurl the entire strength of that corps against the entrenched Greeks who, once again, held the high ground, and blocked his passage to Clisura.*

The objective of the attack was to, at last, break out of the strangling Greek pocket and regain the offensive, attacking toward the mountain pass at Clisura, which controlled the entrance to the Kalpaki Valley. It was in the Kalpaki Valley, in the previous battles in the Pindus and at Metsovo, and around Ioannina, that the six-division Italian Army had been out fought, out flanked and routed back into Albania.

But the Italian Army was no longer six divisions. It was now seventeen divisions, with massive air and artillery. A successful breakout would put it back onto the road to Athens, or at least moving in that direction before the German intervention.

Mussolini himself was on the battlefield to personally watch his legions finally break the Greek line and claim the long-sought victory that would elevate his prestige in The Führer's eyes. On the morning of March 2, he flew to Albania where General Cavallero welcomed him and assured him that he

---

* Often spelled Klissoura.

was ready to attack and was confident of the results.

The Duce wasted no time visiting and inspecting all the forces on the front. He made sure to impress upon the individual soldiers the importance of this upcoming offensive. In the evening while he ate with the senior officers, he harangued them about the importance for the future of all of Italy. This was the golden opportunity for Italy to regain its glorious past and to once and for all conquer the entire Balkan Peninsula and bring it under Italian influence without involving Germany.[1]

General Gambara planned to conduct the assault in two phases along a six-mile front. In the first phase, three infantry divisions accompanied by two Blackshirt* battalions, would smash their collective weight against the center of the Greek defensive line at the Trebessina-Boubessi Ridge, easily identified by the dominant Hill 731. If the Italians penetrated, two divisions followed in reserve to exploit any breakthrough and smash through the breech.

In the second phase, Gambara's forces would assault slightly to the north at Bregou-Rapit Heights, identified by dominant Hill 717, dubbed by the Greeks as 731's watchdog. That attacking force consisted of three lead divisions with two more in reserve. Gambara also had a variety of fifteen independent battalions of Bersaglieri*, Blackshirt, and Alpini# troops to use as he saw fit.

General Cavallero's massing of the Italian Army on the grounds in the center of the extended Trebessina ridge had not gone unnoticed by the Greek High Command. As early as February 10, Greek intelligence had detected the existence of a planned Italian offensive in that area. The morale of the Greek soldiers in their defensive positions was extremely high, and they "had got used to the idea of the impending enemy assault and its repulsion."[2]

The responsibility to defend against this assault fell to B Corps, beefed up to five divisions. From the north along the defensive line from the Apsos River to the Aoos River was the

---

* Originally Fascist paramilitary, later included in the regular army.

* Highly mobile infantry. Name means sharpshooters.

Mountain troops.

XI Division followed in order by the XV, I, V and finally the XVII Divisions.[3]

The XVII Division on the southern end had a particularly dangerous area to cover, in addition to its responsibilities along the main defensive line of resistance; it was also responsible for the dangerous terrain on its left flank. Its flank was not physically tied into the adjacent II Division of A Corps on the opposite side of the Aoos. It ended on the rocky precipice that plunged down into the Aoi Stena, the narrows of the Aoos. XVII Division was responsible for the territory around that sheer northern face and the tiny carriage road that was squeezed between the river and the vertical cliff.

The Aoi Stena was not new to battle and had been recognized as a strategic position by ancient combatants. Armies had been fighting around that critical terrain feature since the beginning of time and was first recorded in 196 B.C. when a Macedonian army held a mighty Roman army at bay by setting their defensive line around the natural obstacle, blocking any entrance to or exit from the Aoos gorge.

Its strategic location controlled the carriage road that ran from the west, through the gorge, to Clisura and then through the pass in the mountains to Greece. The narrow ribbon of the Aoos River meandering through the gorge was dominated on either side by sheer cliffs rising a thousand feet. Throughout the several miles of the gorge, as much as a quarter mile separated the two mountain walls, but at the Greek defensive line at the Trebessina Ridge the mountains pinched together so that the faces of the opposite walls narrowed to just the width of the Aoos and the small road on its north side.[4]

Unlike the similar Proi Madh whose sides steeply led to mountain peaks, the Aoi Stena's walls were virtually vertical, rising like two giant bookends. Proi Madh and Aoi Stena each controlled the only two carriage roads from western Albania to Clisura where they dovetailed together and formed a single road across the Albanian-Greece border.

To make matters worse, Greek intelligence had placed elements of the Italian Centaur Armored Division just four

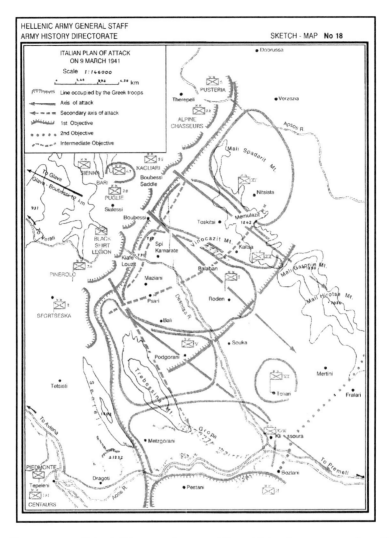

miles west of Aoi Stena, along with anti-tank guns and anti-aircraft batteries covering the road. If Italian armor could somehow manage to mount a single-file armored offensive and smash through Aoi Stena and race to Clisura, the Greek position would be untenable. With overwhelming Italian air superiority to keep the Greek infantry at bay, the Centaur Division could roam freely in the rear, smash supply depots, marshalling areas and ammunition stockpiles, and then attack the Greek defensive line from behind.

In the midst of planning and preparations for the upcoming

Italian assault, the Greek High Command experienced a crisis of their own: a serious crisis of leadership in the ranks of their commanding generals.

The threat of a German invasion was foremost on everyone's mind, and the Greek Army, after all that it had accomplished, realized it would be in danger of being cut off and encircled in Northern Epirus in Albania if the German Army invaded from Bulgaria. The Greek High Command ordered the Epirus Force Army Sector (EFAS) and the Western Macedonia Force Army Sector (WMFAS) to consider contingency plans to withdraw back to the Albanian border.

But in the minds of some of the Greek generals it was not a time for contingency plan, but a time to discontinue the pursuit of the operations in Albania and withdraw back to the homeland. General Papagos dealt with this dangerous situation swiftly. On March 6 he relieved the commander of EFAS, and the commanders of both A Corps and B Corps.[5]

Major General Anastassios Russopoulos, commanding XVII Division, recognized the dangerous situation at Aoi Stena. The Italian Centaurs were immune from attack. The Greeks had no air forces to strike them and artillery was not oriented nor had the range to attack. The tanks were not easily observed and mostly concealed from view.

Russopoulos suggested to his corps commander, the newly appointed Major General Georgios Bakos, a daring plan to eliminate the armored threat by raid. It was dangerous, and any force approaching the road could easily be taken under fire and annihilated by the tanks that regularly patrolled the surrounding area.

Bakos did not like it. He foresaw a possible disaster, a weakening of his own force's ability to guard the line, and a victory for the Italian Army on the left flank, but he reluctantly approved because the danger posed by the presence of Italian armor at such a critical location overrode his worst skepticism.

The raid would have to be conducted over the roughest of terrain interspersed with plunging ravines in the bitter cold. The raiders would require a full battalion along with a company of engineers to descend from their defensive positions under the cover of darkness and make their way between the Trebessina Range and the parallel Senteli Range to the town of Metzgorani. The town would serve as their jumping off point for the attack to neutralize the armored threat.

On the night of March 2-3, the force slipped out of the lines and began the grueling march down the slopes of Trebessina into the saddle between the two mountains, and then moved onto Metzgorani where they occupied the prominent Hill 730 overlooking the carriage road. With night as their ally, part of the infantry moved down to the Aoos, set up a defensive perimeter, and signaled the engineers to come down. The engineers made quick work of the road and in record time dug a ditch over twenty feet wide and ten feet deep, thus eliminating the carriage road as a route for an attack into the Aoos gorge.

But the raiders were not finished. Seizing the opportunity offered by surprise, they then attacked the Italian force that hardly expected Greek raiders in the middle of the night and offered little resistance. The XVII Division's raiders managed to capture the entire force, including the tanks, the anti-tank guns and the anti-aircraft weapons, and guaranteed control of the vital road along the river.

A follow-up attack by the entire XVII Division, in conjunction with an attack by the II Division south of the Aoos on March 7 collapsed the Italian front in that area and advanced the Greek line. It also netted more than one thousand prisoners, field guns, AA-guns, automatic weapons and mortars, and bulging depots of materiel and food.[6]

WHILE GENERAL GAMBARA stood contemplating his objective on that March 9 morning, more than three hundred Italian artillery pieces thundered behind him, lobbing almost a hundred thousand shells into the Greek positions on those imposing peaks.[7]

The western slopes of Trebessina Ridge ran on a north-south axis, perpendicular to the east-west axis of Gambara's planned attack. The Greeks had appreciated the terrain and had meticulously prepared their defensive line. On their left flank, they were unassailable at the Aoi Stena Gorge and the Aoos River.

From the left, the Greek line ran northward with elements of five divisions manning the 7.5-mile line between the two rivers. In the center, at Kiafe Louzit, the ridgeline again plunged down into the Proi Madh Riff. The steep slopes on the other side of the riff soared upward again to form the prominence of Hill 731. Just to the north of Hill 731 were the similar peaks of Hill 717 and Hill 710. The Greek Army could not have chosen a better defensive position.

The Greek I Thessaly Division was in the center and awaited the attack. The division's officers were ordered to hold all captured territory and conduct offensive operations in the form of counter-attacks and close fighting. They were not to withdraw. Forever after it would be known as The Iron Brigade.[8]

The massive Italian barrage thundered and crashed into their positions, but because their line was on the narrow ground and peak of the ridge, many rounds sailed harmlessly over the top. The massed Italian artillery, almost hub to hub, fired non-stop for two hours, churning the forward slopes of Hill 731 and sending geysers of mud, rock and broken trees into the air and severing line communications. The ear-splitting explosions drove the Greek soldiers to seek refuge in the bottom of their fighting holes and trench lines.

During brief moments of respite from the artillery fire, the Italian Air Force dived and pounded the Greek positions and strafed the ridgeline. Over 190 Italian aircraft screamed over the battlefield and beyond the defensive lines seeking out hidden Greek artillery positions.[9]

Gambara and his men watched the spectacular pre-attack bombardment and certainly must have felt that nothing could have survived the pummeling. At 0800 the two-pronged attack force crossed the line of departure and stepped off into the advance.

In the center of the Greek line, Lt. Col. Themistocles Ketseas, whose 5th Regiment was on Hill 731, issued his orders to his battalion commanders, whose soldiers were mostly peasants and farmers.

"Hold your positions at all cost. I'm expecting reports for the tactical situation to your left, right, and up front. Nobody will abandon his position or move to the rear. We shall die here."[10]

Those young soldiers of the 5th Regiment gripped their weapons as they watched the long Italian assault lines far below, moving like ants across the open fields leading to the Trebessina-Bregou-Rapit Line. They could well observe from their lofty perches the Italian advance. It was not long before the effective Greek artillery began ripping holes in the Italian assault formations. Mortars and machine guns also engaged their front line soldiers, but despite the terrible artillery bombardment, elements of the Italian Cagliari Division surged on and managed to reach the rising slopes of the mountain range.

Undaunted, the Italians pressed on. Greek machine guns took a horrific toll, but the Italian line still advanced, ever pushing upward. The whole mountainside crackled with rifle fire and the chatter of automatic weapons. The Greek mortars fired almost vertically because of the ever-decreasing range but still could not stop the advancing line.

Finally, the Greek defenders fixed bayonets. Screaming "Aaaeerra," they abandoned their fighting positions and charged down upon the ascending Italians. The two lines mixed in a swirling melee of flashing bayonets, clubbing rifles, knives, stones and fists. The Italians recoiled and retreated a few steps only to reform and press forward again, and then again and again. Four separate attacks were repulsed, each one with the success first teetering one way and then the other. Finally, at 1630, the Greek line held and the attackers withdrew in the shadow of Hill 731.

To the north, a second Italian attack captured Hill 717 and the Greeks furiously counter-attacked to retake the vital position, but just as it seemed that they might, the Italian forces repulsed them. The Italians then struck at Hill 710, further to the north, but could not prevail, and night fell with the exhausted combatants left to bind up their wounds and remove their casualties. The sun set on the snow-covered battlefield with the Greeks clinging to Hill 731, and the Italians with a foothold on Hill 717.[11] The Greeks rushed reinforcements to I Division lines.

There was only a slight respite for the Greek defenders as the Italian cannonade began anew in the early morning, and again

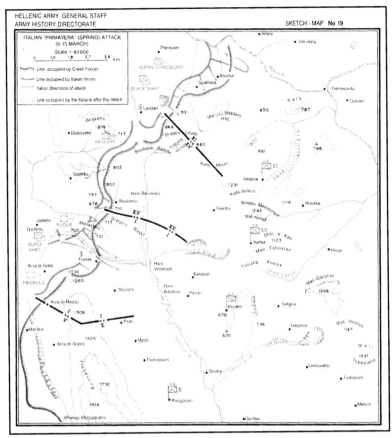

converted the slopes in front of the Greek defensive line into a moonscape. Witnesses claimed that the crest of 731 was shortened by several meters in the bombardment.[12] At 0645 General Gambara's troops again assaulted the Trebessina and Bregou-Rapit heights.

The airplanes struck first and the Italian line again swept up to the ridgeline. The infantry also attacked along the defensive line to the north but launched their main effort against the defenders of 731. Desperate slashing Greeks again repulsed three separate attacks on the line and locked in hand-to-hand combat.

A regiment of the Italian Puglia Division moved along the carriage road just before noon and attempted to envelop Hill 731 from the south, but that effort attracted the fire from all forces north and south of the gorge and was crushed by the intense fire. A second effort met the same fate.[13]

Finally the Italian Army fell back down the slopes and in its wake lay the broken bodies of their dead and wounded. The Greek defenders grimly counted almost 500 of their own casualties. The secondary Italian attacks both north and south of I Division were also repulsed.

Gambara would have to try something other than frontal assaults. Could he possibly slip a force, unseen in the night, through the narrow Proi Madh Gorge and then march toward Clisura and the rear of that entrenched Greek line? It was worth a try.

Two Blackshirt battalions of the 26th Legion were assigned to approach the narrow split of Proi Madh under cover of darkness while Greek attention was occupied by yet more attacks up the slopes of Hill 731.[14] The attackers would attempt to approach and squeeze into the gorge with a march along the carriage path on the north bank of the Desnitsa River, slip past the Greek line, and move toward the town of Hani Vinokazit on the march to Clisura. Once in the rear, the Greek line would be sandwiched between two hostile forces and portend even more danger than a breakthrough on the left at the Aoi Stena. Such a breakthrough would split the Greek line and encirclement of either half of the Greek Army would then be possible.

The general attack began in the dark at 0430 along several points of the Greek line, but once again focusing on Hill 731. It was delivered with the same ferocity as the previous attacks and was met with the same deadly Greek fire. The Greeks had been on one-hundred percent alert and met the Italian assault with a deadly fusillade and an immediate counter-attack that stopped the Italians cold.

Meanwhile the Blackshirts approached the Proi Madh not only under the cover of darkness, but also in a thick fog. But unknown to the stealthily approaching Blackshirts, the Greeks had placed an anti-tank gun detachment in the ravine. The placement of that force might have been because of the previous day's action that attempted to enter the gorge.

The infiltration went smoothly for a while, masked by the battle sounds and the attack on Hill 731, but then something went wrong. Some witnesses said that it was an accidental discharge from an Italian rifle or pistol, but whatever it was, it alerted the Greek forces.[15]

All attention snapped to the action in the gorge. Infantry on the heights delivered fire and mortars into the riff from both left and right. The anti-tank gunners fired point blank into the hapless Blackshirts. Their advance disintegrated into "pandemonium."[16] Italian reinforcements rushed into the fray and into the teeth of the killing field. The shooting went on for hours. Finally, at noon, the Greeks called a cease-fire when surviving Italian soldiers all along the ravine waved white flags.

When the shooting stopped, they came forward with their hands in the air. Sprawled in the riff along the banks of the Desnitsa River were the bodies of 250 Italian dead and an additional 521 surrendered with all their arms and equipment.

Gambara launched multiple attacks along the entire line for the rest of the afternoon. As evening fell, the Greek line still held fast. On the fields in front of Hill 731 the Italian Puglia Division had been broken and rendered ineffective, as well as the Blackshirt battalions, and were relieved from the line. On the night of March 11, the Italian reserve Bari Division took their places.

Shortly after midnight, Bari Division attacked against the I Division at Hill 731 and Bregou-Rapit with heavy artillery support. They were greeted by the same intense Greek fire and repulsed just like their predecessors. Just before dawn the division tried again without an artillery bombardment in hope to catch the Greeks napping. This attack, the eleventh against 731, also failed.[17]

At the end of the fourth day of futile attacks, Mussolini received a disquieting report from one of his army commanders who suggested that the whole operation was a failure and should not be continued. The furious Duce called his senior commanders and tried to impress upon them again the absolute necessity for success before the Germans attacked. The future of all Italy hung in the balance. He then ordered General Priccolo, his air force chief of the General Staff, to place the entire Italian Air Force "at the disposal of the offensive operations [in Albania]."[18]

WHILE THE GREEK and Italian armies battled and maneuvered in Albania, the British began to shuttle both Commonwealth and Polish troops from Egypt to Greece to hopefully establish a Balkan Front, or at least stop a German attack against the Greek Army. The escorted convoys first stopped in Crete, then on to the Greek Port of Piraeus.

Operation Lustre, as the troop movement was called, hoped to land enough forces to take up defensive positions along the proposed Aliakmon Line before the anticipated German attack. British cruisers provided the main convoy cover while on an outer ring Greek destroyers screened for possible enemy torpedo attacks from the east.

On March 11, two Greek destroyers, *King George* and *Psara*, escorted a convoy of three troop transports from Piraeus to Crete. At 1500, a *Psara* lookout noticed a submarine periscope break the surface of the water. She immediately turned into the attack and passed over the point where the periscope had been observed. She made her run, releasing depth charges in a deadly string, the resulting explosions rocked the sea and sent geysers of water high into the air. The enemy submarine dramatically broached the surface, listing badly, but for only a moment and then fell beneath the waves again. There was no further contact with the enemy submarine. Was it sunk? Was it damaged? Whatever its fate, *Psara* had thwarted its attack on the convoy.[19]

But the enemy threat continued. The next day, March 12, a convoy of five empty cargo ships returning to Alexandria was attacked. A British corvette and two Greek destroyers, all under the command of Captain Gregory Mezeviris on board *King George*, escorted the convoy. It sailed in two columns with *King George* covering the port flank and *Kountouriotis* covering to starboard. The British corvette, *Salvia*, was in the van.

Just before sunset, lookouts observed a single plane at high altitude. A short time later, a lookout on board *Kountouriotis* alerted to fourteen more planes flying in a northerly direction toward Crete.

"We thought they were British," said Captain Mezeviris. "However, a quarter of an hour later, the airplanes appeared again behind and at the left, approaching the convoy. I signaled to the ships, 'imminent air attack' and ordered *King George* to sail at full speed toward the cargo ship, *G. Empeirikos* that was lagging behind."[20]

That particular ship had been a problem throughout the voyage and tended to fall behind, and no amount of admonition or scolding or cajoling seemed to inspire the lazy ship as it trudged along at its own leisurely pace. Nor had the captain of the slow vessel signaled mechanical difficulties. Now the enemy aircraft zeroed in on the lagging ship like a lion to a wounded beast separated from the herd.

Three of the aircraft peeled off and flew in a straight line, nose-to-tail, to attack *G. Empeirikos.* The other eleven dispersed to engage the rest of the convoy.

"*King George* opened fire, initially with the stern guns from a big distance against the first aircraft heading toward *G. Empeirikos*," said Mezeviris, "and then against all three aircraft with her anti-aircraft guns."[21]

The enemy plane bore in on the attack and released three bombs. They sailed down and two exploded into the water, but the third scored a direct hit on the slow-moving vessel with a fiery ball and ear-splitting detonation. But the attacking plane did not escape its attack unscathed. It too was damaged by fire from *King George*, and just moments after releasing her bombs the plane burst into flames and fell spinning into the sea.

The second aircraft reversed course, perhaps mindful of number one's fate. But the third continued on its attack path, through the hail of gunfire from *King George*, and bore down on *G. Empeirikos.* The streaks of the tracers from the Greek destroyer seemed to cover the attacking aircraft, but still it came and released three more bombs. One fell harmlessly into the water, but two did not, and again the stricken ship convulsed with the explosions.

"While *King George* was protecting the cargo ship, she was unsuccessfully attacked with bombs and machine gun fire by other aircraft," said Mezeviris. "*Kountouriotis* was responding with intensive fire. The antiaircraft fire of the British corvette [*Salvia*] particularly impressed us."[22]

The convoy was in chaos. The unarmed cargo ships fired

flares to resemble antiaircraft fire to confuse the enemy and hopefully avoid a low-level attack run. *G. Empeirikos* was ablaze as *King George* approached.

"Her crew had abandoned ship. We could distinguish lifeboats in the sea and shouts could be heard," the captain said. "Most of the ship was under water, and after a while she sank. We succeed in saving thirty of the thirty-two seamen. The bombs killed one and another one drowned."[23]

But the damage had not been limited to just that one ship of the convoy. A Norwegian tanker was also damaged and dead in the water. An enemy bomb had split the ship's side and flooded the engine room. The other three ships had fled to the south and had escaped, and the British corvette led them to Alexandria.

The following morning the stricken Norwegian tanker was still adrift, waiting for a tow ship that had been dispatched from Alexandria, and its Greek destroyer stood loyally by. But the enemy also returned to the scene of the battle and made unsuccessful torpedo and bombing runs. The destroyer *Kountouriotis* embarked the tanker crew on board and sailed to safety south of Crete to await the promised towboat. But when it finally arrived, the tanker was not to be found and presumed sunk.

Captain Gregory Mezeviris arrived in Alexandria disheartened. "We were accustomed in the five past months to execute our missions absolutely with no losses," he said. "This first catastrophe of two-fifths of an escorted convoy had distressed me."

He reported to Chief of the British Mediterranean Fleet, Admiral Andrew Cunningham, and the admiral's words were short but lifted his spirits. "Captain, you should realize that in the war you will have losses."

Captain Mezeviris also discovered that the air attack was not the work of the Italian Air Force, but an attack by the Germans, who wasted no time in proclaiming their victory.

"[The] Germans announced that a British convoy was attacked and a ship was sunk south of Crete, said Captain Mezeviris. "[They] even admitted that one of the planes was lost."[24]

UNKNOWN TO ALL but a few, the war in Greece, both on land and sea, was very much a matter of first importance in the confines of an ungainly manor to the north of London. The increased naval activity around Crete and in the waters of the eastern Mediterranean portended something big.

In 1939, during the months preceding Germany's invasion of Poland, British intelligence recognized the inevitability of war and began a program to attempt to break the German code for its encyphering machine known as Enigma. A team of bizarre but brilliant British scholars, Egyptologists, mathematicians, crossword puzzle experts, and a variety of other professions assembled at an oddly built country mansion fifty miles north of London known as Bletchley Park.

The building itself seemed designed by someone who was not quite sure what he had in mind. It seemed to have four different fronts, pressed together, standing side by side, and was a mixture of Tudor and Gothic styles. It had a lopsided look since a large copper dome was not centered, but offset to dominate its left side. Many thought its strange design was perfectly suited for the strange assembly of Oxford and Cambridge scholars and their associates who gathered to solve the Enigma Problem.

Bletchley Park

Theirs would be a daunting task, especially since the Germans were well aware that the British had broken their secret code in WWI.

"It was generally assumed that no civilized nation that had once been through the traumatic experience of having its cyphers read would ever allow it to happen again," said Josh Cooper, head of the Air Section. "It would be a waste of time to work on German high-grade systems."[25]

In the beginning, it did seem an impossible task, but gradually the codebreakers at Station X, as Bletchley was called, made inroads into the complicated cypher machine with its daunting 159 million-million-million settings.[26] But ingeniously, these brilliant minds attacked two of the machines inherent weaknesses: message duplication and operator error. The Bletchley team began to unravel its mysteries and managed, on occasion, to break in and read the Axis mail.

Mavis Lever, one of the codebreakers working under the lead scholar at Bletchley, had been at the University College London working on a degree in German.

"I thought I really ought to do something better for the war effort—I'd train as a nurse," she volunteered.

But the manpower representatives said no; they wanted her for her skills in German. The young girl had instant visions of high intrigue.

"This is going to be an interesting job, Mata Hari, seducing Prussian officers. But I don't think either my legs or my German were good enough because they sent me to GC&CS."[27]•

Her skills landed her at Bletchley, and she described her introduction to codebreaking as scanty indeed.

"I was taken to Dilly Knox's section ... When I arrived he said, 'Oh, hello, we're breaking machines, have you got a pencil?' That was it. I was never really told what to do. 'Here you are, here's a whole load of rubbish, get on with it.'"[28]

She got on with it and eventually developed the skills of a codebreaker. "If you think of it as a ... crossword technique of

• Government Code & Cypher School.

filling in what it might be," she tried to explain. But she also admitted that success was often "inspired guesses."

"You would have to work at it very, very hard ... the magic moment comes when it really works and there it all is, the Italian, or the German ... There is nothing like seeing a code broken. That is really the absolute tops."[29]

Even the doubly tough naval code had periodically been broken, but it was only for quick peeks and usually went dark again in short order as the complexity of the German naval cypher resisted the codebreaker's probing and did not give up secrets for any length of time. But in February 1941 the codebreakers made a major breakthrough and were able to crack into Dolphin, the Enigma system used by the German U-boats.

This had been made possible when the British Navy captured a German ship sailing in the waters of Norway and seized the priceless Enigma key tables from the communications room. These tables disclosed the key settings necessary for the enemy operators and receivers to configure their machines so that the meaningless groups of five-letter gibberish translated into readable words. In the hands of the codebreakers the broken Dolphin cypher had enormous possibilities.[30]

But Dolphin was not the only Enigma cypher to feed information into Bletchley. The codebreakers had also broken Rocket, the cypher used by the German railway. The codebreakers had already detected the movement of masses of German troops to the Balkan area.[31]

On March 24, at the height of all this activity, Mavis Lever was working in the cottage of Bletchley on Italian messages. She was about to have one of those "absolute tops" moments.

"We didn't often know the results of our activities, which messages were important," she said. "The Italian messages were done individually."

Suddenly, before her eyes, in perfectly readable Italian, the printing machine clicked out the decyphered message: "TODAY IS THE DAY MINUS THREE."

"[It] was very dramatic stuff ..." said Lever, "just that and nothing more. So we knew the Italian Navy was going to do something in three day's time. So we worked for three days. It was all the nail-biting stuff of keeping up all night working.

"Then a very, very large message came in which was practically the battle orders ... how many cruisers there were, and how many submarines were to be there and where they were to be at such and such a time, absolutely incredible that they should spell it all out."[32]

Lever ran as fast as she could to her superiors to give them the bombshell. Breaking the code was one thing, but no one at Bletchley was capable of doing anything about initiating action. That information had to be transmitted to the British Mediterranean Fleet anchored in Alexandria. The delicate link from Egypt to Greece for supplies, ammunition and men was about to be attacked, and the loss of that link would doom to failure any hope of "providing succour" to the Greek fighting allies.

The combined Italian Fleet had left the safety of its widely dispersed ports located in Naples, Taranto, Messina and Brindisi. The ships rendezvoused, moving to the southeast to interdict and destroy the British convoys transporting men and materiel from Egypt to the Greek mainland to support against the anticipated onslaught from the massing German forces.

The huge Italian armada of thirty-one ships, including five submarines, sailed from Naples in three battle groups. The *Trieste* Squadron with three heavy cruisers and supporting destroyers was in the van. The massive battleship *Vittorio Veneto* and its supporting ships followed, and the *Zara* Squadron with its three cruisers and destroyers, brought up the rear.[33]

The British Fleet in Alexandria could not just sail in broad daylight without the Italians knowing they were on the move and scaring off the Italian fleet. Admiral Cunningham knew that the British fleet's every move was watched and reported on by the Japanese Consul. If he wanted to take maximum advantage of the intelligence bonanza that had been handed to him to spring a surprise on the unsuspecting Italian fleet, he would have to create a plan to deceive the spies and have a chance to slip the British battle fleet out of the harbor unnoticed.[34]

A round of golf would provide just the answer. Cunningham packed his clubs and an overnight bag and went to the clubhouse where he made sure that everyone saw him tee off and walk the course. If the Japanese Consul was doing his job, the admiral's golf excursion should have been transmitted to the Italian Naval High Command long before he finished his round. The overnight bag translated into an extended outing.

After dark, the admiral made his way back to his flagship under extreme secrecy, and the British fleet of seventeen ships, including two submarines, slipped out of port and into the dark Mediterranean waters. A separate squadron of seven Greek destroyers added to their numbers, and a British force of four cruisers and four destroyers sailing from the Greek port of Piraeus brought the Allied fleet to thirty-two ships.

On the morning of March 28, the cruiser force from Piraeus was in position south of Crete, approximately eight miles to the west of the main force. Cunningham's main force consisted of three battleships, *Warspite*, *Barham* and *Valiant*, and the aircraft carrier *Formidable* that had replaced the damaged *Illustrious* from the Battle of Taranto.

They sailed on undetected because the Italian Air Force had not made a fly-over of the Port of Alexandria that morning. But the Italians did make contact with the cruiser force from Piraeus when a scout plane spotted the ships and shortly thereafter the British cruiser force likewise spotted the Italian *Trieste* Squadron, which opened fire on the British and began a hot pursuit. The British cruiser force sailed away to the east toward the main British force.[35]

But neither side was aware of the presence of the other's main battle fleet. Ninety miles separated Cunningham's battleship and carrier force from the Italians' *Vittorio Veneto*. The brief cruiser engagement broke off around 0900, and the Italians gave up the chase and reversed course, steaming west from whence they had come. The British cruisers, no longer pursued, also reversed course and followed the Italian ships. It seemed there would be no battle.

But at 1055 the Italian cruisers headed to the northwest and met *Vittorio Veneto* sailing toward them. The big battleship saw the trailing British ships and opened fire with her 15-inch guns and drove the British off with some very close near misses. *Vittorio Veneto* began her own pursuit of the retiring British cruisers when a strike force of torpedo bombers from *Formidable* met her. Cunningham, in an effort to not let the chance for decisive action against the Italian fleet slip away, had launched the *Albacore* torpedo bombers in hopes of slowing down the Italian fleet so he could engage them with his main battle force.

The attacking *Albacore* biplanes, a latest replacement for the older *Swordfish*, swooped in on the big battleship but were ineffective and soon retired. But the battleship had spent time taking evasive action against the attacking planes and fell behind the fleeing British cruisers. At 1220, it broke off the pursuit and reversed course, again to the northwest and proceeded on a course to the anchorage at Toranto.

Almost three hours later, at 1509, a second flight of *Albacores* surprised the Italian battleship and attacked again. Squadron leader, Lt.Cdr. J. Dalyell-Stead, flashed along the water to within 1,000 meters of *Vittorio Veneto*, and unleashed his torpedo. As the twenty-one-foot torpedo sped toward its target, Dalyell-Stead could not avoid the deadly wall of fire from the battleship's anti-aircraft guns, and disintegrated, with his two-man crew, into the water.[36]

The doomed plane's torpedo, however, partially found its mark and detonated near the battleship's port side propeller. It ripped a hole in the hull and before the ship's damage control parties could stem the flow, 4,000 tons of water had poured in. But the damage was quickly repaired and *Vittorio Veneto* was underway again at 1642—on one propeller, making nineteen knots.

The crippling of *Vittorio Veneto* was reported to Admiral Cunningham, and he went into immediate action and ordered yet another aircraft launch off *Formidable*, this time with six *Albacore* and two *Swordfish*. Joining the strike force were also two additional *Swordfish* from a squadron based on Crete, whose pilots took off on their own to get into the fray.

At 1936, as night fell, the aircraft pounced on the Italian fleet. Lt. F.M.A. Torrence-Spence flew his *Swordfish* into the fight looking for an opportunity to attack. He was no stranger to attacking Italian ships at night. He had attacked the Italian fleet at Taranto, and had successfully launched his torpedo to strike the battleship *Littorio*, sinking it in the shallow waters of the harbor.

He watched as the aircraft from *Formidable* tried to attack through the protective smoke screen provided by the belching stacks of the circling escort destroyers and the sweeping searchlight beams that sought to illuminate attackers. Even though many of the aircraft swooped in for low torpedo runs, none could find the mark against the furiously firing and maneuvering Italian ships.

Torrence-Spence finally saw a small hole in the obscuring black smoke and dived his *Swordfish* through to find himself on an attack course directly leading to one of the large ships. He released his torpedo and pulled out of his attack glide to gain altitude, and looked back to see the cruiser *Pola* rock with the explosion and slow to a six-knot crawl. The ten attacking British strike force planes, out of torpedoes, returned to their bases.

The Italian Admiral of the fleet, Angelo Iachino, decided to form a protective force around *Pola* and the attending *Zara* Squadron. He ordered the *Trieste* Squadron of cruisers and destroyers to reverse course and sail to her defense. The Battleship *Vittorio Veneto* and the rest of her supporting ships would continue on a course to Taranto. Iachino was totally unaware that the British fleet was not as far distant from his own ships as he had thought but actually close at hand.

In fact, as the *Trieste* Squadron steamed to join the protective force around the stricken cruiser *Pola* and her sister ships, *Fiume* and *Zara*, the British fleet entered the battlefield. British radar detected *Pola* and the rest of the *Zara* Squadron. A signalman on *Pola* actually fired a flare from a Very pistol to pinpoint his position thinking the approaching ships were friendly.

Cunningham immediately went into action and deployed his battleships to engage the Italian force. He ordered the carrier *Formidable* out of the battle line and to the rear, lest she be damaged by heavy fire from the imminent battle.

Warspite, *Barham* and *Valiant* deployed and turned their turrets and prepared to fire broadsides against the unsuspecting

Italian ships with their collective twenty-four fifteen-inch guns. They were at point blank range, even less than two miles. The British destroyers flicked on their searchlights, and the powerful beams illuminated the gathered Italian fleet like animals in the dark suddenly caught in the headlights. Moments later, the roar of the battleship salvos was deafening. Huge sheets of flame leapt from the barrels of those terrible guns as their projectiles crushed the enemy's ships. Within five minutes the two heavy cruisers *Fiume* and *Zara*, were nothing but shredded, burning hulks.[37]

British destroyers darted around to engage the startled Italian ships trying to maneuver to either fight or flee. The Italian destroyers, *Vittorio Alfieri* and *Giosue Carducci* fell before the weight of the pummeling British guns and sank beneath the waves. Within five minutes, Cunningham withdrew his battleships. The destroyers mopped up and collected Italian survivors from the sea as prisoners and departed before dawn for fear of Italian or German air attack.

The Battle of Matapan had cost the Italian Navy 2,400 casualties and the loss of three heavy cruisers and two destroyers. British casualties were the single aircraft and three men of Lt.Cdr. J. Dalyell-Stead's *Albacore* crew. The Italian Navy would not recover. Coupled with the losses at Taranto, the navy was now only a shell of its previous grandeur and incapable of challenging the British Navy, nor stopping or interrupting the vital British transport operation from Egypt to Greece.

Codebreaker Mavis Lever had the final word. The young girl, with visions of high intrigue and gathering intelligence by seducing Prussian officers, had instead intercepted the critical Italian message at Bletchley Park and set the wheels in motion for the entire Matapan drama. She summed up the performance of Admiral Cunningham. "He pulled a real Drake on them."[38•]

---

* Sir Francis Drake: Often credited with heroic action in the defeat of the
  Spanish Armada in 1588.

CHAPTER 7
OPERATION MARITA

JUST BEFORE MUSSOLINI DEPARTED Rome to travel to the battlefield of Albania, he decided to break his self-imposed silence. Since November 18, when he had bragged "we shall break Greece's back," he had not made himself available for public comments. He now stood on the stage of the Adriano Theatre in Rome, cheered on by his Blackshirt loyalists.

"I have come to look you in the eye," he began, "and take your temperature and to break my silence, dear to me especially in wartime."

Four months had passed and he and his armies had not broken Greece's back as he had promised, but Mussolini still exuded an air of confidence. "Soon maybe it will be spring, and as the season may dictate, will come our beautiful season."[1] His Blackshirts roared their approval.

But his Operazione Primavera had not thus far produced his beautiful season or anything even close to beautiful. The Greek Army still stood rock-solid virtually in the same positions and occupying the same ground they had occupied when the offensive began on March 9. Rising above the Albanian battlefield was the terrain feature that had now become the very symbol of Greek determination and resistance, Hill 731, and the Italian High Command realized that it would be on Hill 731 where the decisive battle would have to be fought.

Two attempts to bypass the Greek line had been disastrous: first at Aoi Stena and later at Proi Madh. The Greek line was solidly placed between two rivers, the Aoos and the Apsos, making any Italian attempt at a deep envelopment virtually impossible unless they undertook the hazard of making a double river crossing on either flank.

On March 14, at the front line in Albania, the fighting continued with unrelenting ferocity. Although they had been frustrated by their unsuccessful attacks on the Greek line, the Italian Army prepared for yet another major assault.

Just after midnight they infiltrated small groups into a ravine north of Bregou-Rapit hopefully to approach the Greek line undetected to support the main assault during daylight. At first light, heavy Italian artillery barrages crashed into the Greek lines and continued without interruption until midmorning. The focus of the bombardment was on the right sector of I Division's lines.

At 1000 the barrage lifted and the Italian attack, with two regiments of the Cagliari and Bari Divisions, swarmed up the slopes of Hill 731. For two and a half hours, the fighting mimicked the previous assaults with close fighting and swirling lines, and finally at 1230 the Italians streamed down the hill leaving behind heavy casualties. It was their fourteenth assault against the heights since commencing Operazione Primavera on March 9.

At 1500 they launched their fifteenth assault. Amid the crash and thunder of gunfire, they finally gained the summit of Hill 717 and, for the first time, crawled onto the forward slopes of Hill 731. If reserve forces could push up and continue, they would have finally breached the line. But the Greeks reacted with lightning quickness and formed for a counter attack. They stormed the Italian positions and finally drove them off the hills once again. The Italian soldiers attempted to regroup in the ravine they had earlier occupied, but Greek artillery located them and drove them from that position.

But the Greeks had also been battered. Even as their exhausted soldiers tried to reorganize their sorely tested defenses, redistribute ammunition, and evacuate their wounded, the Italians caught them by surprise and struck again. This time they swarmed up the hill without the telltale pre-attack artillery. Instead a tremendous bombardment was conducted against the rest of the I Division hoping to cut off reinforcements that might be sent from those adjacent forces to the point of attack.

Again the attackers and defenders locked in a death struggle on a battlefield strewn with artillery craters and shattered trees and uprooted trunks. The Italian Air Force ran the last of its 300 sorties for that day in support of the attacks, but despite all efforts, the sixteenth attack on Hill 731 failed like the rest.[2]

The following day an eerie calmness spread over the battlefield as if the land needed a rest. It lasted until 1300 when Italian gunners began their attack again on Hill 731 and the heights of Bregou-Rapit. It was a systematic shelling and lasted all afternoon before stopping. Was the attack finally at an end, or was the long bombardment the prelude to yet another infantry assault?

For an hour and a half nothing happened. Then it began at 2000 with a simultaneous artillery bombardment against the entire I Division front. One hour later the fight had been reduced to close combat and hand grenades, and the Italians finally withdrew. Along the rest of the Greek B Corps line between the Apsos and the Aoos there was only artillery fire. Losses on the slopes of Hill 731 were heavy on both sides. This seventeenth attack and the entire action on March 15 was the decisive day.[3] General Cavallero had convinced Mussolini that there should be a termination of offensive operations so they could attack again at a more advantageous time.

On the evening of March 15, General Papagos issued his Order of the Day:

"The seven-day effort that the enemy is making against you has not shaken you, it has given you a new occasion to prove yet ... your glorious virtues and above all, your faith in the righteousness of your struggle.

"The struggle of over four months, which you are victoriously conducting, has covered you with laurels of unsurpassable glory, The effort of the enemy is crushed, your will remains unbowed and your conviction as to the victory undiminished.

"Our entire army, that you of the central front so gloriously represent and to the history of which you have added new glorious pages, is watching you and admiring you. I address the warmest of congratulations."[4]

The Greek High Command planned to redeploy their forces in the Central Sector to relieve those who had endured the brunt of the Italian offensive. The I Division would be pulled to a position east of Clisura in force reserve. It was during this planning to shift the divisions of B Corps, that the Italians launched their final attack after a three-day lull.

At 0630 on March 19, after an intense artillery barrage, elements of the Siena Division accompanied by light assault tanks maneuvered to the approaches of Hill 731. Despite the steepness of the slopes, the tanks managed to crawl on the southern approach to the hill, dangerously close to the plunging terrain in Proi Madh. The Greeks were shocked to see the small armored vehicles and reacted quickly to encircle the Italians and drove them off at 0740. Over one hundred Italian dead littered the battlefield, and the maneuvering tanks attracted every weapon present. One was destroyed directly in front of 731 and two others maneuvered wildly and plunged into the Proi Madh Riff. Others abandoned the mountainside.

As a parting gesture the Italians vented their frustrations on the damnable mountain by unleashing the largest artillery barrage ever. Whatever of Hill 731 that might still have been standing was swept away.[5]

Three days later, a small Italian detachment, under a flag of truce, approached the Greek defenses in front of 731. Three priests and litter bearers came to propose a cease-fire for six hours to bury the dead. The Greek High Command told the detachment that they would accept with the acknowledgment that it was Italy that had requested the cease-fire, but the Greeks themselves in the presence of unarmed Italian medical personnel would conduct the burial. This was obviously unacceptable to the Italian High Command because they rejected the proposal and resumed shelling.

A true picture of the horror of the battleground in front of Hills 731, 717, and the entire ridgeline between was revealed in a report from an officer who walked the battered terrain. He was not new to battlefields having fought in Asia Minor and Macedonia in other wars. He said, "The macabre and horrifying spectacle in the area between the heights 731 and 717, went beyond all bounds of imagination. The ridgeline between the two heights was covered with corpses strewn in heaps among which mutilated [arms and legs] of the slaughtered fighters protruded."[6]•

In those ghastly piles of slain warriors it was possible to recognize both Greek and Italian warriors locked in an embrace of death. Nor were those sights restricted to the land in front of the two deadly hills. On the slopes above and in the Proi Madh numerous Italian bodies lay as witness to the ferocity of the battle.

The cost in life during Mussolini's spring attack was staggering. To the defending Greeks, over 1,200 men died and an additional 4,000 were wounded. To the attacking Italians the casualties were horrific: almost 12,000 killed and wounded and an additional 8,000 taken prisoner.[7]

On the morning of March 21, Mussolini departed Albania and returned to Rome. His parting words for his officers and men, who had given their final measure, was filled with loathing and was shameful:

"I have summoned you," he began, "for I have decided to return to Rome. I have been disgusted by this environment. We have not moved one step forward. So far I have been deceived. I have deep contempt for all these people."[8]

ON MARCH 25, the government of Yugoslavia signed the Axis Tripartite Pact aligning itself with Germany. This made it likely that an unopposed passage through Yugoslavia would allow the German Army to advance to the Greek border. For Greece this was the worst possible scenario. Their forces were deployed to the east in Albania and west along the Metaxas Line confronting Bulgaria, but now the undefended north frontier was vulnerable.

But the signing of the pact did not sit well with Yugoslavians who protested loudly in Belgrade. One day later there was a

---

• The Italians would later build a monument called "the Sacred Ground" to their fallen soldiers on Hill 731.

revolt and a bloodless coup led by military officers. The Council of Regents under Prince Paul was disbanded and the crown assumed by the son of previously murdered King Alexander. The new government immediately signed a non-aggression pact with Moscow as a refutation of the Tripartite Agreement.[9] The crowds in Belgrade cheered wildly and celebrated in the streets.

On March 27, a furious Adolph Hitler issued his Directive No. 25. He called for the liquidation of Yugoslavia since the revolt "must be regarded as an enemy and therefore completely crushed as soon as possible."[10]

The dizzying events of March captivated the free world. A military journalist wrote:

"No one seemed to know exactly what the celebrations were about. Yugoslavia certainly had no reason to be explosively cheerful: Nazi pressure was putting its last exquisitely painful touches on the Yugoslav body politic. Probably the celebrants were happy because they suddenly realized Yugoslavia's fleeting power.

"For a giddy moment, Yugoslavia was the most powerful nation in Europe. For an hour, Yugoslavia was stopping Hitler ... and in their arrogance they began to think they might even be able to keep Hitler from the Vardar Valley. They had mountains, they had as much nerve as the Greeks, and their bowels were full of a dislike of the Germans and an implacable loathing of the Italians."[11]

But Germany was not motivated by any of these romantic, heroic thoughts. Their military planning encompassed only achieving their objective and that was to secure the Romanian oil fields and eliminate the possibilities of British air raids that could endanger them—made possible by the prospect of Italian failure on the battlefield.

As early as December 13, with the Italian Army evicted from Greek soil and hanging on by its fingernails in Albania against unrelenting Greek attacks, Hitler had issued his Confidential Directive No. 20.[12] It named Operation Marita for the first time and sketched the plan for the seizure of Greece from the northern shores of the Aegean and the Bay of Thessaloniki, with follow-up operations to defeat and occupy all of the country. Twenty-four German divisions were earmarked for the attack.[13]

The Führer wanted the attack to begin and end in May. It was to be a lightning attack to enable the German Army to rid itself of this Greek annoyance and get back to the business at hand and that was to invade and defeat Russia. Five days after issuing Directive No. 20, he issued No. 21: the outline of the plan for Operation Barbarossa: the invasion of Russia. It would commence as soon as the Greek distraction could be mopped up.[14]

But the invasion was not absolutely necessary if there could be some back-door diplomacy and if that diplomacy could somehow work. Germany pursued that option vigorously, hoping to avoid a military operation in Greece. That would be a victory in itself and allow the Russian invasion to begin forthwith and without the loss of any part of the formidable German Army.

On December 17, just the day before Hitler issued Directive No. 21, Germany undertook to open a discussion that might offer a solution to the Greek-Italian conflict. While still proclaiming noninterest in Greece, the German Military Attaché in Athens met with Major Skylitsis, an officer attached to the Greek Army's General Headquarters.

In the course of a conversation on another matter, the German officer suggested that it would be possible to call a truce to the war raging in Albania. The Germans would approve such a move and the Greek interests would also be protected. He told Skylitsis that Greece would not have to give up its hard earned territorial gains, nor its superior tactical position over the Italians, nor would the Greek Army even have to abandon its positions. Under the terms of the truce that he was suggesting, the army would remain in its positions occupying the Albanian territory until the end of the war when all disputes would be resolved.

When Skylitsis questioned the possibility of future Italian attacks to regain lost territory in violation of the truce, the German officer assured him that no such attacks would be allowed because elements of the German Army would position itself between the adversaries. The proposal had much to offer.

Simultaneously through a second back channel, the same offer was made to the Greek ambassador to Madrid by the Hungarian ambassador carrying the message of the German intelligence chief Admiral Canaris. The Greek Ambassador, Argyropoulos, was very impressed and signaled from his office in Madrid that the government should carefully consider the generous proposal. But Ioannis Metaxas rejected the suggestion out of hand. The offers continued even after his death, but the new prime minister followed the lead of his predecessor and rejected all proposals of a truce.

Prime Minister Alexandros Koryzis put the exclamation mark to all back-channel initiatives: "We are fighting!"[15]

Greece indeed was fighting and its forces were mostly in Albania with only four divisions manning the eastern frontier behind the fortified Metaxas Line (Map p. 161). It had not had to worry about its northern border because of Greece's understandings of the intention of its neighbors. Bulgaria had repeatedly stated it wanted nothing to do with the Greek-Italian War and had, in fact, snubbed Mussolini who had pushed for and had expected a Bulgarian supporting attack from the east while he invaded Greece from the north.

Yugoslavia swore neutrality and Turkey went so far as to promise to attack Bulgaria should she support Italy against Greece. Britain was providing air resources and had begun landing troops in Greece's support as part of its guarantee of Greece's territorial integrity. But all that changed with the stroke of the pen. Bulgaria showed its true allegiance to Germany and Adolph Hitler when it joined the Axis on March 1.

Bulgaria easily sold its soul to Germany with the promise of a share of the Greek carcass once it had been slaughtered. Germany would dole out the land and give Bulgaria Eastern Macedonia and Western Thrace as their part of the spoils of war. In return, Bulgaria would allow the free passage of German forces so as to mass on the Greek border, which they did on March 9.

That march through Bulgaria was witnessed and photographed by the world press. One correspondent called it "a river of steel, which runs long and endless, through plains and valleys, mountain passes and towns."[16]

Yugoslavia displayed honor and courage that Bulgaria lacked, refusing to grovel and rejecting the Axis connection. As a result, Yugoslavia was now on Hitler's list of countries to "crush." Greece's eastern and northern borders were not secure.

On March 17, the German Army reported to Adolph Hitler that the 12th Army could launch the attack against Greece by April 1.

Meanwhile, the British Expeditionary Forces continued to land on Greek soil and were warmly and enthusiastically received by the cheering population who now felt they were not alone. It was not uncommon for the Commonwealth soldiers to move along their route flanked by continuous crowds of Greeks, cheering and throwing flowers in appreciation.

Hans Paul Weiner of the 608th APMC (Auxiliary Military Pioneer Corps) landed at Piraeus, just south of Athens, as part of the reinforcing British forces. The rumor was they were going on leave from the battlefields of Egypt.

"But of course we didn't go home," said Weiner, "but joined an enormous convoy of perhaps fifteen ships sailing north to Greece.

"Before we left Palestine we were issued uniforms which originated from the First World War, as the new battle dress was in short supply. The rifles were made in Canada in 1917 with two-foot long bayonets. Only eight rifles were available per section, so the bayonets were given to another eight men and the remaining eight men, mostly elderly, being left with bare hands."[17]

Each rifleman had received just fifteen rounds of ammunition, counted in the palms of each soldier's hands as if they were precious coins. Weiner placed his cartridges in a drawstring bag and hung it from his belt.

"We marched a few miles through the streets lined with thousands of Greeks to great jubilation. The German Embassy was still there and we were warned of the existence of many German spies.[18]

The population shouted, "Yasso, Yasso, Patriote," as the soldiers marched by.[19] Each man knew the dangers inherent in this new Balkan operation, and had been sent off with the words of General Wavell ringing in their ears.

"You shall fight until the last drop of your blood for Greece, exactly as you would have fought for England."[20]

ALONG THE GREEK-BULGARIAN border lay the formidable defensive belt known as the Metaxas Line, built between 1936 and 1940. It served primarily as a defensive line but was built with offensive capabilities in mind. The forts were envisioned to be jumping off points for offensive attacks and raids, much like the Greek positions in Epirus and Albania had been used once they had stopped the enemy attack.

The line bristled with twenty-one forts manned by 10,000 troops, but the war in Albania had stripped away a great percentage of troops that would usually have manned the forts. Each fort was totally enclosed capable of defending in any direction unlike the French Maginot Line that was mostly oriented to a frontal assault. Infantry positions and machine gun enclosures complimented the forts and artillery observations posts dominated the battlefield below.

Each fort carried enough munitions and supplies to support itself for fifteen days. Between the Bulgarian border and the forts themselves, the Greeks had made the approaches part of the defenses. Anti-tank obstacles and trenches barred the path to the forts and mines complimented the barriers. The forts were connected by road networks and were each in communication with each other.[21]

On March 27, Hitler presided over a hastily called meeting to deal with the new Yugoslavian problem. He had intended to launch Operation Marita on March 28, but the Yugoslavian revolt had been an unpleasant surprise. Now he modified Operation Marita and reassigned the appropriate troops to attack Greece and Yugoslavia at the same time. The new date for invasion was set for April 6.

Now the ball was in the Greek-Yugoslav court, and sadly there was little coordination or cooperation. A British visit to Belgrade determined that there was true confusion and anarchy at the high levels of government and military command, and opposing factions had stultified meaningful leadership. A single meeting on April 3 produced nothing but vague intentions. General Papagos urged the Yugoslavians not to waste their time and efforts to their northern border but to join the Greek forces along the southern border. The British commander, General Maitland Wilson summed up the meeting as "the most useless and the least satisfactory meeting I have ever attended."[22]

AT 0515 ON APRIL 6, the 20th German Army simultaneously attacked Greece and Yugoslavia. True to Fascist style, the German Ambassador to Athens presented the Greek Prime Minister a note of war fifteen minutes after the army had attacked. So at 0530, Prime Minister Koryzis began to prepare his message to his people.

It would simply read, "Since 0515 hrs. the German Army that was in Bulgaria all of a sudden attacked our troops on the Greek-Bulgarian frontier. Our troops are defending our fatherland."[23]

The free world press mocked the antics of the Germans and their concocted provocations of war. *Time* magazine delivered this scathing denunciation:

"As usual the announcement of intention to attack came after the attack. At 5:15 a.m. the Germans struck. At 5:30 o'clock the German Minister to Athens, Viktor Prinz zu Erbach-Schönberg, presented a note to the Greek Government announcing that, because of the wicked British, it would be necessary to attack Greece. As usual the German High Command announced that Yugoslav and British troops, having advanced against them, it had been necessary to 'counter-attack.'"[24]

The initial Allied reaction to the German attack was to be expected. It was all bravado. The Yugoslavs marched off to battle singing, and the Greeks now turned their taunts from Italy to Germany. They modified their pledge to throw the Italians into the sea and addressed the Germans whom they pledged to "Throw into the Baltic Sea."[25]

The main thrust of the multi-pronged German attack struck toward the strategic Fort Rupel, one of the twenty-one forts along the Metaxas Line. Artillery fire covered the fort and then *Stuka* dive-bombers, with their distinctive wails from wing sirens, pounded it. After this "softening up" the Germans advanced with their feared lightning attack: motorcycles, mounted infantry on trucks, armored vehicles and assault guns. They even launched a flotilla of eighteen assault boats on the river near the fort.

But the flotilla was brought to a sudden halt. Three boats in the van fell victim to the meticulously devised Greek defenses and became entangled in an underwater wire net. Snagged in the open water and unable to move or maneuver, the crews watched in horror as their boats were first bracketed by the fire from the forts. Huge geysers of water plumed into the air as the fort gunners found the range and then systematically tore the boats to pieces with a pulverizing cannonade.

As the German ground forces approached the perimeter of the fort, the Greek outposts retreated from their exposed positions to the safety within and prepared a welcome for the Germans. The enormous firepower of the forts erupted in full volleys and stopped the German advance cold. Only the most reckless of the enemy attackers were able to set a fleeting foot on the sloping face of Fort Rupel. The defenders had aptly nicknamed the massive fort *Molon Lave.*•

But the Germans were undaunted and although mostly stopped by the fire and defensive positioning of the fort, a few of their attackers managed to infiltrate between Fort Rupel and the adjoining Fort Karatas. Those bypassing soldiers laid down a smoke screen, slipped past six defending pillboxes and maneuvered rapidly to the rear to capture an adjoining town. But the rest of the German force was not able to follow their daring comrades, although no one can say they didn't try. Numerous attempts resulted only in a thinning of their ranks as the relentless fire from the main batteries and machine guns of Fort Rupel ripped huge holes in their ranks. The fort seemed to fire in all directions. [26]

The German air forces dived into the fray and flew close to 200 missions to support the pinned-down infantry, and

---

• "Come and Take It." A taunt to any would-be attackers.

although the fort had prodigious firepower against ground assaults, it was poorly equipped to defend against air attack, possessing only one anti-aircraft gun.

All along the front the Germans tested the Metaxas Line. The brunt of the attack on the eastern end fell upon Forts Istimbei and Kelkayia that controlled the most critical terrain. First artillery and air attacked the strongpoints. More than 165 guns pounded the fort and when the smoke cleared, the skies blackened with swooping, diving *Stukas* that covered the forts with bombs.

The infantry surged forward and managed to set their feet on the sloping surface of Istimbei, but the Greek commander deep inside called for Greek artillery on his own position. The exploding shells swept the Germans from the surface of the fort and the Greeks counterattacked only to be repulsed themselves by a reinforcing German column that had captured adjacent high ground.[27]

The German strategy was to engage the forts and try and squeeze forces between them to move forward and bypass the enormous firepower, but this first day of attack proved to many of the attacking Germans that the forts had indeed been set into a formidable defense. Despite severe losses, the Germans made gains and succeeded to bypass some of the line. Greek infantry sought to withdraw and reposition itself to avoid encirclement while the defenders manning the forts were ordered to defend "to the last man."[28]

On the second day, the German attack pushed even harder against the Metaxas Line. Fort Istimbei held out until 1600 and then surrendered unable to any longer resist the German attacks using flamethrowers and choking gas. At Fort Kelkayia the German infantry encircled the fort and attack teams mounted the slopes and pumped smoke and choking gases through the fort's ventilation devices. While Fort Rupel held out and resisted all German attacks, it too was in danger. Two hundred German infiltrators had encircled it and cut off its communications. Without communication, the fort could no longer direct supporting fires from other positions nor call fire in upon itself. It became an island in the sea of attacking Germans.

At Fort Perithori the combat was ferocious. German infantry

mounted the surface of the fort and forced passage into the underground spaces. The Greeks met the attack with a fierce, slashing counterattack, and after a two-hour engagement of rifle fire, exploding grenades and hand-to-hand combat, the Greek forces annihilated the German attackers. They then emerged from the fort to attack the Germans still on the surface of the fort and drove them off with heavy casualties.

But the Germans were not through with Fort Perithori. In the late afternoon a reinforcing regiment attacked and was driven off, then returned again to attempt an attack with assault guns and infiltrators. But the fort held fast.[29]

Elsewhere the Greek defenses began to crumble. Over 2,000 soldiers of a screening brigade crossed over the Turkish border and were disarmed. The Brigade commander was humiliated by the performance of his brigade and committed suicide.

On the third day, most of the Greek defenses still fought on. Forts Rupel and Karatas continued to unleash deadly fire on the attacking Germans. Forts Maliaga and Perithori had resisted night attacks and continued to repulse further attacks at daylight. But as evening fell, the situation became desperate. Fort Echinos had been encircled and attacked from all directions. The Germans gained the surface of the fort and attacked the ventilation systems by piping in smoke and choking gases. The garrison of 550 men abandoned the fort and eventually surrendered.[30]

The deep infiltration and penetrations by various units of the attacking Germans outflanked the Greek line and placed the entire Eastern Macedonian Field Army in a dangerous position, threatening the city of Thessaloniki to the south. During the evening of April 8, the army withdrew to the east since they were cut off from the west. Because of the dire circumstances, General Headquarters gave permission to enter into negotiations with the Commander of the German forces.

The Greeks sought honorable conditions for their surrender. They requested from the Germans that the soldiers be allowed to keep their weapons or at least have them returned at war's end. But at 2230, the Military Commander of Thessaloniki received a German demand for unconditional surrender of the city before midnight.

On April 9 the city surrendered, represented by a committee consisting of the bishop, the mayor and the chief of police. German Field Marshal Von List agreed to the cease-fire but made no agreement to the Greek request for terms saying that the subject of the return of war supplies and materiel would be determined in the future. The formal signing was at 1400.

The terms were limited to officers able to keep their swords but little more. The Greeks had hoped to include in the Protocol the promise that war materiel would be returned and, most importantly, that no Bulgarian troops would be allowed on Greek soil.[31] The Germans made no such guarantees, but did agree to not send officers and enlisted to concentration camps, and that civil authority would remain intact.

At 1600 the capitulation was over and the Germans ordered the cease-fire. Many Greek soldiers, especially those continuing to fight and holding the Germans at bay, felt betrayed. They sought to escape and evade toward any part of Greece still actively defending.

By April 10 all of the soldiers of the Eastern Macedonian Field Army knew of the cease-fire. There had been 1,000 Greek casualties, but the Germans had suffered three times that number. The Germans were gracious in victory. Marshal Von List acknowledged that "the Greeks defended their country valiantly." He also ordered his soldiers to "confront and treat the Greek prisoners as befits brave soldiers."

Even Adolph Hitler found time to be gracious. In a speech before the Reichstag he said, "among all the adversaries that we have confronted, it was the Greek soldier in particular who fought with greatest heroism and self-sacrifice. Only when the continuation of the resistance was no longer possible and no longer had any meaning did he capitulate."[32]

Although the Eastern Macedonian Field Army had surrendered, the Greek Army in the Albanian Theatre had not. The Western Macedonian Field Army tried to link up with Yugoslavian forces but it was less than effective. A proposed final joint attack against the Italians never materialized, and the German Army, after sweeping the Yugoslavians aside and overwhelming the Eastern Macedonian Field Army, divided into two massive attack teams.

Marshal Von List formed the Western team to attack on a north-south axis from Florina and an Eastern team to attack south from Thessaloniki. The British forces and remaining Greek forces scrambled to form new lines to meet this attack, but they had to cover a front that extended over one hundred miles.

A German advance southward through Monastir would be the most devastating move of all. Not only would it outflank the Western Macedonian forces, it would threaten the rear of the Greek forces still in Albania.

The Germans moved with lightning quickness. They seized Skopje and Monastir on April 8, gobbled up Florina on the tenth and made contact with the Italians. Despite freezing weather and drizzling rain, the Germans moved inexorably forward in the face of stiff Greek and British resistance. On April 13 many of the forces were in danger of being enveloped, especially the British artillery that, nonetheless, remained firing support missions until the last possible moment.[33]

By the fourteenth the situation was grim. The German East and West Teams consisted of two corps of almost eight divisions, half of them armored. The Luftwaffe had total control of the air and, with improving weather, brought devastating strikes along the entire front. The Greek-British forces were hopelessly outnumbered.

The German forces broke through the Clisura defile and poured southward, outflanking the Central Macedonian Forces. By April 16 there was no longer any coherence between British and Greek forces.

The Greek Army was now faced with swallowing an extremely bitter pill and pondered its fate. The rapidly advancing German Army would soon cut off the victorious Greek Army that had devastated the Italians in Northern Epirus (Albania). The Greek High Command had always envisioned confronting a German attack with a partial withdrawal of those Epirus forces to be formed on a new defensive line while keeping the Italians in check. This was now only a fantasy and a paper exercise.

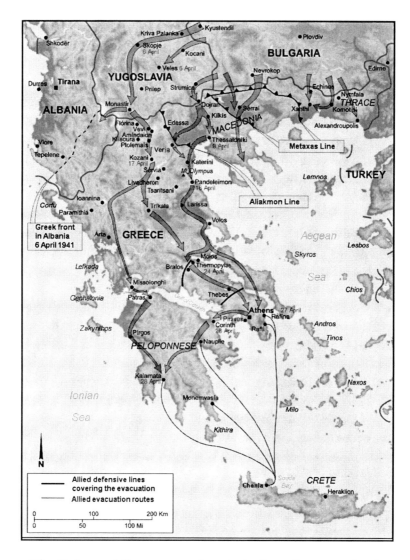

The Epirus soldiers were exhausted after a five-month winter campaign and the proposed orderly withdrawal, while holding the Italians at bay, had been estimated to take one month.[34]

Furthermore the Greek Army in Albania was twenty percent below strength, despite continual reinforcements, and suffered a dreadful shortage of pack animals, which would be required for any withdrawal. Additionally, the army was fifty percent short of weapons at the battalion level. Murmurings among the soldiers and higher officers could be heard that the situation was hopeless. The Commander of A Army actually sent a letter to his higher command recommending capitulation. Officers in B Army felt similarly. They felt withdrawal would lead to a complete breakdown of the army.

The Commander of the Epirus Field Army sent his own letter to General Headquarters filled with the foreboding of doom. He wrote, "... retrograde maneuvers in great depth will not be devoid of the dangers of an inglorious disintegration of the Army." He implored that "a solution be found ensuring the salvation and the victorious prestige of our Army."[35]

The Chief of Staff of the Western Macedonian Field Army was particularly bitter. He wrote, "The opportunity to assume the retrograde maneuver has gone by at the expense of the army, which though victorious was forced to stand as an onlooker, watching the enemy advance on its rear."[36]

On April 16 the morale in the Epirus Army was shattered. Soldiers defied orders and left in great numbers for the rear. Colonel Grigoropoulos reported to General Papagos: "... morale and discipline is extremely critical and getting worse every moment. The Corps leaders painfully foresee we shall not reach the final areas in time. The Army would disintegrate."

He listed other concerns including fatigue, occupation of Greek territories and fear of capture, especially at the hands of the Italians. He concluded: "We believe any further resistance is impossible."[37]

But the government in Athens could not counsel such a proposal. British troops still remained in Greece and were fighting for the country when some Greeks were throwing in the towel. If Greece could expect any support from Great Britain at war's end, they must fight on. The army in the Epirus Front was ordered to fight on to continue its withdrawal and maintain order and discipline.

On April 16, the Italians finally figured out what was happening and attacked but were still not able to break through the Greek defenders despite severe desertion of up to fifty percent of their strength. On April 19 the Italians again attacked but were again stymied despite the full weight of their air forces.

On that same morning Papagos met with British General

Wilson near Lamia. The decision was a formality. The end was just a matter of time. Papagos said, "The time has come for the British troops to deal with their evacuation from Greece in order to avoid any further destruction of the country."[38]

Two days later, King George II called a meeting at the palace in Athens. The political crisis was at hand. Prime Minister Koryzis was there along with Generals Maitland and Papagos and the British Ambassador. The British informed the King that they could hold their ground at Thermopylae until May 6, providing the Greeks could continue to fight in Epirus.

Then the cabinet held its own meeting with the king. The Greeks must fight on until the British could evacuate. Everyone recognized that the situation in Albania was hopeless and the solution was for the government to retire to Crete and leave the generals to work out a truce with the Germans. Prime Minister Koryzis showed the strain of a nervous breakdown as he proposed forming a government with more dynamic members, as if that could be some sort of solution.

Koryzis stumbled out of the meeting, greatly upset, and returned to his home. He went upstairs and locked himself in his bedroom. A shot startled his bodyguards who tried the locked door and then crawled through the transom to find the prime minister sprawled on his bed holding his pistol. In the other hand was an icon of Our Lady of Tinos.[39] On April 20, the Greek Army in Epirus surrendered to the German 12th Army.

General Wavell, having recently arrived in Athens, reported to the king that with the surrender he felt compelled to withdraw his forces as soon as possible. He sent a telegram to Winston Churchill to prepare the world for the announcement that resistance in Greece had collapsed and the Germans were once again victorious. But he cautioned Churchill that British forces were now bottled up between the enemy and the sea and would have to be evacuated once again as they had been at Dunkirk. He concluded his telegram by saying, "Do not wish anything yet said about possibility of reembarkation."[40]

The British Army streamed to the south and southeast toward the ports. In one of those columns was Hans Paul Weiner who had arrived just a few weeks earlier from Egypt. The ship *Ulster*

Prince had brought his company to Greece and now it would hopefully take him away again.

"We waited for a train to take us south, but learned that the Greek railway personnel had all fled, and that the Royal Engineers were occasionally moving a few trains at night because German planes attacked all moving stock in daylight."

So they began to walk.

"We were part of a beaten army in retreat," said Weiner. "We walked endless days in orderly fashion ... It was springtime with beautiful sunshine but very cold nights. On our minds was the thought if the navy who brought us to Greece will be able to pick us up again."[41]

After days of marching, Weiner and elements of the 608th arrived at the port town of Patras and *Ulster Prince* was indeed there to pick them up. But the German Luftwaffe was also there engaged in a duel with anti-aircraft artillery as the diving planes attacked the ship.

"They lost a few planes," said Weiner, "but in the end the ship got a few direct hits and was soon engulfed in smoke and flames.

"Our hopes dashed to nothing, we carried on marching hundreds of miles to the most southerly tip of Greece. The Peloponnes is connected to the mainland by a few bridges over the Corinthian [Canal]. We were lucky and hitched a few hours ride by train and were assured that all bridges would be blown up in good time."[42]

ELFTHERIOS SKLAVOS CONTINUED his strange military odyssey that had begun on the day of the Italian Invasion in October of 1940 when he had been scheduled for discharge but held in service because of the war. A paperwork error had then declared him a deserter before he rejoined his unit and fought the Italians during the winter and spring campaigns. Now the Germans were here.

"An order comes to retreat," he said, "because their planes were mowing people down. We were in charge of the trucks, and we took them, filled them, and started driving down towards

Athens. One of the trucks broke down on the way, so we stopped to see what we could do to fix it. 'Fix it? We don't have time', says the captain, 'The Germans will kill us.' So we abandoned the trucks and took to our heels."

Sklavos and his retreating comrades made it to a small train station.

"There was a train there with about ten coaches attached, and we got on. And more and more people kept getting on until they had to climb onto the roof because there was no more room. And just after we set off, the *Stukas* came down and started firing at the train. So the driver stopped the train, and there were wheat fields on both sides, and everyone ran into the fields to save their skins. And there wasn't just one plane, there were five or six of them—the machine guns kept on—chaos—and they kept firing at us."[43]

When the *Stukas* departed the battlefield, the train moved again and drove until nightfall when it arrived at another station.

"There was just one train there, the last hospital train, an English train. There were no more," said Sklavos. "The others had left and just that one was left, and they were collecting the wounded and putting them on it. We tried to hide in the storage cars, others tried elsewhere, but they threw us all off. They didn't let anyone on. And it was the last train."

Sklavos was frantic. If that train pulled out without him his chances of avoiding German capture would be slim indeed. The situation called for ingenuity, and Sklavos was up to the task.

"Our legs were wrapped with what we called gaiters," he said. "They were just like the swaddling clothes you wrap babies up in ... and each one must have been about five or six meters long. I got in under the train while it was still in the station, and there were some pipes under there for the brakes and the rest of it ... and I went to those pipes, and tied the gaiters from here to here to here, like a hammock for a summer's night.

"And we had some cleaners we used to clean our rifles, and I tied them in, too, and hung up my bag and my gun, and I climbed into this web, ever so slowly, and lay down just like a spider and waited for the train to leave.

"From time to time I saw the feet of the British who were throwing the others off the train, and then the train left with me underneath. And I said, 'Wherever it goes, so do I. I'm saved. And since it's an English train, it's a sure thing.'"[44]

The train traveled miles and miles down the track; how long, Sklavos could not tell as he swayed in his spider web underneath the moving coach with the railroad ties whistling by just inches below him. And then he felt the train slow down and come to a complete stop. Sklavos heard the sound of German aircraft.

"There are mountains on both sides of the track," he said, "and the train came to a standstill in the gorge. And everyone got off—some from this side, some from the other—and went into the fields. I got out, too."

The German *Stuka* strafed the full length of the train but did not drop any bombs; perhaps he had expended all of them, but was shortly just a vanishing speck in the distance. Everyone scrambled to get back on the train. But Sklavos knew he could not get back into his web since that was a delicate operation and the train was already pulling off.

"I moved down towards the end of the train ... to where I'd made my nest ... and I went five or six meters further back, and I saw the wheel, and I counted 1, 2, 3, 4, before the next wheel came along, and 1, 2, 3, 4, and the next wheel passed me.

"So, I counted, 1, 2 - one wheel passes me and bam! I rolled in under the train and grabbed the pipes. I got dragged along the ground, but I manage to pull myself along from one pipe to the next and climb up into my nest. 'Thank God!' I said. The train could have sliced me in two, the Germans could have killed me, or I could have been left behind. We arrived in Athens after a lot of discomfort."[45]

FROM EPIRUS THE PREVIOUSLY victorious Greek Army fell back in disarray. Pvt. Vasilis Kitsikas retreated with a small band of friends.

"And then it was time to withdraw. We stuck together as far as the border, but then scattered. I happened to find myself outside Kalpaki, with another two lads, and they held us there, and wouldn't let us go on ... because the Germans were hammering Florina and were on their way down to Ioannina. When Kalpaki fell later on, we went on to Ioannina where our supply base was. It was chaos there. The villagers had fallen on it like a pack of wolves and so had the soldiers, and between them they'd torn the place to pieces. Someone would take one thing, another something else ... everyone took whatever they fancied.

"And from there we set off on foot, begging along the way ... for bread. And we went past Metsova and we climbed up into Pindus on foot. We climbed over Pindus and got to Kalambaka, and it was there, just outside Kalambaka, that we found the Germans. They held us there for three days. We were in a terrible state.[46]

PTOLEMAIOS KALIAFAS ACTED as a rear guard as his unit withdrew from the Albanian front.

"The Germans attacked. The order was given to retreat and to take up defensive positions behind the old Greek-Albanian border. Me and another two Alpine troops were ordered to stay behind when the others left—we were told to light a fire here and there in the forest, and to fire a burst with the machine gun now and again. And when they sent up a flare we'd leave and catch up.

"One hour passed, then a second. The suspense really was killing us! Three hours went by and four, and then they sent up the flare. It took us less than an hour to catch them up, even though it had taken them four hours to cover the distance. We were really shaking in our boots![47]

Kaliafas and his unit retreated along the familiar ground they fought so hard to win against the Italian Army. Now they were little more than desperate men trying to avoid capture and find food to survive in their escape.

"We got down off the mountains and retreated through Koritsa. Some soldiers broke open the military stores in Koritsa and told everyone to help themselves to whatever they wanted because otherwise the Italians and the Albanians would just take it all.

"I filled my knapsack with cans of food and ships biscuits, but when I tried to lift it, there was just no way. So I said to myself 'I'm not going anywhere with that thing', and I emptied it. I just dumped everything on the spot and filled it with cigarettes instead. I said to myself 'At least I'll not run out of cigarettes before I die.'

"We opened a couple of tin cans and some biscuits and hit the road. I kept finding discarded cans of food along the road the next day. Those soldiers who hadn't used their heads the previous day just couldn't carry them any further ... so for the first couple of days we dined off other people's canned food."[48]

But the Germans were all around, and Kaliafas and his fellow stragglers got off the road and climbed into the mountains to avoid contact. There were rumors of a train leaving from the town of Trikala, so they set their path toward that town. In all their misery of cold, hunger, and pursuing Germans, the thought of escape by train buoyed their spirits.

"We climbed up Mount Kozakas, and then came down again via Porta and went into Trikala where they said there was a train leaving. We had a Hungarian mule with us. There were three of us, and we sold it there for two eggs and a hunk of bread. As the days went by, we found ourselves traveling more and more alongside the Germans. The German trucks drove past but we took no notice of each other. They didn't take us prisoner.

"When we got to the outskirts of Trikala, we found a train with six or seven cars, We found three places and squeezed in. There was gunpowder all round the train from empty shells. It had spilled out of the shells. But the rest of the soldiers who were arriving by the thousands couldn't accept that we were going to leave by train while they were going to have to continue on foot, so they set fire to the gunpowder. It didn't explode, it just burned, but we were scared and got off the train, and of course, they took our places. Then we did exactly the same thing. We lit the gunpowder and they left. Finally, we found out that the train wasn't going anywhere, so we started walking again."[49]

AT 0400 ON APRIL 23, King George II and the Greek government departed for Crete. The king issued a proclamation to his people: "The cruel destinies of war compel us today to depart from Athens, along with the crown prince and the lawful government of the country, and to transfer the capital of the state to Crete."

He went on to praise all Greeks for their heroism and patriotism in the struggle against overwhelming odds and urged all patriots to continue the struggle.

"Greeks, do not be discouraged, even at this painful moment of our history. I shall always be with you. God and the right of the cause will help us to achieve the final victory with all means, despite the trials, the sorrows, the dangers, which we have suffered in common and shall suffer in the meantime.

"Be courageous, the good days are to come. Long live the nation."[50]

The cease-fire between Greece and Germany went into effect at 1800 on April 20. According to the terms, the German Army was positioned between the Italians and Greeks. The Greek forces were compelled to withdraw to the old Greek-Albanian border from whence the Italians had first invaded and to which they had been driven back in full retreat by the victorious Greeks.

The Greek soldiers were to surrender their arms and then go home. The officers were not to be considered prisoners of war. But all that changed overnight. On April 21 the Germans trotted out a second protocol that labeled the officers and soldiers as POWs and their surrendered supplies and arms were labeled "spoils of war" not subject for negotiation at the end of the war. Part of those supplies and equipment were to be given to the Italians. The border would be determined later.

On the next day, the Germans added insult to injury inviting the Italians to be signatories to the truce as well. Mussolini was furious that the Greeks had surrendered only to the Germans, and on Hitler's orders the formal signing had to be repeated two days later.[51] On April 23 General Papagos resigned, and one day after that, the less-than-courageous Bulgarians invaded Greece. On April 27 German tanks entered Athens.

The retreating British scrambled to stay one step ahead of

the pursuing German forces. The withdrawal plan called for evacuation from ports to the southeast of Athens and from ports on the Peloponnese. The British retreating to the Peloponnese had to negotiate the crossing of the Corinthian Canal that separated the Peloponnese from the mainland of Greece.

The crossing at the narrow isthmus was a prime target of the Germans. If they could cut the crossing they could bag the entire retreating British force before they could make it to safe harbor and rescue.

The Germans deployed tri-motored aircraft to drop 800 parachutists to seize the isthmus and the bridge. On April 26, after engineers first landed in gliders, the parachutists jumped on either side of the canal while close supporting aircraft bombed British positions. Despite numerous casualties, the Germans managed to frustrate British intentions to blow the bridge to stop German pursuit by capturing the bridge intact. But before they could cut the fuses and remove the firing devices, the British detonated the explosives with their own fire causing serious damage to the bridge.[52]

Kalamata was the end of the line on the Peloponnese. With the Corinthian Canal in German hands, there was no turning back, and salvation and rescue was only possible if a soldier could make his way there.

Hans Weiner and the 608th APMC was on the road to Kalamata. They had marched all the way from the Port of Patras after the Germans sank their ship. As they passed the small town of Arfara, just thirty kilometers north of Kalamata, anxious Greek eyes watched their retreat, knowing the Germans could not be far behind.

Six-year-old Konstantin Georgountzos had rushed to the top of the hill by the church to see what he could see. He and his family and friends of the family had an excellent view of the valley.

"A colonel of the Hellenic Army came with us to the hill," said Konstantin. "He was a member of the General Staff of our army and close advisor to the then Chief of the Hellenic Army, General Papagos, who successfully conducted the war against the Italians. Just a few days before the Germans entered the city of Athens, Papagos dismissed his staff and retired himself, so the Germans would not take him prisoner on active duty.

"First we saw the German planes hitting targets in the not-far-away Kalamata harbor. Later we saw the first motorcyclists and later the tanks and other vehicles. With some of the other children we walked to the main road leading to town. We saw the invading soldiers and observed them at close range."[53]

Just down the road from young Konstantin, Hans Weiner was frantically hoping for evacuation.

"We arrived at the coast near the small fishing village named Kalamata," said Weiner. "Here the countryside and beaches were full of an array of hundreds of abandoned army vehicles. In the midst of all this was a column of 100 brand new lorries. They were dark green and all had the same mileage. They must have arrived in Yugoslavia by train from the CSR (Soviet Union) and their only trip was from Belgrade to Kalamata. These lorries were full of wooden crates containing millions of dinar notes. We had heard that the entire Yugoslav government was evacuated from this beach some days before. I took a 1000 dinar note as a souvenir."[54]

Weiner and the entire British force on the beach spent the next few days dodging air strikes from German planes.

"No more Greek, seaworthy, fishing or rowing boats were to be found. During the night the area became as busy as an anthill. Under cover of darkness small navy vessels came to pick up remnants of a destroyed army. These boats had to anchor some distance away as the beaches were too shallow.

"After some nights of waiting, it was our turn. We had to wade in single file into the sea up to our waist, in pitch darkness. Members of the first two sections got away when the order came to turn back since the boats were full and had to be away before daylight." Weiner's commanding officer called all sergeants together, thanked everyone for their service and shook everyone's hand.

"He informed us that all organized resistance and movements were stopped and that everybody was on his own.[55]

Weiner realized that he would have to fend for himself and gathered with a small group that was collecting maps, compasses, and other paraphernalia and preparing to do just that.

"This group of about a dozen men sprang into action. A corporal who was in the First World War and whose mother tongue was Greek ... found a villager to act as a guide on a ten hour drive and march over a mountain ridge to another hidden bay away from all the ravages of war, where we could find a boat to escape. For this service he demanded a very large sum of money."[56]

Weiner's group selected a small pick-up truck from among the hundreds of abandoned vehicles on the beach and started down the road that after some miles became very steep and narrow. The men often dismounted and pushed and guided the small truck lest its outer wheels slip off the primitive road and send all plunging into the deep canyon. Eventually the road became impassable and they continued on foot.

As evening fell, the party rested for a while before the final push to coast. They had collapsed with exhaustion along the trail, but when they started to move again the village guide had disappeared.

"We had to carry on with the help of a compass but as it was downhill we knew that the coast could not be far away. As soon as we passed little fields and olive groves, we also noticed that we were not the first in this bay. Other troops had taken all our promised fishing vessels days before and lots of war paraphernalia was left lying about."

Two men from the team swam out to retrieve a large wooden boat, but returned empty-handed and visibly shaken.

"They reported that the boat was riddled with bullet holes," said Weiner, "and that inside, half filled with water, were the bloated bodies of two high ranking officers moving with the swells of the sea.

"I sat under an olive tree and must have dozed off for a while when I was wakened by a commotion nearby, which sounded like: 'They're here, they're here'. The next moment I saw a German soldier with the swastika painted on one side of his helmet, sitting astride a motor bicycle, and had a small machine gun pointing in my direction. We were surrounded by hundreds of bikes.[57]

On April 29 The Germans took 7,000 British prisoners at Kalamata, including a large contingent of New Zealanders. The rest fled into the hills. With this surrender the British operation in Greece ended. Almost eighty percent of the 50,000 men sent to Greece had been evacuated. On May 3, Field Marshal Von List led a parade through downtown Athens. The triumphant Germans rode in the front and the Italians followed. The Greeks stayed in their homes. The British had lost almost 12,000 men, along with 8,000 vehicles and 200 aircraft. The Germans lost 5,000 men but seized virtually all of the Greek arms and materiel.

On May 2, Adolph Hitler decreed total freedom to the Greek officers and soldiers. Greek units, still intact, disbanded.[58]

British General Archibald Wavell wrote in his summary of the action: "The whole expedition was something in the nature of a gamble, the dice were loaded against it from the first."

He also wrote from his headquarters in Crete, "It seems unlikely that the enemy will attempt a landing in force in Crete from the sea. An airborne landing is possible but not probable since the landing force would be isolated without sea support."[59]

But General Wavell did not know that Adolph Hitler had issued his Directive No. 28 on April 25 initiating Operation Merkur (Mercury,) calling for the invasion of the Island of Crete.[60]

CHAPTER 8

OPERATIONS MERCURY AND SCORCHER:
LAST STAND IN CRETE

As THE GERMAN ARMY SWEPT to the south and overwhelmed the Greek mainland, their conquest was not the reign of terror that many had predicted.

Ten-year-old Dimitri Tsaras, having fled with his family from the eastern frontier at Drama at the beginning of the Italian War, developed a feeling of comfort and safety in his new home in Stalida in the center of the country along the eastern coast. He was far away from the Albanian war in the northwest and twice as far from the hated Bulgarians in the northeast.

"At the time of the Italian War, our feeling was that we were going to be okay. We were going to win and we were going to survive. The Germans attacked during April, Easter week, and the Bulgarians attacked*, and they didn't break through the lines, they broke through Yugoslavia where we didn't have the army to guard those places but I don't think we could have stopped them anyhow.

"What we had was the Metaxas Line which was similar to the Maginot Line but we had better fighters than the Maginot had. The Germans broke through Yugoslavia and came the back way, and that was the end.

"We were aware of the attack the day it started, but we were not aware of the seriousness, and my family's first concern was what had happened to my father. He was back in Drama."

---

* Bulgaria invaded Greece on April 24, 1941, hoping to gain land claims in Western Macedonia.

The families of Stalida had left their houses and huddled in bomb shelters to protect themselves against menacing planes as the German onslaught began.

"It was night and we were in shelters to protect from planes overhead," Tsaras said, "and the sirens had gone off and all the shelters were public things, and were dug like trenches with some cover over them, and we were sitting there with candles. There was a blanket in the entrance so it kept the light in."

The family huddled in the soft light of candles and prayed for their own safety but most importantly for the safe return of the elder Tsaras.

"And my mother was there and my sister and my brother and aunt and a few others, and the blanket was raised up and an old fellow with big whiskers walked in and said in Greek, 'Mrs. Tsaras, you will not believe what I have brought you.' And he stepped to the side and in stepped my father. It was beyond description. When I looked at him I thought I was seeing a ghost. He had been sick, he hadn't shaved in days and his cheeks were sunken in. It was a celebration."

The elder Tsaras had known his family was in Stalida, and despite the attacking Germans and the jams of traffic and frightened refugees on the roads, he had made his own evacuation plan.

"He only had the clothes he was wearing," said Dimitri. "He was able to get to a port, and get into a boat, and my father hated the sea, he'd get violently sick. The boat was escaping, and he went to an island, and from that island got to another boat."

As the Germans raced across Greece, terrible stories preceded them.

"The rumor mill was tremendous," said Tsaras. "The Germans are killing, the Germans are doing this, the Germans are doing that, so my father said we need to move. We need to go up to the mountains, to wait for things to settle down.

"He got a couple of horses or mules, from where I don't know, and loaded things that we had—bedspreads and edible things like flour, pasta, macaroni—and we went up to a little monastery. It was a single church with some sleeping quarters like a long cabin and was very, very crude. It was just walls and a roof overhead and dirt floor, but the surrounding countryside was beautiful and picturesque.[1]

After a while, the German threat seemed overblown and the Tsaras family moved back to the city.

"It was a strange thing," said Dimitri. The Germans did everything they could to say they were friends and that they didn't come in as occupiers. The enemy, they stressed, was the Italians."[2]

PTOLEMAIOS KALIAFAS'S FIRST encounters with the Germans were also strange. He had retreated from the Albanian Front and when there was no train to take him any further south he and his comrades started walking. And they walked for miles and miles, stragglers from a ghost army. Sometimes they walked in the company of the German advancing columns with the German soldiers paying scant attention to them.

"By then, we were in a pitiful state," he said, "unshaven and filthy, the only clean bits on our whole bodies was where the sweat had formed little gutters in the grime. Little grooves of sweat. It didn't matter. Our trousers were in shreds. And we were covered with fleas. You had to be constantly crushing them between your fingers.

"We arrived at Karditsa where there was a hotel, and the manager wouldn't give us a room, because of the fleas. As we continued on our way, we saw a little shop with eighteen individual cream custards and rice puddings in the window. We went in ... we had some money ... 'How much? Here you are, close the door' ... and we sat down and ate them all. We really stuffed ourselves, but we weren't finished yet.

"We found a room in a four-story house, a funny, narrow little building, and since it was still early and our stomachs were full, we went down to check out the town. There were Germans there."

It was a bizarre setting. The victorious German soldiers were part of the population that mingled and walked in the streets, and in their midst were the local people, still operating their shops. Bands of Greek refugee soldiers, all in the same condition as

Ptolemaios Kaliafas with their clothes in rags and their bodies infested with fleas, roamed about like lost children. The German soldiers observed them in wonderment. How could this be the army that had devastated the Italians?

"There was an outdoor cinema, semi-outdoor really, and we decided to go and see a movie," said Kaliafas. "And all the soldiers ended up going to the cinema. It was three and a half drachmas a ticket and as soon as we got in, before the film started, we started up singing something everyone was singing at the time: 'Mussolini, you old fart, we're gonna tear you all apart. Your Italians are so tough, but it's obviously just a bluff.'

"We heard machine gun fire. The Germans wanted to break us up. They didn't fire at us, just into the air to scare us. The shots did no harm, but the crush and the panic to get out was no fun."[3]

IN ARFARA, ON THE PELOPONNESE, where the Germans had pursued the retreating New Zealanders of the British Army to the most southerly port of Kalamata, things didn't look too bad. The entire Georgountzos* family had seen the whole episode unfold before their eyes.

The columns of the British Army filed endlessly past their village toward Kalamata and evacuation, and the entire family stood along the roadside watching the procession. The British had been confident of their escape since the German Army would not be able to cross the great canal at Corinth once the bridge was blown. But the Germans launched a surprise glider-borne and parachute attack on the British defenders holding the bridge, captured it and were again in hot pursuit.

Nineteen-year-old Dennis Georges had left Athens on the day the Germans invaded since the school he was attending had closed. He was determined to make his way to the family farm in Arfara.

---

* Some in the Georgountzos family later changed their names to the more easily pronounced Georges and will be referred to by that name.

Dennis Georges was a hero in both the Greek Resistance during the second World War (for Greece) and in the Korean War (for the U.N. Forces). Here he is in 1948 doing intelligence work.

"We had to make our way back to the village because there was nothing to eat and there were no jobs as businesses closed," he said. "I and another friend of mine took the train to go to the village, because in the village we had a farm, and we could have something to eat. When we left Athens we came to the Isthmus of Corinth and the German airplanes were coming and bombing and firing their machine guns, and the British were trying to protect the canal from the German invasion. And a *Messerschmitt* came and machine gunned the train to try and put it out of commission. We all ran out and jumped into this big hole and there must have been a hundred other people in the same hole.

"The Germans were bombing the highway, and I was in the hole all day, and the British soldiers were there to protect the bridge across the Isthmus, and they had anti-aircraft guns firing at the attacking German airplanes. And one of the gun crew leaders of the guns firing at the planes, what do you think he was doing while firing? He was shaving! That's right, shaving. Unbelievable! He was cursing the Germans and firing and shaving. That was the British influence which they had. They were trained to take care of the empire.

"This was the first time I saw dead people, and the train stopped because it could go no further, and I and the other two or three fellows with me started walking toward the village which was 160 miles away from the Canal. We left Corinth on a Friday evening and followed the tracks and walked all night, and the next days and arrived in Arfara on Tuesday morning."[4]

Dennis Georges had raced ahead of the German Army and joined his family in Arfara just days before the enemy columns arrived. He watched the drama of the last battle with the British unfold with his cousins and siblings. From the family's lofty perch on the hill by the church they had an unobstructed view.

As the last of the British column began to pass, six-year-old Konstantin Georgountzos watched two New Zealand soldiers take up positions on the right side of the road on a small rise and set up their machine gun to cover the road. They were there only a short time before the head of the German column approached with its motorcycles in the lead. The New Zealanders delivered a stream of automatic weapons fire on the German column stopping it in its tracks and forcing it to deploy.

The Germans maneuvered along both sides of the road trying to outflank the deadly gun, but the New Zealanders had selected their ground well and kept the attacking enemy at bay. They held their ground for several hours and each minute of time that they bought meant a chance for additional rescue down the road at Kalamata. Finally, toward dusk, the Germans got the upper hand and surrounded and overran the position, killing the two defending New Zealanders.

To the people of Arfara, this terrible scene was their first look at the German Army. But days later, after the British ended their evacuation efforts and had surrendered, Konstantin watched the Germans bury their dead.

"I still remember a military cemetery the Germans erected outside of Kalamata and their soldiers moving small trees from the land near our home in the village in order to decorate the cemetery. Then things stabilized and my father returned back to his position in the city and our country began life under triple occupation and was divided between the Germans, the Italians, and the Bulgarians, and with that began chaos and the crumbling of our society."[5]

THE EVACUATION OF THE ALLIED forces from Greece to the Island of Crete had been staged on five successive nights beginning on April 22. The Royal Navy had used six cruisers, nineteen destroyers and numerous smaller transports and other vessels to accomplish a second Dunkirk.[6] But Admiral Cunningham's ships had not gone unscathed. He had lost two of his destroyers to the German Luftwaffe during the evacuation, and the German air forces scattered his ships and those of the Greek Navy with constant combat air patrols. Dealing with the Italian air forces had been one thing, but the German Luftwaffe revealed the Allies' Achilles Heel.

"The first heavy bombing of the Port of Piraeus by German aircraft on the night of April 6 showed the inefficiency of our anti-aircraft defenses," said Captain Mezeviris of the Royal Hellenic Navy. Our anti-aircraft batteries surrounding the Naval Station of Salamis and at Elefsis had succeeded to repulse the rather feeble attacks of the Italian airplanes ... the anti-aircraft defense was completely insufficient to repulse a vastly larger German attack.

"In addition, our destroyers had minimum anti-aircraft weaponry and were not equipped with multi-barrel machine guns, which is the only effective weapon against German dive bombers. Even more serious was the scarcity of anti-aircraft ammunition. The destroyers were ordered not to fire unless directly threatened."[7]

Because of the continuous threat of German fighters and bombers, the British Navy was forced to disperse and the Greek ships were reduced to continuous sailing trying to hide behind small islands to avoid detection. On April 22, the Greek destroyer *Hydra*, under the command of Captain Mezeviris, prepared to sail to Crete and then on to Alexandria, Egypt.

"Since the morning we had changed positions several times, but nowhere could we become invisible," said Mezeviris. "I asked Commander Pezopoulos if he had any ideas about what to do until the time we sailed to the rendezvous point. He said, 'whatever is destined to happen, will happen.'

"At 1730 an enemy reconnaissance aircraft appeared. To confuse it, I ordered to change course ... and when the plane disappeared, I returned to our previous course. Twenty minutes later, seventy airplanes were sighted. Thirty-five of them separated and headed toward *Hydra.* I ordered full speed and continuous zigzags, and then [we opened] fire when the first squadron entered our firing range.

"The planes were diving, releasing their bombs from low altitude and at the same time machine gunning, aiming at the bridge. It was raining bombs around the ship and water jets were flooding her up to the upper bridge. Two anti-aircraft batteries went out almost immediately and the third one jammed. After a while one of our engines, and then the other one stalled. Weaponless and immobilized, the ship was at the mercy of the foe."[8]

In London, Winston Churchill tried to focus on the bright side of this tremendous ordeal. He signaled General Wavell: "I congratulate you upon successful evacuation. We have paid our debt of honour with far less loss than I feared. Feel sure you are waiting to strike a blow. Enemy's difficulties must be immense."[9]

Judging from the speed of the German preparations to invade Crete, the difficulties must have been less than "immense." In short order the Luftwaffe had wrested control of the sea in the waters around Greece from the Allied navy, and had occupied Greek bases for their airborne and transport regiments. Two *Fliegerkorps*, VIII and IX, would conduct Operation Mercury. The VIII Corps would provide the support aircraft—fighters, bombers and reconnaissance planes—while the IX Corps would provide the paratroopers.

VIII Corps was massive indeed. It sported sixty recon aircraft, 280 bombers, 150 dive-bombers and 180 fighters. The German plan called for 22,750 men to assault the Island of Crete. Ten thousand paratroopers would follow the spearhead of 750 men in gliders in the initial assault and once the airfields were secured, 5,000 more troopers would land in transports and 7,000 would land by ship.[10]

While the German airborne threat was not to be ignored, those forces were still airborne forces with all their inherent weaknesses. They were limited to what they could carry in on their backs, or land in gliders or drop in containers. They would have to begin as single soldiers and hopefully regroup rapidly to form a fighting force, and they were very vulnerable to ground fire. Their landing zones offered no concealment and an opposing force might easily surround the landing area and inflict enormous casualties before they would even have a chance to fight. Their ability to be effective was linked to reinforcement and rapid resupply.

Churchill, far removed from the potential battlefield, recognized these weaknesses. He signaled his thoughts to General Wavell.

"It seems clear from our information that a heavy airborne attack by German troops and bombers will soon be made on Crete ... It ought to be a fine opportunity for killing the parachute troops."[11]

The German parachute invasion would be limited to terrain along the northern coast of the 160-mile wide island. The island was wider than it was long. From north to south it was only forty miles but its southern shores were separated from the north by an enormous, lateral mountain spine with peaks as high as 7,000 feet. Crete had only one airfield at Heraklion and one port that could handle two small ships simultaneously at Suda. It had two flat landing grounds at Maleme and Retimo, and its main road connected the villages along the northern shore. Only two mountain tracks led across the giant peaks to connect to the southern shore.

The 10,000 Greek soldiers that had been evacuated from the mainland formed the Greek Expeditionary Force, but they were lacking the arms and materiels of a fighting force. While many soldiers had their individual weapons and small amounts of ammunition they had carried with them, there were few crew-served weapons and no guns or vehicles. Efforts to resupply these forces upon arrival in Crete were largely unsuccessful due to the presence of the constantly patrolling Luftwaffe. Only 3,000 tons of ammunition out of 27,000 tons shipped escaped the German bombs as did half the guns and engineering materiel.[12]

On May 1, General Bernard Freyberg, commander of the 32,000 British Commonwealth and 10,000 Greek Allied forces on the island soon realized the precarious state of his army. He signaled to General Wavell:

"Unless fighter aircraft are greatly increased and naval forces made available to deal with seaborne attack, I cannot hope to hold out with land forces alone, which as a result of campaign in Greece are now devoid of any artillery, have insufficient tools for digging, very inadequate war reserves of equipment and ammunition. Forces here can and will fight, but without full support from Navy and Air Force cannot hope to repel invasion. If for other reasons these cannot be made available at once, urge that question of holding Crete should be reconsidered."[13]

But because of secret intelligence in London that revealed and detailed the entire scope of the German airborne operation, optimism abounded. On May 9 the Chief-of-Staff signaled concerning Operation Scorcher: "So complete is our information that it appears to present heaven-sent opportunity of dealing enemy heavy blow ..."[14]

Freyberg set his defenses to protect the northern coastline including the airfield and landing areas at Heraklion, Retimo and Maleme, and the port at Suda Bay. He made a pragmatic assessment of his situation to defend against the German attack to General Wavell:

"I feel sure we should be able to stop him if he attacks after the sixteenth. If however he makes a combined operation of it with a beach landing with tanks, then we shall not be in a strong position ..."[15]

General Freyberg put on a strong face against these overwhelming odds. He certainly knew his chances were slim. His Anglo-Greek forces were barely equipped, facing an enemy who had overwhelmed all opponents with hardly a setback. It would be easy to criticize the entire idea of defending Crete, but what were the alternatives? There were none, unless one considered abandoning Crete and pulling back to the western desert in Egypt as an option. The consequences of that were self-evident: loss of control of the Mediterranean, German air forces now in range of Allied forces in Egypt, and conquest and enslavement of 400,000 Cretans.

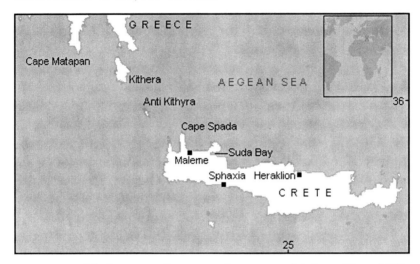

It would be equally tempting to criticize Churchill's seemingly overenthusiastic messages and demands from London to his beleaguered forces and their generals on the battlefield. But Churchill's job was to lead and inspire confidence in these the darkest of hours. He could have avoided the entire situation that had begun in October of 1940 by simply abandoning Greece to the Axis powers. He could have surrendered early and left Greece to its own fate, but Greece had been his only Ally in the entire free world to face the fascist might with him.

His messages from London might sound more like those of a charlatan, far removed from the battlefield and out of harm's way, foolishly ordering his doomed army into a battle. But he was not. He had stood with France and escaped at Dunkirk and he and his countrymen had endured the Battle of Britain, alone, and had fought the enemy in Norway and in the desert and were now fighting them at sea in the Battle of the Atlantic. His homeland was being bombed and smashed on a daily basis. The dark forces of Fascism were on the march to conquer Europe, and he was facing this irresistible force with only one small ally, Greece.

At the time that he sent optimistic and cheery messages filled with bravado to his generals, he was under fire himself on his own battlefield, London. On the night of May 10 the Germans bombed London in a heavy raid and those bombs found the House of Commons, smashing it. Liverpool, along with other British ports, was hit and fires from burning buildings lit the skies. The light from this conflagration could be seen for miles.

Still Churchill would not be mentally ground under by the enemy. "All my information points to 'Scorcher' any day after seventeenth. Hope you have got enough in Colorado* and those there have the needful in cannon, machine guns and A.F.Vs (Armored Fighting Vehicles) ... I should particularly welcome chance for our high-class troops to come to close grips with those people under conditions where enemy has not got his usual mechanical advantages and where we can surely reinforce much easier than he can ... "[16]

Churchill's optimism encouraged Wavell who answered, "We have stout-hearted troops keen and ready for fight under stout-hearted commander and I hope enemy will find 'Scorcher' red-hot proposition."[17]

THE GERMANS ATTACKED CRETE at 0530 on May 20, beginning with massive bombing runs on the airfields at Maleme and Heraklion. A second wave of planes swept British defensive positions at 0715.

"It's a terrifying sound, a terrifying ordeal to be on the receiving end of a *Stuka* dive," said Arthur Douglas of the 106th Royal Horse Artillery. "They seem to be diving straight at you, like as if it's me that they are coming for.

"One morning, the *Stuka* raids stopped. The *Messerschmitt* raids stopped, and there was sort of an eerie silence. It was quite strange because your ears and your nerves had gotten so used to this continual bombing and strafing that it was totally strange to see the sun and hear the silence, and you could hear the silence and it was so lovely. But it didn't last for very long when a

---

* Code name for Crete.

different noise came."[18]

On the heels of the fighters and bombers came the 493, three-engine *Ju-52* transports with the first waves of paratroopers and towing seventy gliders. The crews of the sixty-eight anti-aircraft guns scattered along the 160-mile width of the northern Cretan coastline did not have the luxury of blazing away at the approaching air fleet. Shortages of ammunition dictate fire discipline.

The British defenders craned their necks skyward to see the streams of jumpers and supply packs exiting the transports amid the black puff of exploding shells delivered by the ground batteries. The parachutes blossomed in all the colors of the rainbow, each color meant for easy identification. White was for weapons and ammunition, yellow for medical supplies, pink and violet chutes indicated officers and NCOs so that the landing troops could rally to their leaders. One mesmerized British soldier described it as if it were "balloons coming down from the ceiling of a dance-hall after a party."[19]

The Cretan people also gazed up into the sky at the strange sight of the first airborne assault in military history.

"I was up in an olive tree watching them come down," said Kaliopi Kapetanakis. "I was only fifteen years old and I had no idea what I was seeing. I told my friend, 'the whole sky is full of umbrellas.'"[20]

Seventeen-year-old Chrissa Ninolakis could not believe her eyes. "It was something for me, a fascinating, spectacular sight. And then, immediately the cries from everywhere, 'the Germans are coming. The Germans are here.' And then I was afraid. But the Cretan spirit is always the same and the people went down to fight."[21]

As the German paratroopers hit the ground in the Maleme area, they rushed to form into fighting teams. One of the weaknesses of airborne forces is the fact that each man lands separately and needs to find his fighting team to reorganize. Typically a German paratroop squad or section might consist of eight men with semi-automatic or automatic weapons, two snipers, and a three-man machine gun crew. Special teams would be armed with light anti-tank weapons and flamethrowers.

German paratroopers in Crete

The initial waves of paratroopers suffered heavy casualties, partly because their daylight descent under their canopies presented a lucrative target to the defenders, but mostly in their mad scramble on the ground to locate para-packs of ammunition and equipment.[22] By early afternoon, the Germans had little to show for their operation and were isolated and pinned down.

The second wave prepared to depart from the Greek mainland, but all was not smooth at the airfields. The planes had to be refueled by hand, the choking dust from air activity formed a permanent cloud over the airfields and vital communications necessary to coordinate the gigantic airlift was in a shambles thanks to Greek partisan activity jamming and cutting telephone lines. This confusion resulted in the fighters providing air cover departing long before the transports were able to get airborne. Instead of the transports departing as a unit, they were able to take off only in small isolated groups.[23]

Because of the poor coordination at the Greek airfields, the protecting German fighters used up precious fuel waiting for the transports, translating into shortened time over the battle areas. In many cases the ground forces had no air cover.

The paratroop drop was scattered and part of the drop landed in a less defended zone, running into enraged civilians armed with farm tools, clubs, stones—anything that could kill the invaders. They provided substantial resistance along with the forces of the Greek Gendarmerie. The Germans were forced to break contact and fall back to more defensible positions.

All across the island the Cretan population rose up to participate in the attack, and many German paratroopers found themselves fighting for their lives, surrounded by civilians wielding knives and swinging clubs.

"Everyone—men and women, great and small—ran to the nearest scene of action to attack the enemy, armed as they were," said George Psychoundakis, a twenty-one-year-old shepherd from the village of Asi Gonia, far removed from the main roads. "[They had] guns that anyone would have sworn were taken from some museum. The villagers had kept them for many years in holes and caves and now, all eaten up with rust, they really were almost archaeological specimens."[24]

At the end of the day, the German paratroopers were clinging to small defensive positions and the three airfields all still remained in British hands. They had suffered more casualties than Germany's killed-in-action since the beginning of the war.[25] The issue was very much in doubt.

On the Greek mainland, the ports of Piraeus and Thessaloniki were hubs of activity. The German seaborne forces had embarked on their transports and weighed anchor to begin convoys to Crete, escorted by Italian destroyers. The naval invasion consisted of two flotillas, the first was to land on May 21 at Maleme, and the second to land the following day at Heraklion. These flotillas were made up with sixty *caiques* (small landing vessels) and seven transport ships. The Italian escort force had two destroyers and twelve torpedo boats accompanied by smaller vessels and minesweepers.

While the term flotilla technically described the German naval force, its makeup was hardly first class or worthy of the title. A German soldier described the caiques that made up the flotilla as "an assortment of scarcely seaworthy Greek coasting tramps and some larger rusty death traps."[26] Notwithstanding that dismal description, the "death trap" flotilla would be the only lifeline for the paratroopers now pinned down in Crete. Reinforcements, heavy equipment, ammunition and other materiel necessary for the successful pursuit of the attack on Crete were contained in the holds of these caiques.

The British Navy whose mission was to protect the forces on Crete had a daunting task. They had no air cover since the last aircraft had been withdrawn from the island and the aircraft carrier *Formidable* was reduced to only four operational aircraft. As such, Admiral Cunningham issued orders for the fleet to patrol north of the island only during the hours of darkness and to retreat to the south of Crete during daylight to avoid patrolling German aircraft.

In the darkness of early morning of May 21, twenty-five caiques of the first flotilla, laden with German support troops, ammunition and supplies for the beleaguered paratroopers on Crete, ventured out into the Aegean Sea. But rumors of the British fleet patrolling nearby caused the small group to return to base. Later during the day they set out again, at about the same time that the British fleet moved to a position north of Crete to block the route of a potential German seaborne invasion. If the British fleet made no contact, then during the night and early morning of the twenty-second and twenty third, Admiral Cunningham ordered it to sweep to the north toward the Greece mainland to try to locate those forces.

About midnight, part of the British fleet, patrolling eighteen miles to the north of Malame discovered the caique flotilla, with the Italian destroyer *Lupo* escorting. *Lupo* went into immediate action and accelerated to lay down a smoke screen in an attempt to hide and protect the defenseless caiques. But the destroyer's efforts were in vain, and British warships pummeled *Lupo* with 6-inch guns, scoring eighteen hits. With the Italian shepherd out of action, the British fleet pounced upon the caiques like hungry wolves on sheep, and destroyed all but three that managed to escape the murderous fire. But, in victory, the British fleet had expended a large part of their anti-aircraft ammunition and withdrew toward Alexandria.

At 1000, another force of the British fleet sighted a second group of caiques, which was the second flotilla, escorted by another Italian destroyer, *Sagittario*. The flotilla sighted the warships, executed an about face and raced to the north with the British Navy in hot pursuit. But in their pursuit, the British ships became dispersed chasing down the scattering small ships, and in their separation lost their concentrated anti-aircraft defensive fires.

The German Luftwaffe swooped in and attacked the dispersed British ships and from 1000 until noon conducted bombing and strafing attacks like a swarm of aroused hornets. The cruiser *Naiad* was hit and forced to reduce her speed. The destroyer *Greyhound*, in hot pursuit of a fleeing caique, was itself attacked and sunk by fighter-bombers. Two destroyers, *Kandahar* and *Kingston*, raced to the scene to pick up survivors but were themselves soon under attack from the relentless German aircraft. The two destroyers could take only a few men aboard before they were driven off the rescue scene and reduced to throwing life floats to the men swimming in the water.

Two additional cruisers, *Fiji* and *Gloucester*, responded to the frantic calls for help from the stricken ships and raced to the scene. But *Fiji* had only eighteen percent of her allotted AA ammunition and *Gloucester* was just slightly better off with thirty percent.

Ted Garner was on board *Fiji*. "Our ship was one of Britain's fastest and most powerful cruisers and we were relentlessly dive-bombed from dawn to dusk, until her shell rooms were emptied of AA ammunition.

"The attack had begun at dawn. As the sun rose, sixteen *Ju-87s* appeared, flying against the hot, blue sky. A fierce barrage met their dives and their bombs went wide. A half hour later, a second formation closed over us, one plane swooping so low that we could see the tires on its landing wheels turning with the force of the dive. The noise of our guns was too great for us to hear its engines. We saw the bombs, small and black at first, falling, increasing prodigiously, now with fins that turned the air into a shriek. We crouched. The explosions rocked the ship. One bomb threw up a wave that drenched the bridge with black water. All about us, the sea gave up fountains of water sparkling in the sunlight. One bomb splinter cut through seven bulkheads."[27]

Both *Fiji* and *Gloucester* eventually joined *Greyhound* on the bottom of the sea. German aircraft also blasted *Warspite*, the heroic battleship at Matapan, and early on the twenty-fourth Admiral Cunningham ordered the entire British fleet to withdraw to Alexandria.[28]

He had sustained severe losses and in his attempt to retreat to Alexandria he suffered more. Just off the south coast of Crete, the Luftwaffe spotted some of the withdrawing British fleet and again attacked. The destroyers *Kashmir* and *Kelly* sank in minutes.

Signals Officer Edward Dunsterville was on the bridge as he watched a German plane attack and drop the fatal bomb. The bomb detonated and Dunsterville held on to whatever he could as the *Kelly* immediately listed. "I was clinging on as long as I could, then I was swept down, came up too near the propellers for comfort and went down again." He finally surfaced to find "a lot of us bobbing about and we found bits of wood to hold on to."[29]

During the three-day battle with the German Luftwaffe, the British Navy lost two cruisers, four destroyers, and one battleship was put out of action. Additionally two cruisers and four destroyers were severely damaged. Cunningham had to signal Churchill in London, "Unable to reinforce or supply Crete except by fast warships at night."[30]

One final attempt to reinforce Crete was made on the night of the twenty-fifth, but again the Germans discovered the force and swept in to destroy it. *HMS Glenroy* signaled the disaster: "Unable to continue operation tonight. One third of landing craft out of action, part may be repaired tomorrow. All army petrol burnt or overboard."[31]

The German aircraft seemed to be everywhere. The carrier *Formidable* was struck and damaged as well as its escorting ships. On May 27 the Germans struck and severely damaged the battleship *Barham*.

Crete was doomed. By May 23 the German paratroopers had established an effective airfield at Maleme and were landing troop-carrying aircraft every three minutes. Those aircraft then took off again to reload with more reinforcements.[32]

On the twenty-seventh, Wavell signaled the bad news to Churchill: "Fear the situation in Crete most serious. Canae front has collapsed and Suda Bay only likely to be covered for another twenty-four hours if as long. There is no possibility of hurling in reinforcements. Reinforcement has steadily become more difficult on account increasing enemy air force and may now be considered impossible."

He continues:

"Telegram just received from Freyberg states only chance of survival of force in Suda area is to withdraw to beaches in south of island, hiding by day and moving by night."[33]

King George II and the Greek Government evacuated Crete to Alexandria, Egypt on the evening of May 25[34] and during the last three nights in May. The British evacuated 18,000 of the 32,000 British soldiers sent to Crete.

The path to evacuation was a tortuous one. It was impossible to attempt any rescue along the northern coast since the German ground and air forces prowled the entire area. That left the stony southern coast as the only other option, and it was a meager one. The beach at Sphakia was just a sliver of sand in the shadow of a steep mountain slope to the north. The track across the mountains leading to Sphakia was nothing more than a path.

The retreating forces would have to negotiate their way from the olive groves in the north, up and across the bare and stony mountains. The descent would be little better. A scrambling, stumbling series of steep tracks with the soldiers sliding and grabbing at scrub bushes for balance to the tiny beach below.

Some rested by day in the shade while those who were more anxious pressed on in the heat with little water. General Freyberg later called the path the *via dolorosa.*"[35]

The 5,000 British soldiers left behind faced surrender or evasion in the rugged hills of Crete. For Arthur Douglas the announcement of his fate came on June 1.

"They said, 'that's it lads, they've given up, capitulated. And the Germans have taken over the island from today. There's no more ships, the navy has lost too many, they're not taking any more off the island, and from now on, you'll be prisoners of war.'

"And shortly after he spoke, a German officer came down,

in shorts, and he wore knee-length boots, and he had a huge revolver dangling in his hand and he spoke absolutely perfect English, and his expression was, 'to you the war is over.' The buckle of his belt had the words, *Gott Mit Uns,* God is with us, and I turned to Lance Ferguson and said, if God's on his side, who's on ours?"[36]

During the next three months, 600 evaders were able to find their way to the Middle East.[37] Many of the Greek forces were taken prisoner or attempted to melt into the Cretan population.

Casualties in the British Navy were particularly high. Over 1,800 men had been killed in the German air attacks. Three battleships and an aircraft carrier had been badly damaged.* Nine other ships had been sunk and thirteen others damaged. Wavell had aptly described Germany's total air supremacy as a "box barrage of bombing aircraft."[38]

Germany had not escaped without horrific casualties to their airborne forces. The Battle of Crete had been the first complete airborne operation ever attempted. The German records listed 6,116 casualties including 2,131 wounded, but other records indicate that number to be very low.[39]

Winston Churchill thought the casualties around 15,000 since there were 4,465 marked graves at Maleme alone.[40] And British and Greek forces had reported on May 22 that they had buried 1,250 Germans at Heraklion.[41#]

Whatever the casualties, Germany would never again attempt an airborne operation. The German commander, General Kurt Student called the Battle for Crete, "the Tomb of the German Parachutists."[42] But with the fall of Greece and Crete, the last free European territory now fell under the iron fist of the Fascist powers. A contemporary historian perfectly described the final withdrawal from Crete and Greece's plunge into the unknown.

---

* HMS *Formidable* was so damaged by German dive-bombers it was sent to United States' repair docks.

Other Allied soldiers also reported burying 900 German bodies at Rethimnon.

"When darkness fell upon May 31, 1941, and mercifully hid from the German bombers the ships bearing the last soldiers that the Royal Navy could evacuate from Crete, the Hellenic people entered that dark night of the soul ..."[43]

CHAPTER 9
OCCUPATION, STARVATION AND RESISTANCE

WHEN THE LAST BRITISH SHIP sailed for Egypt, the island of Crete was left to her own destiny. Marooned British and Commonwealth soldiers took to the hills to escape the hands of the victorious German conquerors and were hidden by the loyal Cretan peasants. Those peasants who had fought side by side with their British allies now sought their own safety in the obscurity of their tiny villages as rumors of German atrocious behavior preceded the actual arrival of the enemy occupying forces.

German General Julius Ringel, who had commanded the 5th Mountain Division, had posted a memo to his forces that authorized retaliation against civilians:

"The Greek population, in civilian dress, has taken part in the fighting. Any Greek civilian captured with a firearm in his hands is to be shot immediately."

But Ringel's memorandum went much further than retaliation against Cretans who had fought for their homeland. It further stated: "Hostages are to be taken from the villages. If acts of hostility take place against the German Army, these hostages will be shot."[1]

George Psychoundakis recalled: "They began to burn down villages and torture the inhabitants, loading them like beasts of burden and killing them with appalling torments. The Germans proved themselves to be, in every way, utter barbarians. They were avenging, they said, their slain brothers-in-arms who now filled the whole island with graveyards."[2]

To consolidate their power and disarm the population, the Germans approached each village with an interpreter and took up a non-threatening position, usually in a small coffee shop. From there they summoned the town leader to come and sit with them. When the Mayor had arrived and introduced himself, the first question asked was whether the people of his village had taken part in the attacks against the German parachutists. In Asi Gonia, where George Psychoundakis lived, the Mayor said that his people had not and that the village was too far removed from the battle area, and had hardly even known that a battle was taking place.

Seemingly satisfied, the German officer then asked if the town possessed any weapons. The Mayor then denied any weapons saying that all weapons had long been given up to the army for defense, but hastened to add that there were a few "fowling-pieces" around. The Germans demanded that even those had to be turned over, and any hiding of weapons would be dealt with in the harshest of measures. Those measures included executions. For each weapon hoarded, ten men would be shot and their houses burned to the ground and families turned out.

Thus was revealed the hideous face of Nazism, and also the embryo of the Resistance. "The villagers thought it would be wise to hand over a few rotten and harmless guns, any old iron to deceive the Germans ... The good ones were hidden away as carefully as sacred relics," said Psychoundakis. "There were plenty, because when the English retreated to Sphakia for possible evacuation, even small boys had gone down to the seashore and the valleys bringing rifles back with them."[3]

ON THE MAINLAND, especially in Athens, the initial introduction to the German occupiers was similarly non-threatening. German sentries continued to salute former Greek officers and sang the praises of the Greek soldiers. The Italians were initially the bad guys.

"The Italians would go in forays out to try and find the Resistance people, and they would go and surround the whole village, and they would go into the village, and they would take everything from the homes, even cooking utensils, and they would start coming back to their base. The word would get to the mayor of the town, and he would go to the German commander and say, 'You're supposed to be our friends. Look what they are doing!' The commander would send his officers in a German car and turn the Italians around and send them back."[4]

The new Greek puppet government had been formed by Greek generals, led by General Georgios Tsolakoglou, who had capitulated in Epirus, and now sought favor with the conquerors. Tsolakoglou had somehow rationalized honor into his decision to capitulate.

"I found myself before a historic dilemma," he said. "To allow the fight to continue and have a holocaust or, obeying the pleas of the army's commanders, to assume the initiative of surrendering ..."[5]

But the pleas of the army's commanders, to which Tsolakoglou referred to as his justification to proceed with the idea of surrender, were actually only the pleas of two other wobbly corps commanders in the Army of Epirus and the Bishop of Ioannina. This committee hardly qualified for the label of the "army's commanders." Tsolakoglou's "historic dilemma" as to whether "to allow the fight to continue" was neither his dilemma nor his decision to make. In fact, Tsolakoglou's superior, the actual commander of the Epirus Army, General Pitsikas, had flatly refused to entertain such an idea for capitulation when that self-appointed committee had first approached him with their ideas. In fact it was Pitsikas who had frantically signaled the prime minister that urgent help was needed to continue the fight: "In the name of God," he had pleaded, "save the army from the Italians."[6]

But his pleas had fallen on deaf ears, because although Prime Minister Koryzis promised Pitsikas there would be a "favorable solution to the matter within the course of the day," it was not forthcoming. Koryzis's solution to the crisis had been to succumb to the temptations of depression and despair and shoot himself.

So as a reward for his mutiny and capitulation, Tsolakoglou*
was appointed prime minister by the Germans and served well
to relay German orders and demands to the Greek people and
became the official German mouthpiece.[7] On the surface things
did not look too bad. The conquerors proclaimed that German
occupation meant safety and prosperity for all Greeks. But
no amount of cajoling, feigned courtesy, ceremonial saluting,
could sway most Athenians that a dark day had truly arrived in
their city, and the conquerors were really the proverbial wolves
masquerading in sheep's clothing.

Each day Athenians were painfully reminded of the fact that
the Germans had ensconced themselves on their land. They
were the lords and masters. High above the city, for everyone to
see, the red Nazi flag with its swastika flew from the most sacred
of Greek land, the high hill of the Acropolis.

* At war's end, Tsolakoglou was tried by a Special Collaborators Court,
found guilty and sentenced to death. That sentence was commuted to life
in prison, where he died in 1948.

ON THAT FATEFUL DAY of defeat and occupation, April 27, the Germans had arrived and paraded as victorious conquerors and passed to the review of General List. First came the German motorized armored scout cars followed by other armored units. Because of the insistence of Mussolini, Italian soldiers were also included in the parade.

While the German unit commanders sat tall in the turrets of the scout cars, the Italian soldiers were parading in trucks, jammed in like sardines, seated on benches four across and six deep with their bayoneted rifles held vertical to their sides.[8] German infantry followed the mechanized units, all in the shadow of the Acropolis.

The Germans had sent a motorized unit to that spot that overlooked the entire city and from which the blue and white flag of Greece snapped in the breeze. It was at that stony outcropping, directly in front of the Parthenon that they would ceremonially raise their conquering flag.

The German commander ordered the young Greek Evzone, Konstantinos Koukidis, who was the guardian of the Greek flag, to "retire" the Greek colors. Perhaps the Germans made that "generous" gesture to curry favor among the Greek citizens and to present themselves as compassionate occupiers and not appear as harsh masters. Or perhaps it was just a common courtesy among soldiers and a follow-up to Hitler's orders to treat Greeks with respect. But whatever the reason, Koukidis was given the opportunity to lower his country's flag with respect before the new flag would be raised.

Greeks who could witness the event wept, just as citizens of other countries had wept as the irresistible German Wehrmacht had ground their nations under. Koukidis lowered the flag and unhooked the blue and white banner from the clips on the rope halyard. He then reverently wrapped the flag about his own body, as if it were a shroud, and, in a final act of defiance, hurled himself off of the edge of the stony outcropping to his death far below. He had struck the first blow against tyranny in the eventual rebellion.

The Germans raised their flag, but the fire of resistance had been kindled and it wasn't long before others, following the spirit and inspiration of the self-sacrificing Koukidis, rose to defiance. Three days later, on April 30, two students scaled the northwest face of the Acropolis, in the dead of night, to rip the accursed Nazi flag from the pole. Manolis Glezos and Apostolos Siantas braved capture and certain execution to pull off their heroic feat and inspired not only Greece, but also the rest of the free world.[9]

Rigas Rigopoulos wrote, "Just a glimpse of the Nazi flag with its swastika flying over the Acropolis was enough to upset us ... the enemy uniforms filled Athens, the black boots and the heavy stomping that echoed loudly in the night silence, the shouts and orders heard in a foreign language—all these ... created a suffocating atmosphere ..."[10]

The Germans quickly posted the rules of conquest. There would be a curfew: no one on the streets after 2200. All firearms to be turned in within twenty-four hours. No radio could be tuned into any foreign station and, of course, it was forbidden to shelter any British soldier left behind. All violators were to be executed. Greeks ignored such proclamations and the Germans at first issued only warnings to the rule-breakers.

"We eagerly waited each evening near the radio," said Rigopoulos. "Between the noise of the interference produced by the enemy to neutralize the Allies' broadcasts, we distinguished with difficulty the beloved signal ... three dots and a dash: The letter "V." The sign of Victory ... The radio broke our isolation, animated our spirit of national pride, and reinforced our souls' resistance."[11]

Greece had been divided into three parts for occupation. The Germans needed to bring in the Italians and Bulgarians to free the bulk of their forces for the upcoming assault on Russia, Operation Barbarossa. Hitler defined Germany's interests in Greece as securing supply and communications routes to the German air bases in Greece and the island of Crete, safeguarding copper in northeastern Serbia and protecting shipping routes on the Danube.[12] Of course, there were the oil fields in Ploesti, but those were now secure since the British had been driven out of the country and their navy had been dealt a severe blow in their Crete operations.

The Triple Occupation of Greece by the Axis Powers (1941-1944)

Legend:
■ German Occupation Zone
■ Italian Occupation Zone (occ. by Germany after Sept. 1943)
■ Bulgarian Occupation Zone
☐ Bulgarian occupation (under German control) from July 1943
■ Dodecanese Islands (Italian possession since 1912)

In an ironic reversal of roles, the Italian Army that had barely survived annihilation at the hands of the Greek Army, now assumed the role of principal occupiers of the land. The Germans maintained control of the key city of Athens, Eastern Macedonia, Eastern Thrace and two-thirds of Crete, and gave control of Western Macedonia and Western Thrace to Bulgaria.

But despite their heroic struggles against the giant, totalitarian powers of Italy and Germany, and the world acclaim and admiration that Greek courage and fighting spirit had garnered, for the Greek population it all came down to occupation and survival. Hunger and Want became Greece's new enemies. No amount of glory for their mighty struggles could diminish the fact that their new fight against these two new, unassailable enemies would be a matter of survival. George Kotsonis remembered it well even though he was only four years old.

"In their opening act in the Greek drama the Germans gathered and stole all foodstuffs they could find in Greece to feed the German Army. This act created the famous famine of

1941 that spread out all over Greece and especially in the urban areas. Thousands died of starvation, especially in Athens where the garbage cars in some cases were picking up dead bodies from the streets. When I complained to my mother that I was hungry, she used to say 'wet your finger with saliva, dip it in the salt, and eat it'. I am not quite sure whether that recipe worked out as intended."[13]

The Germans literally looted the cities. Stores had nothing to sell and despite possessing money or wealth, there was nothing to buy and barter became popular.

"When you saw your first person lying dead on the street, you gathered around and were horrified and did not know what to do," said Konstantin Georgountzos, who was six years old. "When you saw the second one, you paused and observed. When you saw the third one, you quickly walked past."[14]

"The Germans had entered Athens and paraded like conquerors in Syntagma Square," said Philippos Mavrogenis. I was just a little kid, and I remember going and staring open-mouthed at all that stuff. And then it was the Occupation and a time of great trials for the Greek people ... especially for us here in Athens, in the capital ... and people were dying of hunger, they had nothing to eat ... nothing at all. There was nothing ... the Germans had taken everything for the German Army, and us poor wretches here would sit around with empty stomachs, trying somehow to find something."[15]

Mavrogenis was thirteen and remembered the cruelty of the black marketeers preying on the misfortune and plight of starving people.

"They were, from round about Athens, and they'd bring in a little wheat, or corn, or something like that. Four or five kilos, and for that you'd have to give them a house. And those 'gentlemen' made a fortune out of those people's houses, because people were dying."[16]

"I found myself in the soup kitchens," said Chrysoula Korotzi, and [you would not believe] the things that happened! People would wait in line to get their share, which would just about keep body and soul together ... because everything was carefully rationed. And there wasn't any bread to be had. The bread we had, well, it was, and at the same time it wasn't, bread. It was made out of broom seeds, and was like mud that they stuck on a piece of grease-proof paper, and they'd give you some with your ration."

Those who had died from starvation were able to serve their loved ones who were still living in a macabre way.

"Because people wanted one more portion, they'd hide their dead ... they didn't register their death, but who was going to ask questions back then? When if you went out onto the street in the morning in this neighborhood, you'd see dead bodies on the streets with swollen bellies, and kids with their bones sticking out, and them dead, too. And the town hall would send a cart round every morning, the Council truck, and they'd throw those people into the back, just like you would a side of beef. I'll never forget it, them just lying there ... and them picking them off the street."[17]

"There was rain, misery, hunger, and my father going to collect snails," said Tasos Zografos. He got wet, caught a cold, which turned into pneumonia and they took him into the public hospital. He loved fish, but where could I find fish? But the taverna had some for the Italians, and I thought I'll slip a couple of fried fish in my pocket to take to my father when I went to see him."

Zografos entered the tavern and tried to make his way to the table where he could pinch the fish, and thought that maybe in all the talking and chatter, he could take some and escape unnoticed. But he was not good at remaining unnoticed and after transferring his pilfered prizes to his pocket, the Italians caught him.

"Of course, it wasn't just the fish that left the taverna," he said, "... so did I, and for good. That was when the struggle started and I mean that quite literally—for survival: four younger brothers and sisters, and a mother with no chance of finding a job because, at that time, women didn't go out to work. And now with my father ill, it was up to me to get the whole family through this. I had a little trolley, and I'd move stuff from place to place.

"One time a German stopped me to carry his stuff to Larisis

Station. It must have been two or three kilometers away, but we made it. He took his stuff and got ready to leave. I asked him 'money?' and he gave me a kick. The Italians would give you a crust of bread."[18]

In Athens, the Germans forced shop owners to display pictures of Adolph Hitler. If the German occupiers were intent on good relations with the occupied population, this was an act guaranteed to ensure failure.

Rigas Rigopoulos daydreamed and imagined "if all over Athens every window with the hated despot's picture would break at the same moment, every heart would fill with satisfaction and new strength against the depression of slavery." The young man, however, went further than just daydreaming. He contacted his friends at the university.

"Stavros and his fellow chemical engineers would have to design and build small explosive devices with elastic suction cups that would break the shop windows' glass thirty seconds after adherence without causing harm to passersby," Rigopoulos said. "Experiments went on for several days ... but unfortunately did not produce the desired results. The suction cups came off with the explosion without breaking the five-millimeter thick glass."[19]

But daydreaming and reality were two different things; and reality was: starvation. The most unlikely events became sources of possibilities for food. Garbage cans were the first to lure passersby to examine for meager hidden treasures. Then they became territorial possessions to be fought for just as a lion stakes out his territory against all intruders. Hunger turned people into animals, into collaborators, into betrayers. Many Greeks testified that hunger was worse than death.

The occupiers themselves sometimes turned out to be a source of unexpected, discarded nourishment.

"I remember the Germans peeling potatoes," said Zografros. "It was drudgery in the army to peel potatoes, so the peelings were very thick ... food for us. And we'd go and pick them out of the rubbish, wash them and make a potato soup. When the Germans caught on to us, they'd go and piss on the rubbish ... as if that made any difference—we'd still take them and wash them.[20]

During that first year of occupation, an estimated 100,000 Greeks died of starvation, especially in the large cities where obtaining food was no easy task. It was not that the Greek harvest had been a disaster—it had been approximately seventy-five percent of the previous year's crop—it was the government and the occupiers that could not provide the necessary support to bring the harvest into the flow of vital material to sustain the Greek population. Those in the rural areas generally had enough to survive and even barter with their excess for other necessities. Those in the cities bartered everything, including priceless personal possessions, just to survive.

"People were starving," said Dimitri Tsaras. "I remember at one point my mother traded our good china, one hundred pieces of china that my father had bought for my mother in their younger years from Czechoslovakia, with his initials and her initials on it, traded it for two containers of olive oil, and one container turned out to be bad."[21]

People tried to survive with the black market where even the occupiers plied their trade. "We had a German soldier, Karl, who would walk to our house and he would bring a sack of potatoes and we would give him whatever money, or whatever fruit we had.

The plight of the Greeks, although initially slow to evoke public outcry, eventually did and the Axis Powers engaged in a colossal game of finger pointing. True to form, Adolph Hitler used his incompetent junior partner, whom he had allowed to participate at the signing of the Greek surrender, and whom he had allowed to march in the victory parade in Athens amid great ceremony, to take the fall in the court of public opinion. After all, was it not Italy that was in charge of the occupying force? Everyone knew that.

On May 31, even in The Duce's own country, an article in the magazine *Minerva* had carried a Greek slogan that had The Duce hopping mad. It said, "No greater misfortune can befall a country than to be governed by an *old* tyrant." Was there any question as to who was in charge of Greece, and who was responsible for the current debacle and deaths of the Greek population? Wasn't the conquest of Greece just what Mussolini had always wanted?

Did not Italy go to war in 1940 to accomplish that very goal? Even though the Italian Army had stumbled around and had to be rescued by Adolph Hitler's army, was it not The Führer who then graciously handed Greece over to his friend to bask in the glow of victory? Hitler was on very solid ground in the blame game.

Ten days later, Mussolini's pot boiled over. He was still smarting from his continued status as second fiddle, a status that had originally led him to bite off more than the could chew in Greece, and a status that now seemed destined to paint him as the great pariah in this current Greek situation.

"I am thoroughly disgusted with the Germans since the time List signed an armistice with Greece without our knowledge and the soldiers of the Casale Division ... found a German soldier barring the road and robbing us of the fruits of victory ..."[22]

Count Ciano thought this tirade was "Mussolini at his best."[23]

But Mussolini was not finished with his grousing. "Personally I've had my fill with Hitler and the way he acts. These conferences that begin with the ringing of a bell are not to my liking. When people call their servants, they ring a bell. And besides, what kind of meetings are these? For five hours I am forced to listen to a monologue that is quite pointless and boring."[24]

So there was no question as to who was in charge, and if Hitler was seeming to be moving to a position of "it's not my responsibility," and was happy to continue to extract food supplies from the beleaguered people of Greece and send those supplies to his troops in North Africa, then it was going to be The Duce who was going to have to explain starvation to the world.

But The Führer did not get off scot-free. *Time* magazine exposed Hitler to its readers as the master of the techniques of sacking a city and its people. It seemed that the principal of Athens College had witnessed the plundering of the city and had written an article in which he stated that "the Nazis stripped Greece of not only food, automobiles, bicycles and furniture, but carried off even doorknobs, locks & keys." It also appeared that the Italians were at least trying to send some foodstuffs to Greece, but it was the Germans who were the problem. "Mussolini sent 1,000 cases of milk to Greek babies who needed it desperately," the magazine reported, "ten cases were distributed, then the Nazis followed the old Nazi custom—'borrowed' the remaining 990."[25]

On top of the Acropolis, the authorities had, in order to not entice open revolt, allowed the flag of Greece to fly. Of course it did not fly alone and was flanked by the Nazi swastika and the flag of Italy. The Greeks labeled it, "Christ hung between two thieves."[26]

Worldwide, the Axis was wearing out its welcome and the world was showing more resistance. In occupied Yugoslavia, "Bomb-loving Serbs and Croats loosed so much explosive at Germans, Italians and at each other that officials announced: 'Whenever those responsible for a plot are not apprehended, hostages will be executed instead.'"[27]

By September, the influential world media had flushed out the really bad guys and it wasn't the Italians. "Two million Greek children will lack goats' milk this winter," reported *Time* magazine. "A quarter of the population faces death by famine. German soldiers, moving out of private homes in which they had been billeted, took away the beds, leaving carefully made-out receipts."[28]

But the Germans had washed their hands of all the misery and death of the Greek people. Johann Von Plessen, the German minister to Rome, instead lambasted the Italians saying, "in Greece, people are starving and that [Italy] is responsible for whatever may take place there."[29]

Mussolini exploded at the accusation. "The Germans have taken even their shoelaces from the Greeks, and now they attempt to lay the blame for the economic situation on our backs."[30]

By October the starvation of the Greek population was a horrifying reality. The Italians feared that revolt would begin any day. Bread rations had been reduced to ninety grams a day.*

---

* Approximately three ounces.

The duality of command of the Axis occupiers, and the confiscation of grain shipments by the top-heavy bureaucrats and those first in line to pilfer the life saving supplies, ensured starvation at the end of the pipe. Mussolini's advisors warned that anything could happen in this atmosphere of hunger "from epidemics to ferocious revolts on the part of the people who know that they now have nothing to lose."[31]

The Duce ordered that 7,500 tons of wheat be shipped at once but that was miniscule compared to what was needed. The Italians themselves did not have enough and the pursuit of the war had pushed Italy past its ability to feed even its own population at a proper level.

"The Italians, too, are tightening their belts to the last hole," said Ciano. That last hole in the Italian belt was given a special name by the disgruntled population. Said Ciano, "It is the one the Italians call the 'foro Mussolini'—'the Mussolini hole.'"[32] Other Italian officials believed the Greek "rebellion will begin when the first children starve to death."[33]

The Greeks continued to die by the tens of thousands during the winter of hunger of 1941-42. By the end of January, the Italians realized that they were powerless to stop the ongoing catastrophe. "We can give very little," admitted Ciano, " but our means of transportation to get it there are even less."[34]

Ships of the Italian merchant marine had been sunk in record numbers and convoys never failed to attract British attacks. With the departure of the German Luftwaffe to the Russian front, Great Britain was again able to rule the skies and seas.

"We have given up trying to get convoys through to Libya," complained Ciano, "every attempt had cost a high price, and the losses suffered by our merchant marine reached such proportions as to discourage any further experiments."[35]

The futility of attempting convoys against the British fleet was never more apparent than on November 9, 1941. The Italian Army in North Africa needed supplies and materiel for their expedition against the British, but was being strangled on the battlefield since few supplies could break the blockade.

Ciano wrote: "A convoy of seven ships left, accompanied by two 10,000-ton cruisers and 10 destroyers, because we knew

... the British had two battleships ready to act as wolves among the sheep. An engagement occurred ... All, I mean *all*, our ships were sunk, and one or maybe two or three destroyers. The British returned to port after slaughtering us."[36]

When the Italian command tried to put a better face on the convoy disaster by claiming an imaginary sinking of a British ship, no one believed it. A next day claim to having damaged a British warship simply because photographs showed it moored next to a dry dock drew howls of scorn.

"This is equivalent to declaring that a man is probably slightly dead because he has gone to live near the cemetery," scoffed Ciano. A humiliated Mussolini called it the worst day of the war and said, "I have been waiting for a piece of good news for 18 months now, and it never comes."[37]

The Italian failures translated directly into misery for Greece. There were no ships to bring food to the occupied land, even if there had been food. Mussolini's government faced a 500,000-ton grain shortage as winter approached in 1941, and the only resolution to the problem was to again humble himself to Hitler and ask to "borrow" some food.

"Mussolini cannot make up his mind to write to The Führer to make this request," said Ciano, "and I can understand this. If we could do without this help it would be most fortunate, but it seems ... it is absolutely necessary. Even those responsible for domestic order believe that any additional food restrictions would surely cause disorders."

The Italian apprehensions concerning the threat of rebellion due to starvation, oppression and hatred of the Fascists was founded in fact. The free world press hammered out a steady drumbeat of atrocities as they leaked out from behind the Fascist wall of occupation. One report stated:

"The volleys of firing squads beat like doom in the cities of Europe: 117 shot in Yugoslavia, 32 in Paris, 18 in Poland, five in Berlin, five in Belgium. These were deaths announced by the forces in occupation. How many more died unrecorded, only whispers told."[38]

There were other reports about the Warsaw Ghetto: "Bare statistics from Warsaw's ghetto bore eloquent testimony to

Poland's suffering. Normally twice as many persons are born in the ghetto as die there each year. In June of this year only 396 were born. Four thousand, two hundred and ninety died."[39]

An alarmed Ciano wrote about the Greek catastrophe: "If we continue on the present course the most complete bankruptcy will take place within two months. Greece can no longer yield anything for the simple and clear reason that it has nothing ... Hence we face uprisings and disorders, the size of which is impossible to estimate accurately at this time. But nothing can make the Germans change their absurd and idiotic attitude, and the worst of it is that we Italians must suffer 80 percent of the consequences."[40]

THE FIRST MAJOR ATTACK of the rebellion came not against the Italians occupiers, or the hated Germans, but against the Bulgarians, arch enemies of Greece since the 1913 partitioning of Macedonia after the 1912-13 Balkan War. It was the Bulgarians that the late Prime Minister Metaxas had so distrusted and against whose threat of invasion he had oriented and constructed the massive Metaxas Line of fortifications.

Like the German occupiers, the Bulgarians instituted a program of tyranny against the Greek population, including eviction from homes, land confiscation, displacement, and economic exploitation, as well as an attempted "Bulgarization" of the occupied Greek territory. Bulgarian was made the official language, forcing many to flee to the German zone and those fleeing exposed property rights and businesses to the eagerly awaiting occupiers who pounced on the opportunity.[41]

Rumors of rebellion permeated the air and were whispered in private conversations. Early in September some Resistance forces managed to conduct first raids against German occupying forces.

On September 22, 1941, partisans, or Andartes, ambushed a German vehicle on the road between Thessaloniki and Serres. Whatever successes that might have been claimed by the partisans were instantly forgotten and paled in the aftermath of the German's bludgeoning retaliations and reprisal that included the incineration of all the houses in ten Greek villages on Mt. Kerdyllia, and the rounding up and execution of the entire adult male population in those villages.

One week later the rebellion launched its first mass uprisings, later to be known as the Drama Event. On the night of September 28-29, 1941, bands of armed Andartes launched simultaneous attacks on the Bulgarian forces occupying the towns of Doxato, Agios, Athanasios and Horisti, all in the District of Drama. The attacks caught the Bulgarians by surprise and by morning the Bulgarian forces had withdrawn from Drama. The partisans took over control. Bulgarian authority seemed over.

But it was only the beginning. The Bulgarian forces used a two-day respite to reform, rearm, regroup and refine their plans to brutally put down the rebellion. Their ensuing attack was swift and overwhelming. Bulgarian forces swept with lightning quickness through Drama in a great wave of mass terrorism and indiscriminate shootings and butchery. Anyone on the streets was shot, and arrests of leaders and sympathizers were quickly followed by summary executions. Even the peasants in the fields were not spared from the all-consuming Bulgarian attack.

In hot pursuit of the rebel forces, the Bulgarian Army targeted villages and houses for attacks by fire, including artillery. Peasants were rousted out and beaten to give information about the Andartes. The Bulgarian soldiers, unleashed on this orgy of destruction, set fire to many villages after looting and pillaging and rounded up anyone unlucky enough to be in their paths.

The Bulgarians especially targeted the town of Doxato where the Andartes had first launched the attack. All males between sixteen and sixty fell before the firing squads and the town was torched. The excesses went on for days and when it was over no one knew how many Greeks had died, but the estimates ranged between 5,000 and 15,000. Entire communities were displaced, and women and children left to the ravages of homelessness, predators and starvation. Any abandoned property was confiscated and given to Bulgarian settlers eager to claim the land.

Following the Drama Event, 90,000 Greeks were forced from their homes in Eastern Macedonia, and the occupiers set up what they called "Greater Bulgaria."[42] Galloping inflation, food shortages, a collapsing service industry no longer able to provide fuel, and the necessities to sustain life above the level of privation and poverty forced many Greeks to desperation. The offer to go to work for the Wehrmacht in Germany was a particularly bitter pill to swallow, but for 10,000 Greeks it was the only thread of life left to grasp.

The end of 1941 and the onset of a fierce winter found all of Greece under foreign occupation and subjected to the rules of oppression. But the great cities like Athens were additionally embraced in the grip of famine and death. Everyone was employed in the occupation of survival. It was a daily battle that had to be won so as to be available for the next day's struggle. It was in that atmosphere that the seeds of rebellion, first planted at Drama, would be able to flourish and grow.

In Athens, the letters EAM[*] and ELAS[#] began to appear on walls next to old graffiti and next to the previously scribbled words "OXI, OXI" and the letter "V" for Victory, all written during happier times. The Communists' hammer and sickle also began to decorate the walls.[43]

---

[*] Ethniko Apeleftherotiko Metopo (National Liberation Front).
[#] Ellinikos Laikos Apeleftherotikos (Hellenic People's Liberation Army).

CHAPTER 10
TERROR AND REBELLION

IN JANUARY OF 1942, the idea of resistance and rebellion against the conquerors was not foremost in the minds of most of the Greek population. Daily survival was. There had been a few attempts by loosely organized bands of fighters to attack the slave masters, but the harsh reprisals by the Germans and Bulgarians that had followed those first feeble attempts had brutalized the population and terrorized them to the point that they withdrew into themselves, refusing to give any sustaining help to the resistance fighters. Cut off from the support of the population and tracked down in a relentless anti-guerrilla campaign, the Germans, by October 1941, could report total control in their zones of occupation.[1]

In Athens, control was the easiest for the occupiers. Nighttime on any street in the huge city had been transformed into a world of darkness, presenting a ghoulish scene of shadowy figures creeping and stumbling along in the freezing weather to find some sort of shelter or relief from the ever approaching grip of death. As each gray dawn broke, many of those who had, just the night before, stumbled along as walking skeletons, now lay in contorted heaps on the sidewalks and streets. Their stiff emaciated frames became the object of the cart that rolled each day to pick up those who had succumbed. They were, "scraggy remnants of bodies now extinguished, having used up all their reserves of their flesh," observed Rigas Rigopoulos.[2]

"Little children, like ghosts, with skin stuck to their bones, with eyes bulging out of their sockets, with hands and feet swollen, eagerly searched the trash at street corners to find something to eat."[3]

As the sun rose, the rest of the population faced the new day, some with more hope than others. Those who had jobs went to them. If any line formed promising the opportunity to buy or barter for something of value it quickly lengthened to the point that latecomers knew there would be no chance for anyone except the lucky few at the front.

A little flour or some olive oil or the chance for a tiny piece of meat fetched enormous value, not in money because it was worthless* and grew more worthless with each passing day, but from property and the institution of barter.

"That is how we came to lose our piano," said Rigopoulos, "[and] some gold family jewelry, a big sewing machine, and all our copper kitchen cookware, just to get some foodstuffs to help us celebrate Christmas and take courage for the new year."

He had managed to buy, at a great price, a piece of a lamb from a black marketer and reveled in the thought of the happiness it would bring his family, especially his invalid father, during this time of Christian joy. As he hurried home, he carried the precious package, clutching it tightly, befitting the valuable possession that it was.

"I couldn't resist feeling the lamb inside the package," he said. "By the time I got home, I had managed to tear off a little piece with my fingers. And I felt sheer delight as I chewed the raw flesh in the streets."[4]

The Greeks who lived in the countryside were infinitely better off than the city dwellers, although "better off" still meant hunger and privations. Alkicee Georgountzos's grandmother lived in Kalamata, on the southernmost shore and far removed from Athens, but she still had to sell her house to obtain twenty kilos of olive oil.[#5] The Georgountzos (Georges) family had all gathered on the family farm in Arfara, on the Peloponnese, just north of Kalamata.

Dennis Georges was the second oldest male, but his older brother was in the police force so he worked the farm with his father, and was a leader of his family of two younger brothers

---

* The drachma had been so deflated that it cost 500,000 for a loaf of bread.

Less than 45 pounds.

and sister. "We worked the farm," said Dennis, "so that we would have food to survive. We produced okra, beets, and potatoes and other crops."[6]

It was at Arfara where Greeks had witnessed that long line of British soldiers retreating toward Kalamata, and evacuation, in front of the attacking German Army. For many Greeks it was their first opportunity to help fight against the Germans, and many of them assisted the marooned British and hid some of those left behind.

Historically, Kalamata and the southern Peloponnese had been a crossroads of invading armies against Greek defenders. Its single road leading to the Corinth Canal, and then to Athens, was an ideal place to first meet the enemy and then fall back, first to defensible mountain positions and then to the natural moat of the Canal. Invading armies coming from Kalamata had to pass along that certain route.

But the conquerors had not come from the south through Kalamata. They had come from the north. They had been forced to negotiate the Canal, with great difficulty to pursue the fleeing British. The British had used the single road, winding through the land overlooked by formidable mountains, to their best advantage to avoid capture and to evacuate the greater portion of their army. Those mountains were perfectly suited for future guerrilla operations, and the main road was perfect for ambushes.

Above the village of Arfara, high up on the face of the mountain and barely noticed by the naked eye, were the ruins of a long-ago settlement. That ghost village was over 1,000 feet above the valley and consisted of partially standing houses and stone walls. It had at one time been the homes of the Georgountzos ancestors until 1821, when the Turks were finally driven out. The Greeks had been forced to live high in the mountains while the dominant Turks occupied the choice lowland. But now in the face of an occupying army, those old ruins and tumbledown houses beckoned as a hideout to partisans in a resistance movement. The long, steep, switch-backing, stony path up to the old village offered a perfect opportunity for warning of an approaching enemy. For any pursuing Germans, that long uphill trek meant entering a world of an enemy with hundreds of eyes watching from every cave and from behind every rock. It would be a daunting challenge.

Life in Arfara under occupation was a life mostly under Italian rule, not German, and as twelve-year-old Konstantinos Georgountzos said, "We did not fear the Italians, it was the Germans who everyone feared, but they only came around several times a year, but when they did they were very organized, to try and defeat the partisans. They would surround the town and sometimes they would stay for an hour and sometimes they would stay for a week."[7]

But the fire of patriotism burned in the villagers around Arfara and the people whispered among themselves about forming a resistance. Nineteen-year-old Dennis Georges (Georgountzos,) the older brother of twelve-year-old Konstantinos and cousin to six-year-old Konstantin, was chosen as the leader.

"The people began a movement and said, 'let's get rid of the Germans,'" said Dennis, "and before I realized it, the youth around Arfara had formed a resistance and they elected me as the leader. And they called me the 'master' of twelve to fifteen villages. It was 1941 and I was nineteen years old and this section I was involved with was influenced by the Communists in the Resistance.

"So we got some guns and started abusing some Italians, and played hit and run with the Germans. We progressed our techniques against the Germans and, one time, I went into the village and sat down with my father, whom I loved to listen to, and after a long talk, I decided to stay overnight rather than return to the field, and slept in his house. In the morning, I heard the sound of many boots of soldiers outside my house. I got up and my sister was there, and she was fifteen, and I put my hand on her mouth and said, 'don't talk, there are Germans outside.'

"I slipped out and hid myself and the Germans searched from house to house, and room to room, and they couldn't find me and I left the village and headed for the farm. I was moving down there and the Germans had surrounded the village, and I was running and some German who was up high saw me running and he called to me, 'Kom, Kom,' as the beckoned with his fingers, but that only made me run faster.

"The German didn't shoot me, only because they had not completely surrounded the village, and they were not supposed to shoot until they saw the green flare that says, 'The village is surrounded, Let's move in.' They didn't shoot me because they didn't want to alert the village that they were surrounding it."[8]

There was no shortage of weapons in the area of Arfara and Kalamata since the British had abandoned huge quantities of materiel in their frantic attempt to escape in May 1941. The Italians were the loosest of gatekeepers, and preferred to play at kickball with the Greeks, and chase and befriend the local girls. They were very good at looking the other way, and the people of Arfara were able to get some of the excess harvest from their orchards and vineyards to Athens to barter for other necessities.

"It was never a problem," said Dennis's cousin, Konstantin. "People were bringing to Athens provisions for the large population of the city and bribing the Italians in order to transport the goods and sell them to the black market. It was a simple rule: if you had five boxes of grapes, it was one for the Italians and four to Athens."[9]

In the Spring of 1942, Dennis was making runs to Athens to swap foodstuffs for other necessities.

"I used to take potatoes, figs, raisins, and olive oil and go on top of the train to go to Athens and sell it, but the people had nothing to give you except their clothes. The only way to take merchandise to the big city and try and sell it was to put it on top of the train. But how do you put it on top of the train because other people are on top of the train? Everybody was pushing and shoving each other. I had fear that someone would pull you off the train, and sometimes there was rain and sometimes there was snow. Sometimes you had to go through tunnels, all while on top of the train.

"One time a fellow was sitting up higher and sometimes in the tunnel some stones are jutting down lower than most of the others, and one hit him and threw him back into six others, and they all fell off the train and I was fifty feet behind them, and I was very afraid."[10]

But between his farming and train-top travel to Athens with

his precious cargo, Dennis ran his guerrilla bands with a cool dexterity and continued to "abuse" the Italians and Germans. But there were many close calls. On one occasion in 1942, the Germans managed to maneuver a force, unseen, very close to Arfara. When they were finally spotted, they were already in the town.

Dennis's younger brother, Konstantinos, usually sounded the alarm with the church bell, or used a large horn through which he shouted, "the Germans are coming, the Germans are coming." But this time, the village had been caught off guard, and the youngster had to make quite a run up the hill to the church, and when he breathlessly arrived, he jumped on the bell's rope and rode it up and down making the bell peal its late warning. But by that time, the Germans were on top of them.

Everyone ran for cover. But the road to safety was blocked. The encircling Germans barred that long, steep path that ascended to the ancient ruins on the face of the mountain. It was every man for himself, and Konstantinos also ran, but the Germans were not interested in a twelve-year-old boy. They were interested in the Resistance's leader, his older brother, so Konstantinos was able to watch from a safe distance.

The partisans ran for their lives, ducking and darting to emergency hiding places, long-planned for just such a surprise. Konstantinos saw Dennis lift a board covering a well that had been dug to collect rainwater. He watched his brother slip into it and pull the board back over the top to conceal himself. Dennis wedged himself inside, pressing against the sides with his arms, legs, shoulders, and hands to support himself. Then he could only hold his breath as the Germans walked right over him.

"But a small boy from the neighborhood also saw Dennis slip into the well," said Konstantinos. "He was a boy about five years old, so when the Germans came, he had seen Dennis, and he went up to one of them and said, 'Uncle German,* Uncle German, Dennis is hiding in the well!'

---

* The use of the word "Uncle" is a common term of respect, especially for Greek children to their elders

"But the German soldier was unmoved and paid no attention to the little boy, so he said again, 'Uncle German, Uncle German, Dennis is hiding in the well!'"[11]

Of course all the German soldier heard was the little voice saying Greek words that sounded like, "BABA DZHERMAN, BABA DZHERMAN," followed by a string of equally indecipherable words telling him to look in the well. Dennis's secret hiding place remained secret.

ALTHOUGH THE GERMANS had been the most reluctant of warriors to become involved in Greece, and were there only because of the gross incompetence of Benito Mussolini and the Italian High Command, the fact that they had come to Greece as conquerors and occupiers meant that they brought with them their master race dogma and their plans for the resolution of the Jewish question.

For the most part, except at Thessaloniki, the Jewish question was not a dominant theme at first. Perhaps Hitler's call for treating Greeks with respect so the Germans might be accepted, not as conquerors but as friendly occupiers, might have temporarily masked the hideous face of Nazism.

In a campaign of appeasement and false promises, the German commanders who arrived at the Jewish community at Didymoticho, in Eastern Macedonia, actually comforted the 900 Jews residing there by reciting just the words the fearful Jews wanted to hear. The commander announced, "that they were in no danger whatsoever and that they would enjoy equal rights with no discrimination or action against them."[12]

But that masked face of Nazism eventually was peeled off and revealed itself in its full horror, and would claim the lives of eighty-six percent of Greek Jewry, including all but thirty-three of the 900 from Didymoticho.

In Thessaloniki, where 56,000 of the 77,000 Jewish population lived, the oppression was almost immediate. Two days after the arrival of the Germans, the three Jewish newspapers* were

---

* *Le Progress, L'Independent* and *Messagaro*.

forced to close down and all their supplies, equipment, and presses confiscated. The conquering Germans evicted Jewish families so their homes could become military offices and barracks, and the Jewish community's Administrative Counsel was disbanded and, by April 1941, the archives seized and shipped off to Germany. On July 11 all male Jews were herded into the Plateia Elftherias (Liberty Square) and publicly humiliated, then designated as forced laborers.

Within weeks of the initial oppression, the *Sontercommando Rosenberg* arrived and set up shop to perform its shameful function. Its business was to target prominent wealthy Jewish figures and their property, as well as well as property of the Jewish community, for plunder. The Rosenberg Commandos conducted raids of all Jewish establishments including homes and businesses, schools, libraries and synagogues, to confiscate anything with religious value. In the booty were rare manuscripts and books that would find their place in a new home in Frankfurt for stolen Jewish treasures: the Nazi Library for the Investigation into the Jewish Question. Its director, Dr. Johann Paul, was able to proudly boast that in the span of a couple years, he had accumulated 10,000 of these stolen Jewish treasures.[13]

Amid this grisly and barbaric work of those dedicated to murder, extortion, confiscation and cruelty, life in Greece went on, and the large port cities became great arsenals and supply and transportation centers for the German *Wehrmacht*. Infantry, artillery and armored units arrived in Athens to be staged, detailed and loaded aboard ships for further transportation to Libya and Rommel's Afrika Corps fighting in the desert.

The Greek population could only watch as their country became a stepping stone for further German conquests. But until mid 1942, the dream of resistance and the desire to strike back at the accursed enemy was just that, a dream. Slowly the Communist EAM and its combat arm the ELAS were able to provide the leadership to recruit and organize a resistance movement. In less desperate times, ELAS might not have had Greek freedom fighters flocking to its call, because that organization was hard core Communists with an eye ever on power, especially for the future. In keeping with its commitment to its global ideology, the Germans were not the only enemy. Greeks who fought the enemy and did not believe in the Communist dogmas were equally dangerous and had to be liquidated also.

It was convenient for ELAS to mask their international goals and to pass themselves off as an organization interested only in national patriotism, Greek freedom and a nonpolitical motivation. It was easy for patriotic Greeks to temporarily overlook the dark side of ELAS since they were a fighting force on Greek soil in a position to confront the accursed enemy. It was also true that the legitimate Greek government was not on Greek soil and that they were in exile and nowhere to be seen. To the common Greek citizen, they had fled the country to the safety of London and Cairo and they had abandoned the rest of the Greek population to endure this living hell at the hands of the conquerors. So ELAS was the most available option for Greek patriots wanting to strike a blow for freedom against the murderous invaders.

"I heard about the huge organization ... EAM," said Rigas Rigopoulos. "Some proposed that I take part in this movement which, from the beginning, seemed to have solid foundations and many resources. Various friends of mine were already members ... the fact that many who spoke to me about EAM were known leftists, made me suspicious ... The EAM matter required careful observation."[14]

IN ADDITION TO THE SPECTER of starvation that had become a common scene in the daily lives of Greek citizens, Fascist brutality soon became a way of life. It was all too common to witness Greeks arrested in the middle of the night, dragged from their houses, loaded on wagons and hauled off to their executions.

"I saw my first execution done by the Italians," said Dimitri Tsaras living in Stilida. "They were brought to the cemetery and executed by the *carabinieri.* We were youngsters. Then the local Italians came and started firing in the air and we took off

---

* The National Italian Police force.

running. I saw a lot more in Lamia, and there we could see an open truck with a dozen Greeks on it, singing their patriotic songs, surrounded by German soldiers, going to their execution because a German soldier had been killed. The rate was ten to one."[15]

The Germans and the Italians cultivated their own cult of informers, traitors and collaborators to subvert the Resistance. Information from an informer often translated into a midnight raid to capture the denounced person or the appearance of a sudden roadblock and barricade to snare rebellious individuals or units.

"The Germans and the local Blackshirts* would block all the roads together," said Kitina Kakkava, who had one brother in the political organization and another in the mountains with the guerrillas. "They'd seize all the men on the streets and herd them together into the square, and there'd be an informer there, one of the local Blackshirts, and he knew who was with the partisans up in the mountains, with the Resistance, and he knew who their parents were, too. And he'd say, 'Him. Take him.'

"One day the partisans killed one of the local Blackshirts. The Germans and the Blackshirts burned a whole city block to the ground—seventeen houses—and the people didn't even have time to get a handkerchief from inside. And they seized nine men and one Italian who was a teacher that had been sheltered. And the next day they lined them up in the square and shot them ... all nine Greeks plus the Italian. And my brother Panagiotis said 'Kitina, go and see what's happening.' So I go down into town and I head for the square to take a look, to see what's been going on from close up, and they wouldn't let us get very close, but I saw the corpses down there in the square.

"The Germans didn't go out into the villages, and neither did the Blackshirts. Every now and then, they'd organize a raid on a village ... they'd burn houses down and kill people. They used to say, 'you know, there are partisans in that village, and the people there shelter and feed them' ... that sort of thing. And the Germans would go there with the local Blackshirts, and set

---

* Italy's Fascist paramilitary thugs.

fire to houses and kill people."[16]

The Italians were quite different.

"They were just a group of youngsters with guitars who danced all the time," said Yiorgos Zervulakos. They'd sell a rifle or some bullets now and again to some rebels they were in contact with. I don't think they really wanted anything to do with what you'd call war.

"I was with my family in a village called Geraki, and when the occupying forces arrived, the village was put into the Italian zone. So a group of ten Italians came and set up a 'carabinieri' headquarters in an old mansion house from the last century, a four-floored stone building almost like a castle."

"These Italians were on very friendly terms with the people in the village, and there were two olive presses in the area, and the Italians imposed a tax and collected the oil in some big tanks. So, when they'd collected lots of oil, the guerrillas came down from the mountain with the animals they'd taken from all the surrounding villages, and they loaded them up with the oil and took it away.

"But the devil had his hand in it and these [ELAS] guerrillas killed three of those Italian kids. The next day a company of Italian troops came from Sparti for reprisals. 'You killed three of ours, so we'll kill three of yours.' The Italians summoned the priest, the mayor, and the schoolteacher and asked them to hand over three Greeks for execution. The three heroically put themselves forward."[17]

But while they were locked up on the upper floors, those three hostages began to talk among themselves and plan a different alternative.

"And the priest got inspired and remembered that the Italians had an informer in the village who they used to ferry information, and he said, 'Let's hand over Thimios. Let's get rid of him once and for all. The Italians will kill him and we'll get rid of him, and we'll get out of this alive. Who else?'

"They had noticed someone limping round the square, a blind, crippled beggar who wasn't from the area, begging for bread in those hungry times. So, that's the second one, 'Now, who can be third? Let's give them the village loony!'

"Now, the village lunatic's madness was of a very specific type. He was this guy called Vasilis, a little short and fat, and he always wore a long greatcoat, which was dyed black. It almost went down to his ankles, and he never wore trousers underneath, and whenever he met a woman in the street he'd open up his coat and flash his wares. That's how his madness came out. 'Let's give them Vasilis.'"

The three were turned over to the Italians who assembled the entire village to witness the execution, all because the ELAS guerrillas had killed the three Italians while confiscating the olive oil.

"The whole village was there," said Zervulakos. "All the women and children, and the school kids lined up because we had to see how bad people get punished. So, the priest went up ahead with a cross, mumbling what priests usually do, and then there was the poor beggar from foreign parts who wasn't limping any more, and was suddenly cured of all his ailments, and behind him was the informer, Thimios, who was cursing the Italians, the Germans, and anyone else he could think of for their 'ingratitude, their meanness, and what sort of a life is this?' And Vasilis brought up the rear in his long coat. He walked along proud and completely indifferent.

"They lined them up at the front of the wall and raised their rifles. An officer had drawn his sword to give them the signal, and just then, just before the bullets struck, Vasilis opened up his coat!"[18]

THE ELAS RESISTANCE fighters bore a striking similarity to the hardcore Communist and Gaullist fighters that populated the Resistance in occupied France. Those fighters had developed a bad reputation for causing death and wanton destruction to innocent people just to be able to claim that they had killed some of the enemy with no regard for the guaranteed, harsh reprisals by the Germans.

"There was an awful lot of what terrorists do," said Tony Brooks, a clandestine saboteur with the British SOE (Special Operations Executive) in France. "There was throwing of grenades to get a headline and to force the security authorities to make reprisals, arrests, take hostages and so on, and therefore, in the Lyon Area, the Communist Party spent their time lobbing grenades into cinemas, cafes, *soldatenheim** and mixed cafes where there might be quite genuine French people talking and five or six Germans drinking beer and laughing.

"They would just lob a grenade through the glass window, possibly not even kill a German but then there would be twenty people arrested and so on, merely to keep pressure on."[19]

The British SOE was a secret service of the Ministry of Economic Warfare whose weapons were sabotage, propaganda, and guerrilla-type attacks. The service had been formed in July 1940 and its mission had been tersely and unmistakably stated by Winston Churchill: "set Europe ablaze." That meant to attack Germany and Italy by all means available to enhance the total Allied war effort. It included raising, training and organizing Resistance forces to sabotage and disrupt the enemy's capability to wage war.[20]

In France that meant underground networks and clandestine saboteurs, and an armed resistance cell, the *maquis*. In Greece, the tactic was open guerrilla warfare against the Germans and Italians, but there was more. Rival guerrilla factions, vying for supremacy and future political posture, often fought each other. They engaged in a deadly struggle for power, and that struggle became as much of a threat to the innocent Greeks as the conquerors themselves.

"One day some ELAS boys killed three Germans," said Philippos Mavrogenis. "The Germans were going down Vouliagmenis Street on their way to the airport. And they [ambushed] them, and then they shot a fourth German on a motorbike who managed to escape with his life and inform the Kommandatura.

"And two trucks packed with fully armed Germans arrived, and made no distinctions whatsoever. If they saw you, they killed you. They left no one ... they killed 250 people that day. Anyone they found walking along the road was shot dead, and

---

* A German soldiers' cafe.

that was the end of it. In one café the customers didn't have time to go to their homes, and seven of them hid behind a fridge. In goes the Germans and executes all seven of them on the spot. It was a blood bath. And what had those ELAS men achieved? They killed three Germans, but they killed 250 of us."[21]

But the SOE assessment of the capabilities of a Resistance in Greece had not been quite accurate. Operations against the occupying forces and their sympathizers would not be limited to simply guerrilla warfare. Individual Greek patriots, fired by the spirit of rebellion, sought out trusted accomplices to form small resistance units and to implement their own plans to disrupt the conquerors and conduct their own private war.

Rigas Rigopoulos wrote: "From day to day, we felt resistance around us spreading and swelling: underground publications, spying, formation of partisan groups, sheltering of British soldiers, protection of Greek patriots, caring for Greek children, organizing escapes."[22]

Some of his friends and acquaintances had already formed resistance groups preparing for future action against the enemy. The Army of Enslaved Victors and the Pan Hellenic Union of Fighting Youths (PEAN) were already up and running. Underground newspapers sprouted up everywhere and were passed from hand to hand.

Inspired by his own dream of resistance, he formed the Hellenic Patriotic Society that he codenamed, 5-16-5, the numerical position of the first letters of *Elliniki Patriotiki Eteria* (EPE) in the alphabet. His was an ambitious project to find and work with cohorts to collect vital information about "unit movements, loading of war materiels, defensive constructions, fuel stores, and movements of merchant and ships of war."[23] He managed to secure a wireless from a secret operator whose principles had been arrested and who had continued to keep the set active with routine check-ins with his control.

Armed with the priceless wireless set and a network of ingenious observers, Rigopoulos submitted an enormous amount of information that was surprising to British Headquarters in Cairo. The amount of data that poured into Service 5-16-5 for further transmission to British Headquarters was enormous. The dimensions of a German position might have been accurately measured, right under the noses of the soldiers, by a Greek youth innocently pedaling his bicycle along while counting the number of pedal revolutions. Later, those pedal revolutions were converted into wheel revolutions, and then converted into linear meters.

There had been no limit to the number of willing eyes able to observe all facets of daily occupied life, to count trucks, tanks, and German buildings, and to observe and sketch designations and emblems painted on the side of German vehicles. What had been needed had been a method of assimilating this mountain of raw data and, more importantly, the ability to transmit the information to where it could be useful, and acted upon. Service 5-16-5 provided this ability.

But that was just the beginning. A contact with a Greek patriot, Alexander Kairis, working as a civilian in the German Headquarters of Southern Greece, brought a treasure trove of information about shipping and convoys, cargoes and escorting war ships, and routes, speeds and destinations.

"We had a finger on all the movements at the Piraeus harbor,"[24] said Rigopoulos. "Many ships whose departures and journey details we had announced were torpedoed by our submarines or sunk by Allied planes. We verified that fifty-five were destroyed before they reached their destinations."[25]

Unfortunately this amazing resistance organization, 5-16-5, did not escape the ever searching eye of the Germans, or their relentless pursuit. In April 1943 the organization was penetrated and quickly collapsed with many operatives captured or forced to flee and hide. Alexander Kairis, the Greek patriot who risked his life in the lair of a German Headquarters to provide the vital shipping and convoy information, did not survive the war. He was discovered, arrested and sentenced to death. He was executed by firing squad on November 2, 1943. Reportedly, part of his last words to the Germans were, "You are dishonest cowards, violators of human freedom."[26]

KOSTAS PERRIKOS HAD founded the Pan Hellenic Union of Fighting Youths (PEAN), and his group's target was a particularly repulsive collection of Greek traitors and collaborators. It was the National Socialist Patriotic Organization (ESPO), comprised of Nazi sympathizers who set about trying to raise a Greek fighting force to stand with the German Army and fight for the Reich on the Eastern Front. ESPO offered jobs in Germany to work in the military industry. A large poster on the mezzanine of their office building called for recruits: "Greek youth, join the pioneer of the New Order."[27]

Perrikos's eight-man demolition crew took on the responsibility to attack this hated group of traitorous Greeks. Their offices were on the second and third floors of a four-story building in downtown Athens. Perrikos's team was two technicians, four university students, a coffee shop owner and a woman.

There was a bonus target for Perrikos's group. On the fourth floor, the German Field Police had an office, but there were also innocent Greeks conducting business within the confines of this building, including a law office, tailor's shop and a dentist. Unlike the murderous ELAS, Perrikos was not willing to sacrifice the innocent to attack the tyrants. He planned his operation for Sunday when the innocent shops would be closed and only the ESPO would be present, conducting a regular weekly meeting.

PEAN's weapon would be a ten-kilogram* homemade bomb with a six-minute fuse delivered to the site in a basket carried by the woman and covered with green leafy vegetables.

In a corner of a hallway on the mezzanine level, there was a small ledge, not very wide, close to the ceiling. It was not wide enough to accommodate the bomb's bulkiness, but it was the ideal location since it was directly beneath the offices of the ESPO. The problem of the bomb's falling off of this ledge was quickly solved by wedging a board on a forty-five degree angle between the bomb and the floor to hold it in position on the narrow ledge.

---

* 22 pounds

At 0900 on September 20, 1942, the saboteurs rendezvoused near the building, carrying concealed pistols and the bomb in the basket. The ESPO meeting was in full swing, its offices were packed with its members. But there was a snag. One of the law offices was open and four people were conducting business. So the team waited. Surely the law office would close soon. But it did not.

"We wait an irritating two-and-a-half hours," said Takis Mihailidis. "Two-and-a-half hours holding a 10 kilogram bomb, revolvers at the ready, in the center of Athens, to spare the lives of four innocent people."[28]

At 1130 the ESPO meeting was beginning to break up and the team knew it had to attack or call off the operation. Would they ever have such a golden opportunity again?

Fortunately, at just that time, the four people in the law office also departed. Like clockwork the saboteurs each moved to positions to perform their designated tasks. They placed the bomb, ignited the fuse and made their escape just minutes before noon.

At exactly 1203, Athens was rocked with a jarring explosion and a rising cloud of black smoke from the building collapsing onto itself. The Germans sounded air raid sirens, and it was pandemonium with police, fire trucks and curious people racing to the scene to see what had happened. It took the fire department two days to put out the fires and to secure the site.

The explosion killed twenty-nine ESPO members and wounded twenty-seven more. Forty-three German soldiers also died. Unfortunately, one innocent priest died when he happened to pass the building just as the bomb exploded. After the blast, the ESPO disbanded and no such organization was ever formed again.

Six weeks later, the Germans closed in on PEAN and arrested Perrikos and nine of his associates. He was executed by firing squad with four others. A fifth died in a concentration camp, and Julia Bilbas, the woman who had carried the basket of leafy vegetables, was sent to Germany and later beheaded with an axe.

FIVE DAYS AFTER the blowing up of the ESPO headquarters in Athens, the Greek Resistance pulled off one of the great sabotage events of World War II. It was designated Operation Harling by the British and for the first and only time during the war the Communist ELAS and Nationalist EDES* guerrilla forces fought together.

Operation Harling's objective was to sever the main supply route of the Germans in their continual effort to resupply their forces fighting in Egypt. That supply route was the single-track, north-to-south railway down the center of Greece to the Port of Piraeus near Athens. It covered 300 miles, but in that journey had to cross three east-to-west mountain ranges.

High speed was out of the question and the train snaked its way through many tunnels and over three truly spectacular viaducts over the Asopos Gorge until it reached the narrow plain leading to Athens. Over the Asopos Gorge was the southernmost Papadia viaduct. The center was the Asopos Viaduct and the northernmost bridge was the Gorgopotamos Viaduct. Destroying any one of the structures would halt the Germans ability to effectively move materiel to the Port of Piraeus.

The plan was for three British sabotage teams of four men each to parachute into Central Greece with their arms and explosives and forage off the land, making contact with the Andartes for the assistance they would need to accomplish their mission. The British anticipated that the Greeks would be willing to provide help and, once the mission was completed, Cairo would initiate plans to evacuate the strike force.

On September 28, the British made the first attempt to insert the teams, but were unsuccessful when no landing lights appeared to mark the drop zones. Two nights later the teams were inserted but the drop was scattered and they became separated and, although two of the teams found each other in a week, the third team was missing.

Greek peasants could not provide any information about the whereabouts of partisan guerrillas, so the British planned to recruit their own supporting force from the locals nearby. But

---

* EDES: The Greek Democratic National League (non-Communists)

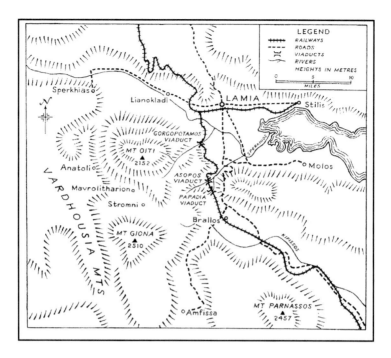

on November 14, six weeks after the initial jump, the third team showed up and, by good fortune, were accompanied by eighty rough looking bearded Andartes, carrying a variety of arms. Their leader was the legendary ELAS commander, Aris Velouchiotis.

Several days later, British Major C. M. Woodhouse had found Napoleon Zervas, the guerrilla leader of the EDES forces that were engaged in a fight with Italian soldiers, and Zervas immediately committed forty-five of his best men to the mission. Both groups were eager to join the action, and the British placed Zervas in overall command of the combined Andartes force.[29]

The British reconnoitered the supporting viaduct structures from their base camp and hideout on the slopes of Mount Oiti to the west of the viaducts and concluded that the Gorgopotamos Viaduct should be the target. A copy of the blueprint of the spans of the viaduct was invaluable, and the team studied it carefully. The entire viaduct consisted of seven steel spans crossing almost 700 feet from end to end, and the track curved in a slightly leftward arc as it crossed the gorge. The spans rose over 100 feet above the riverbed and were supported by five stone piers and two steel piers. The sappers decided to attack and cut the two steel piers to collapse two sections of the bridge.

The approach to the river bottom and the bridging supports was not a long march from the cover of Mt. Oiti. There was sufficient ground cover to offer a concealed approach to Gorgopotamos that the other sites lacked. More importantly, the Italian reinforcements to react to an attack on the bridge were positioned farther away from the target than they were to either of the other two spans. Even though there were eighty permanent men garrisoned at Gorgopotamos, the closest Italian mobile reinforcements were several miles to the north.

The sappers carried 500 pounds of explosives. Captain Arthur Edmonds, one of two New Zealanders on the force said, "The same result could have been achieved with one-tenth of the total charge, but we were in the dark as to the size of the bridge members until we reached the target."[30]

The Simplon-Orient Express on the Gorgopotamos viaduct.
The saboteurs used this photograph which, with the print on the
next page, was the only information available before the operation.

Images courtesy of the New Zealand Electronic Text Center

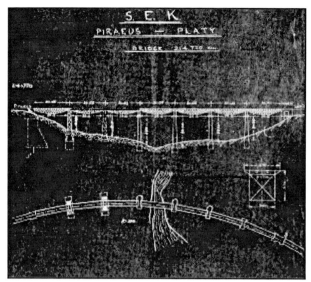

**The original blueprint of the plan and
section of the Gorgopotamos viaduct.**

The plan was to attack at night under cover of darkness. The British detailed two eight-man teams of partisans to go in first and cut railway and telephone communications, then position themselves to intercept any reinforcements trying to enter the demolition zone. Eighty Andartes would attack the main garrison and a smaller twenty-man force would attack the northern defensive positions.

The demolition teams would remain several hundred yards upstream of the viaduct and wait for a white light from the northern end, and a red light from the southern end indicating the garrison had been eliminated or controlled. A green pyrotechnic flare was the signal for withdrawal.

In total darkness, with the moon not rising until late, the strike force began its move down the mountain to the lowlands. The only sound was the men sliding and scraping along as they felt their way down, holding on to the tails of the mules and grasping one another for balance as they moved in a long serpentine line.

At the Gorgopotamos River they stopped and deployed for their assigned missions. The Andartes moved off into the attack on the garrison and it wasn't long before the countryside reverberated with the sound of an enormous firefight. But that attack, anticipated to last only thirty minutes, was still going strong after forty-five and then sixty minutes.

Then the signal came. The demolition teams went straight to the piers, cut the protective wires around the base of the steel supports, and set the charges. Within thirty minutes, the sapper leaders blew the whistle to take cover and ignited the fuses. The men moved a short distance away and pressed themselves flat to the ground. The earth convulsed with the detonation. Showers of red, metal shards mushroomed in the sky as the spans twisted and plummeted to the ground.

Two spans were down and a third twisted badly. A second set of charges soon brought down another span and a pier, and the green flare rocketed into the sky just as the Italian reinforcement train arrived to the gunfire reception of the Andartes.[31]

Both EDES and ELAS were winners. Their rival underground papers were only too happy to regale the heroic exploits of their fighters to the detriment of the other side. Recruiting soared as young Greek patriots swarmed to join the Resistance ranks. The German supply flow to North Africa was stopped and interrupted for the seven weeks it took to rebuild the spans of Gorgopotamos.[32]

Gorgopotamos viaduct after November 25 attack

For the Greek population it was a moment of sheer joy in the face of a terrible ordeal. There were few resistance attacks in all of WWII that could compare to the spectacular success of the blowing up of the Gorgopotamos Viaduct.

As a result of the mounting resistance successes against the German occupying army all over Europe, Adolph Hitler secretly declared a war of annihilation against the Resistance and all saboteurs and their supporters. In an October 18, 1942 order, not revealed until after the war, and introduced at the Nuremberg Trials, Hitler wrote:

"From now on all enemies on so-called Commando missions in Europe or Africa, challenged by German troops, even if they are to all appearances soldiers in uniform or demolition troops, whether armed or unarmed, in battle or in flight, are to be slaughtered to the last man ... Even if these individuals, when found, should be prepared to give themselves up, no pardon is to be granted them ...

If the Germans conduct of war is not to suffer grievous damage through such methods, it must be made clear to the adversary that all sabotage troops will be exterminated, without exception, to the last man. This means that their chance of saving their lives is nil."

Hitler gave further instructions for the necessity of absolute secrecy of his criminal directive. There were only twelve copies made and the recipients were only those at the highest level of command. He wrote:

"This order is intended for commanders only and must not, under any circumstances, fall into enemy hands."[33]

IN ARFARA IN THE BEGINNING of 1943, Dennis Georges' guerilla bands began their attacks. He was now twenty years old.

"I had orders to go along the road that led past Arfara to Kalamata because the Germans would be passing a convoy of six trucks," he said. "We would set up along the highway to 'abuse' them. We carried Thompson submachine guns and the ambush force would be seven others and myself. We went there and set up until the Germans would come, and on the other side of the road from us I set up a man with a machine gun. He was an experienced soldier.

"We went there at night because we didn't want to move in the day, because we didn't want people to know where we were going, and it was around one o'clock in the morning, and it started to rain, pouring down and running down your shirt and drenching all your clothes, and finally we saw the trucks coming.

"They had told us there would be only about five or six, but there were fifteen trucks, so we all spread out to cover all of them. When they came close we all shot and threw hand grenades, and some of us ran forward and jumped on the trucks, and threw hand grenades in the trucks."[34]

The Germans who did not die in the trucks poured out in great confusion. The ambush had originated on the east side of the road, and the shots and explosions made the natural tendency for the survivors to run away from the turmoil to the west side of the road, and that is when the experienced soldier with the machine gun opened fire and went about his deadly work. A few Germans escaped and could be seen running back to the north.[35]

"We captured five or six, and then I went to a nearby village," said Dennis, "to some relative and took off my clothes and built a fire, and while standing naked, held up my wet clothes and tried to dry them."

FLUSHED WITH THE ELIXIR of success, especially at Gorgopotamos, the British High Command sought to turn up the heat on the Germans' ability to move vital supplies through Greece. It also sought to impede the arrival of war materiels for use in fortifying the Greek mainland against a future possible

Allied invasion. A Balkan Invasion was very much in the Allied deck of cards as an invasion site.*

Gorgopotamos had been only the second choice as a target to interdict the railway line that was the main supply artery for the German Army. The target of choice would have been the even taller Asopos Viaduct south of Gorgopotamos. But even with the assistance of the EDES and ELAS guerrillas, the three teams of British Commonwealth saboteurs, many New Zealanders, were not strong enough to undertake the effort. But the target had not been forgotten.

In May 1943, Brigadier Eddie Myers, who had been a colonel and team leader during the attack on Gorgopotamos, thought an effort against the massive Asopos Viaduct was possible and ordered planning to begin for an attack on the "soapy one," the code name for the viaduct derived from the sound-alike Asopos. Fittingly, the name of the new operation followed the soapy theme and was called Operation Washing.[36]

The Asopos Viaduct was gigantic. Its sheer height and engineering majesty was breathtaking as it rose 330 feet above the riverbed, spanning the gorge from a point where the track suddenly appeared out of a mountain tunnel, traveled 600 feet, and just as abruptly disappeared into another mountain tunnel on the other side. Three massive stone piers supported the rail tracks approaching the edged of the gorge, and two sets of steel framework legs held up the 264-foot arched span that actually crossed the sheer drop into the gorge. The entire viaduct seemed to defy the forces of gravity and appeared to cling precariously to the steep slope of the mountain.

Most everyone agreed that the Asopos Viaduct was unassailable. The Germans certainly thought so, as did the local Greeks. During daylight the German garrison had full view of all approaches to the bridge, and at night powerful searchlights swept the ground in all directions, including the tiny foot tracks on the mountain that crossed the tops of the tunnels.

---

* Allied intelligence had gone to great lengths to convince the Germans that they planned to invade Greece while it planned to invade Sicily.

But Myers, who had been a colonel and a team leader in the assault on Gorgopotamos, felt that a successful attack could indeed be mounted against Asopos. He felt if it were properly planned and adequately manned with the forces available in the

Asopos viaduct

area, including the guerrillas, the operation could be attempted with a reasonable hope of success. He therefore assigned Captain Charlie Edmonds, the British liaison officer working with the local Andarte anti-Communist guerrillas under the command of Colonel Dimitrios Psarros, to begin reconnaissance and planning for the operation. Edmonds set up his headquarters in a position that would be most secure and virtually immune to discovery or attack by the enemy. He headquartered in the village of Anatoli, 6.500 feet in the air on the northern slope of a mountain overlooking the lowland and the viaducts.

The plan was hardly off the ground before it seemed doomed to failure. The Communist leader of the ELAS guerrillas, Aris Velouchiotis, attacked and captured Psarros and demanded under the threat of death that Psarros and his men join the ELAS forces. This was a serious violation of the understanding he had with the British to not attack approved rival guerrilla forces. Myers was furious and immediately signaled British HQ in Cairo that all support and supplies to Velouchiotis should be immediately stopped. The ELAS leader had not expected such a reaction and after a second thought agreed to join forces with Myers to attack Asopos.

But Velouchiotis did not have the last word when it came to deciding what the Communists would do or not do. His decision to commit his forces to the Asopos operation was clipped by his superior, General Sarafis, who in turn answered to the EAM Central Committee. EAM nixed any ELAS participation in Operation Washing.

"I explained that this could not be done," said ELAS General Sarafis, "... because such an action against the Germans, who had fortified themselves with concrete artillery and machine gun emplacements, barbed wire entanglements, searchlights and ambushes, could have no hope of success unless at least 1,500 men were used, with artillery and machine guns ... I explained that, as military commander of ELAS charged with the direction of operations, I was of the opinion that the action had no chance of success ..."[37]

The refusal by the ELAS guerrillas to provide the vital manpower necessary to ensure the possibility of success of Operation Washing was a bitter pill to swallow for Edmond's clandestine saboteurs. The frustration vented itself in cursing and throwing things about, but when that subsided each man's thoughts slowly drifted to an ever more satisfying thought: let's damn well do it on our own.

It was Captain Geoffery Gordon-Creed and Lieutenant Don Stott who first approached Edmonds asking permission to present this bold thought to Myers for his approval. Stott's reputation for fearlessness was legendary. He had been a sergeant in the artillery fighting in Greece, and had been left behind, like so many others, when the Germans overran the mainland. The Germans had taken him prisoner, and he soon found himself in an outdoor stockade surrounded by barbed wire.

But captivity did not suit Stott or his comrade, Sergeant Bob Morton, and in broad daylight, with the astonished guards watching, Stott and Morton raced to the wire carrying makeshift poles and vaulted over, followed by a hail of bullets. They evaded the German's attempts to recapture them, acquired false passports, and managed to maneuver around with the help of the loyal Greek population. Three failed attempts to sail for Egypt found them still trying to hide on the Greek mainland until they managed to make contact with the organized underground that finally evacuated them to Cairo to begin their careers as saboteurs.[38]

Eddie Myers was very interested in the idea, and Captain Edmonds was more than enthusiastic to tell him about the chance to pull off a major sabotage operation that everyone had declared "impossible." This impossible mission's main ally would be the secrecy of stealth.

"The only way it could be done by stealth," explained Edmonds, "would be by following the stream down the gorge. That is, practically speaking, impossible, and because the Germans regard it as impossible, a determined party just might succeed."[39]

It wasn't just the Germans who thought it was impossible. So did the local Greeks who were very familiar with the impassible gorge and German defenses. The German commanders had meticulously inspected the gorge from both ends and the plunging falls and sheer walls convinced them that no man-made barrier could have been built that would be a more formidable obstacle than this creation of nature. Not withstanding the overwhelming negatives, Myers gave Gordon-Creed and Stott an enthusiastic go ahead to launch Operation Washing. Within the hour, the two officers, with a third man, were off to recon the gorge.

But it wasn't long before that recon team was back at headquarters, explaining to Edmonds that the gorge was every bit the obstacle everyone had said it was. They had not gone far before a plunging sixty-foot waterfall stopped them cold.

Even if it were possible to proceed past the falls, it would still take the team days to even reach the area of the Asopos Viaduct. Their report graphically described the treacherous approach to the target:

> "For the most part the gorge was only a few yards wide, with sheer cliffs rising to a thousand feet above the stream. The sun never entered the gorge, and the only passage for most of the way was through the freezing cold water or along the steep cliff sides. The heartbreaking barriers were the waterfalls, with side walls worn smooth as glass, and the deep pools into which the water fell. Loose rocks from the cliff faces kept shooting down into the stream."[40]

But Edmonds was undaunted. On May 21, 1943, two years after the German Army had overrun Greece, a tiny party of eight men, equipped with 340 feet of plaited rope, explosives and necessary supplies, marched to the Asopos Gorge to attempt the "impossible task." Captain Gordon-Creed led the team and Lieutenant Stott was their most able guide. At the first waterfall where the recon party had turned back, they stashed their supplies in a dry area. The heavy loads and extreme exertion had exhausted them and they rested for the rest of the day.

On the twenty-third, using their new ropes, they descended the sixty-foot falls into the pool below and trekked forward in the icy water until they were again blocked by a second waterfall, requiring another strenuous descent. The following day's progress in the frigid water was very slow, and the team hoped that if there was a third waterfall, it would be the last. They collapsed for the night.

As they began anew the following day, Stott and Morton went ahead to reconnoiter but shortly returned to the main party very disappointed. They had indeed reached a third falls. The water plunged over a fifteen-foot wide ledge and dropped forty-feet into the pool below. Since they had used all the rope and there was no way to negotiate the smooth perpendicular sides, they could not proceed. Stott also reported that they had still not seen the viaduct even though they had traversed fully two-thirds the length of the gorge.

Reluctantly they again stored their supplies and explosives and turned around to retrace their steps through the torturous passage. On May 28 the ragged team again stood before Captain Edmonds reporting on their unsuccessful venture.

"When they returned to my headquarters," Edmonds reported, "their appearance told the tale of their hardships. Their knees were cut and bruised from scaling the falls, their clothes were torn and ragged and most of them looked worn and exhausted."[41]

Neither Myers nor Edmonds were discouraged by this new setback. They were even more determined to renew their efforts and ordered special materiel from Headquarters Middle East at Cairo. This included more rope and grappling hooks, axes, rope ladders and anything else that might be handy to negotiate the gorge.

On June 15 they were again ready, but this time the sabotage team would be even smaller, only six men. The new plan called for three men to force their way through the gorge and to proceed to the area of the Asopos Viaduct. Upon arrival in the vicinity of the bridge, Stott would dispatch a message back to the rest of the team waiting at headquarters at Anatoli, and Captain Gordon-Creed would then lead the rest to rendezvous at the target area.

Stott's team took off loaded down with all the special equipment from Cairo and headed for the gorge. The other two members of his team were a former motor transport driver, Charlie Mutch, who also had never managed to escape Greece, and a displaced Palestinian Arab soldier named Khouri. They quickly negotiated the first two falls and prepared for the third one that had previously stopped the team.

"Our first day was spent in felling a tree about half a mile back and floating and pushing it down the river," reported Mutch. "The roar of the stream stopped the sound of the axe. The tree was about seventy feet long and had branches every three or four feet. After having it well tied back it was let over the waterfall, and to our joy it reached the bottom with about three feet to spare at the top."[42]

The men scrambled down their tree ladder and proceed to

swim and wade in the cold water of the pool and stream below. Stott went ahead as the point man. They had traveled in the neck-deep water for almost 400 yards when Mutch and Khouri saw the lieutenant swimming back toward them. He excitedly reported that he had seen the viaduct and it was only another hundred yards ahead.

Gaining some dry ground, Lieutenant Stott scribbled out a message for Captain Edmonds and ordered Mutch to retrace his steps and bring it to him. At headquarters, the Captain was delighted to read:

"I got down the big waterfall, found it was the last and suddenly when I rounded the bend I came face to face with 'Mrs. Washing' herself. There was a lot of activity going on and workmen were swarming over the viaduct strengthening it to carry heavier loads and making a deuce of a din, rivetting I think. They have scaffolding erected all over it and ladders leading up from the bottom. I was taking all this in when I looked down at the stream and saw two workmen only about 10 yards away from me working with their heads down getting stones out of the stream. Luckily they didn't see me and I quickly got out of sight. These workmen come down from the railway line by some steps cut in the north cliff side, and we should be able to get up this way. Please send Geoff, Scotty and Mac immediately. The job's in the bag. I am going off on a recce of the road south of Lamia while the others are coming. Yours, Don."[43]

Gordon-Creed's team met Stott's team in the gorge on June 18. They maneuvered all the explosives and materiel into a spot closer to the target and then hid themselves to wait for nightfall. Clad only in their uniform shorts and hiking shoes, the six men shivered in the cold waiting for the moment to attack.

Finally, well after dark and after the construction crews had stopped their work, silence settled on the bridge and the six-man team shouldered the explosives and hiked them up the steep slopes leading to the base of the viaduct. The tangle of barbed wire that had surrounded the four steel pylons supporting the 264-

foot arched span had been folded back during this construction, and the team moved right onto the base platforms.

In short order, busy hands fixed the charges to the four steel legs of the span and stretched detonating cord between each of the four charges. The team kept a cautious eye on the shadow of a German sentry pacing back and forth along the tracks and, just out of sight, they could hear other German voices murmured from the garrison buildings. At one point, a sentry's patrol route took him right past Gordon-Creed hiding at track level, and, as he passed, the Captain brought down a stout piece of lumber on his head and the soldier fell off the bridge into the gorge below.

Lieutenant Stott's team began to withdraw while others continued to fix the charges. It was important to gain a vantage point to see the results of the attack and he could only gain that point high up on a mountain. Mutch and Khouri withdrew with him to prepare the path for the hasty withdrawal once the team had lit the fuses.

"What a mad scramble it was swimming and climbing ropes," reported Mutch as he retraced his steps. "While going up one rope ladder my arms gave out on me and I fell back about twenty-five feet and knocked myself out, and got a bad knock on the shin. I came to about fifteen minutes later hearing Khouri calling to me from the top in the darkness."[44]

At midnight the work of setting the charges was finished and the saboteurs started five chemical fuses, one was all that was necessary, but five left nothing to chance. The explosives were set to detonate in an hour and a half, allowing the team time to escape. In the darkness, the withdrawal was agonizing. While the falls had to be descended when the team approached the target, they now had to be ascended on the way out. As they climbed and trudged and swam, their anxious eyes stole glances at their watches as the minutes ticked by. But when an hour and a half had passed and each man had expected to hear the explosions, nothing happened.

Fifteen minutes later everything was still silent in the night. The only sound was the rushing water. Then twenty minutes went by and still nothing. After all their effort, was this going to be a failure? Had the Germans discovered the charges and disarmed them? Could all five fuses have been faulty? Should they stop their headlong withdrawal and begin to retrace their steps to try and salvage the mission? Twenty-five minutes passed, and they stood still in the cold water, and suddenly a bright flash illuminated the gorge. The team heard no explosion since the roar of the water, crashing over the falls, drowned all sound. Standing in the waist-deep water they faced the bright light and then turned to each other and congratulated themselves. Operation Washing had succeeded.

IN THE DAYS FOLLOWING the attack on the Asopos Viaduct, the Germans looked internally to find the culprits. Certainly no outside force could have possibly made such an attack. The entire garrison force was the prime suspect as well as the workers and laborers. The officers in charge and other key personnel in charge of security were shot, and it was five days before the Germans discovered a rope ladder in the vicinity.

They began an emergency construction effort to rebuild the viaduct to get the supply trains moving again and in five weeks, they had done just that. A new span was ready to lift into place, and a giant boom swung it up and over the gorge. But as the engineers worked to connect it, something went wrong and it slipped and teetered and crashed down into the gorge on top of the wreckage of the old viaduct. The bridge was not back in operation for another five weeks. The saboteur's blast on June 20, 1943, had disrupted the German supply line for almost seventy days.[45]•

• The six members of the team were all decorated, with Lieutenant Scott recommended for the Victoria Cross. But he was finally awarded the DSO (Distinguished Service Order) as was Captain Gordon-Creed. Scott did not survive the war and drowned in Borneo in 1945.

CHAPTER 11
DARKNESS AND LIGHT

THE PERSECUTION OF THE GREEK JEWS had two faces. At Thessaloniki, the oppression of the population and the implementation of the Nazi plan for the Final Solution had begun almost immediately after occupation. But in Athens, things were different. Athens was under Italian authority and the Italians had no anti-Semitic laws, so it was only natural that Jews from all over occupied Greece flocked to Athens to melt into the general population, partially protected by the sheer numbers of the great city.

Such was the case of Moissis Gattegno's family. As the German occupation of Thessaloniki began in 1941, things changed drastically for this eight-year-old boy and his family. His father had been a prominent and prosperous jeweler, but in a matter of days the Germans converted Alvertos Gattegno into a homeless destitute man.

The German tactics to accomplish this "conversion" were standard. They came to his shop and "bought" his valuable stock of jewelry, paying Alvertos with German Occupational Marks, which were worthless. Then they confiscated his home and most of his furnishings, forcing the family to find refuge, with the few things they could salvage, in the abandoned house of a friend who had fled to Athens. But hiding from the Germans meant constantly moving.

"So we ended up in this laundry room," said Moissis, "and three or four people came every night and blackmailed my father."[1]

A family friend was their only hope of salvation, and he had

246

them "arrested" so he could issue false IDs and change their names, and move them eventually to Athens where they hid and began to try to escape to the Middle East. By February 1944, Alvertos had painstakingly acquired papers for his family and even paid for a boat to smuggle them out of Greece to Turkey, but at last the boat's captain betrayed them to the Germans. Months of horrible privations followed, first in the Chaidari concentration camp in Athens, and later in Bergen-Belsen.

Zak and Louisa Soussis and their four children were a wealthy Jewish family living in Athens prior to the war. But after the Germans overran Greece and occupied the land, Zak heard the disquieting news about the fate of Jews in Thessaloniki and, like many other Jews in Athens, tried to obtain false IDs bearing Christian names for himself and his family. Knowing that the Germans confiscated all the stock from seized Jewish stores, he took his stock and gave it to his non-Jewish friends for safekeeping.[2]

AT THE VERY TIME that the Soussis family struggled to hide from the ruthless Germans, an event, far removed from Athens, unfolded that would greatly affect their lives and the lives of millions of others caught up in the struggle of WWII. At 1730 on September 8, 1943, on the eve of the major amphibious attack onto the Italian mainland at Salerno, General Dwight D. Eisenhower, the commander of the Allied Expeditionary Force, signaled a sensational message to the world:

"The Italian Government has surrendered its forces unconditionally. Hostilities between the armed forces of the United Nations and those of Italy terminate at once."[3]

Italy was out of the war, and most of the world cheered, but with Italy out of the war, for Greeks who had been under Italian occupation, this was bad news. The Germans moved to quickly occupy Athens. Gone was the more lenient occupation. On September 20 the newly arrived military commander of Athens, SS General Jurgen Stroop, welcomed Dieter Wisliceny the head of the Rosenberg Commando, who had successfully carried out its program of confiscation and theft of Jewish assets in Thessaloniki. Stroop himself had commanded the forces that had put down the Jewish rebellion at the Warsaw Ghetto, and was now determined to carry out Hitler's well-instituted anti-Semitic programs of the Final Solution.

Wisliceny's first order of business was to summon the Chief Rabbi of Athens, Elias Barzili, to his headquarters. He ordered the rabbi to present to him exact figures, documentation and other vital data concerning the Jews in the city. This information was to include: names, professions, and addresses of Athenian Jews; a list and data of foreign Jews, and also Italian Jews who had obtained papers under Italian authority; data of all Thessaloniki Jews who had fled to Athens; and names and data of people who had assisted Jews to flee to Palestine. Jews would also have to come to the Synagogue and register.

Wisliceny announced that Rabbi Barzili was also to form and preside over a new *Judenrat*,* and was expected to provide names and data on those who would sit on this council with him. Their first order of business would be to create a Jewish Police Force to enforce Nazi orders, and the council would also undertake to create and issue new ID cards for Athenian Jews.[4]

The Judenrat was a diabolical invention of the German extermination machine. It was composed of compliant Jews whose duty was to assist and to set into motion the machinery that would provide slave labor to the Germans and to assist, by providing information, in the effort to round up and deport Jews, eventually to extermination camps. Jews who balked or were squeamish about serving on the Judenrat and carrying out these duties were replaced by those who were more "compliant." Those who were replaced could expect to be shot or find themselves on the trains to extermination.

Chaim A. Kaplan, a veteran of the Warsaw ghetto wrote in 1941 to describe this odious council: "The Judenrat, in the language of the Occupying Power—is an abomination in the eyes of the Warsaw Community ..."[5]

---

* German for "Jewish council."

After receiving his instructions, Rabbi Barzili left Wisliceny's headquarters a very shaken man. He contacted a number of Greek authorities but no one could help him in his dilemma. Several prominent Jews made an appeal to the quisling Greek government now under the new quisling leader and collaborator, Constantine Rallis. Rallis showed the depth of his cowardice and traitorous enslavement to the Germans by proclaiming to the rabbi that the fate of the northern Jews of Thessaloniki had been brought about by their own illegal, subversive activities, as if to suggest that the Jews of Athens would be safe if they would just cooperate with the Germans.*

Only the Greek Orthodox Archbishop Damsaskinos Papandreou, offered any solution, and that solution was one of reality: in desperation, the Jews of Athens must run for their lives. He had seen the Nazis in action in northern Greece, and knew that only flight could offer hope against capture and inevitable extermination.

Rabbi Barzili played for time and informed Wisliceny that some of the records were missing. It would take a few days to compile a complete list and he used the time to destroy any remaining Jewish records. His supporters had him shave off his beard, gave him a new identity card, and sent him packing to the mountains and to the safety of the Resistance. The Germans had been thwarted for the time being.[6] There would be no lists at this time, and no Judenrat.

The Greek archbishop, however, disregarded his own safety and continued to fight actively to help the hunted Jews. He denounced the German barbarism and instructed his priests to state the Church's position in their sermons. He initiated the creation of several thousand false Baptismal Certificates and other identity papers to aid the persecuted Jews, and supported Athens Police Chief, Angelos Evert, who provided over 27,000 false IDs. He ordered convents and monasteries to shelter them, and for priests to appeal to their communities for brave Greek

---

* At war's end, Constantine Rallis was convicted as a traitor and collaborator and sentenced to life in prison, where he died in 1946.

families to hide them in their homes. Over 600 priests were rounded up with the Jews for such actions and deported.[7]

Archbishop Damaskinos of Athens and all of Greece.

But the archbishop was not finished. He eventually carried his bravery right into the face of the enemy itself. In a lengthy public letter he appealed to the Germans to honor the terms of the treaty they had signed. In part he said:

"The Greek Orthodox Church and the Academic World of Greek People Protest against the Persecution ... The Greek people were ... deeply grieved to learn that the German Occupation Authorities have already started to put into effect a program of gradual deportation of the Greek Jewish community.

"According to the terms of the armistice, all Greek citizens, without distinction of race or religion, were to be treated equally by the Occupation Authorities ... Today we are ... deeply concerned with the fate of 60,000 of our fellow citizens who are Jews ... we have lived together in both slavery and freedom, and we have come to appreciate their feelings, their brotherly attitude, their economic activity, and most important, their indefectible patriotism ..."[8]

Stroop was furious with the letter. The archbishop was becoming a real nuisance and a threat to the smooth running of his command. He threatened the archbishop with death in front of a firing squad, but Damaskinos was not intimidated and was unmoved by the General's threats. He would have the final word.

"Greek religious leaders are not shot," he replied to the general in a display of cold-blooded courage, "they are hanged! I request that you respect this custom."[9] Stroop was speechless, and his swagger and abuse was reduced to irrelevance and impotence in the presence of Damaskinos.

While many in the Greek community succumbed to anti-Semitism and denounced their Jewish countrymen, there were many acts of heroism among non-Jews to help the persecuted Jews of Greece. Perhaps none more heroic than that performed on the island of Zakynthos in the Ionian Sea. There were 275 Jews living in Zakynthos, all of whom survived the Holocaust largely because of the heroism of two men: Mayor Loukas Carrer and Bishop Chrysostomos.

Following the usual protocol of demanding a list of Jews from the leaders of a community, the Germans also demanded a list from Zakynthos's Mayor Carrer. He refused and the Germans made a second demand, this time at gunpoint. He left to compile the death list, and returned with Bishop Chrysostomos who presented the list to the German officer.

"Here are your Jews," the Bishop declared. "If you choose to deport the Jews of Zakynthos, you must also take me and I will share their fate."

When the German official scanned the list he found there were only two names on it: Mayor Carrer and Bishop Chrysostomos.*[10]

ZAK SOUSSIS NOW frantically scrambled to hide himself and his family from the new German occupiers. A wealthy friend offered him a hiding place at his mansion, and Zak, his wife and four children occupied the gardener's house. But their refuge was short lived when the Germans commandeered the mansion and the Soussises found themselves living under the very noses of the enemy. They moved to another hiding place.

---

* Mayor Carrer and Bishop Chrysostomos were named Yad Vashem as "Righteous Among the Nation" for their heroism.

But it was Zak's brother who created the next problem. Samuel Soussis's family was arrested after being denounced by the landlady of the house in which they were hiding. Zak was frantic, and in an act of desperation, hoping to influence the Germans and gain Samuel's freedom, he did the unthinkable: he went to the synagogue on March 24, 1944 and registered, as Jews were supposed to do every Friday. While he was there, the Germans raided the Synagogue and arrested everyone who showed up and imprisoned them in a concentration camp west of Athens.[11]

Zak managed to send his family a few notes and those notes along with his watch and gold ring were all the family had of him. Louisa had been waiting for Zak when he went to the synagogue to register, and she saw the German raid and the arrests. She moved the children, Sylvia, Alvertos, Daisy, and Marios, from the house just in time to avoid the German party that came for them. A few days later, Zak and the rest of the Jews arrested at the synagogue were herded onto trains and deported to extermination camps.

Louisa was left alone with her four children to escape and evade from the monster that sought to devour them. Young Marios said of his mother, "From that day on, housewife Louisa was transformed into a furious lioness, who would do anything in order to save her children from the rapacious birds of prey of the Third Reich ... the Germans never managed to find us.

"I remember walking in the fields that night, my mother in front, Sylvia and Daisy behind her, followed by Alvertos carrying me on his shoulders. We had nothing but the things we could carry, a few bundles of clothes and nothing else. We carried the fear of the persecuted in our hearts, the anxiety ... Like a new Moses, my mother led her small tribe of Israelites to the Promised Land."[12]

LIFE ON CRETE under German and Italian occupation had been no different than life on the Greek mainland. The Germans ruled with an iron fist. Early on they had executed any Cretans whom they suspected might have fought against the attacking paratroopers. In June 1941, during the first month after the battle, they executed over 2,000 and they would execute thousands more during the occupation. They carried out the first mass execution at the town of Kandanos.

"We heard about the village, Kandanos," said George Tzitzikas, a Greek soldier now on Crete, fighting the Germans for the second time. "The Germans destroyed the village completely: burned it, killed all the people. The Germans erected a sign saying, 'this place used to be the village of Kandanos. We destroyed it because they resisted German troops.'"[13]

Leslie Newton, a British Commonwealth soldier, was one of the 5,000 soldiers stranded on Crete, and was in a small outdoor compound as a German prisoner.

"We were herded in there and guarded by a few paratroops, and some of the women used to come round there and throw bits of bread to us, feeling sorry for us, and also quarts of water. Some of the officers there took exception to this, and warned them, in German, that if they didn't go away, they would shoot. That was the saddest moment when these three paratroopers just opened up with their pistols and shot them. The [women] didn't have all that much bread ... but they gave it to us, and I think we have to be very thankful that they did so."[14]

"Everything was sad during the occupation," said seventeen-year-old Stelios Anezakis. "We had misery all of the time, nothing but misery. All of the possessions we had in our lives, and suddenly in an instant, everything was gone. No house, nothing to cover yourself, nothing to eat. Nothing."[15]

German General Alexander Andrea commanded the occupation forces on Crete and wasted little time letting the population know that he was in charge, and that any notion of resisting the German rule was futile. He posted his dictum for all to see:

"Germany has the power to enforce her will in your land. God help those who resist."[16]

"The Germans captured Crete and they spread death and destruction and fire all over Crete," said George Tzitzikas. "They aimed to destroy the spirit of the Cretans, and have the Cretans submit to them. But they failed, they failed miserably."

"It was almost romantic to get involved in the resistance. The younger children were so proud ... they knew the dangers. They knew that the Germans were killing without asking."[17]

This total commitment to resistance by the entire population meant that the entire island was a giant spy network. Everyone watched the Germans, reported on their every move, and communicated with each other and with resistance fighters. As on the Greek mainland, the shortage of German troops to man all civil positions, especially those providing services to life on the island, meant that locals had to continue in those positions, and that meant more eyes and ears to pry into the inner workings of the Germans and their movements and more vital information to successfully attack them.

However the price of this dangerous spying and resistance was not cheap. The Germans slaughtered anyone they so much as suspected was involved in such activities, and destroyed homes and burned villages in retaliation. Executions were a common occurrence and few families were spared the heartbreak of watching a relative shot to death before a firing squad. But those executions were events that the condemned used as a stage for their martyrdom, and an opportunity to make their final acts of defiance. They sang patriotic songs while standing in front of the firing squads and uttered memorable last words. They left notes scribbled on their prison walls, and, more often than not, those last words were, "Long live Greece; long live Crete."

This cycle of death and destruction led the guerrillas to also conduct a war without mercy. Among the guerrilla bands, their hatred for the Germans and their fast hit-and-run tactics led to a "take no prisoners" mentality. German soldiers and guerrilla fighters were committed to a war of annihilation.

"After a fight, Bill Moss told me to execute our prisoners," said Eleftherios Skoulas. "I was not a man who could do such a thing. It was not in me. So I gave the instructions to Manolo, who was a hard man, and told him to do it."[18]

This undaunted, patriotic outpouring of courage was not lost on the Germans who witnessed it. Even General Alexander Andrea, who commanded the occupational forces, was moved to say:

"The courage of Cretans facing the firing squad is

legendary. Cretans turn to mythical figures. They are so
proud during their tragic moment of death that one can
hardly fail to admire their courage. When executions
were to take place, I would leave my desk and walk out
to the balcony, just to watch and admire those proud
people. Nowhere else have I witnessed such defiance to
death, such love for freedom, than on Crete."[19]

The resistance fighters in Crete started from a very different
position than had the embryonic resistance fighters on the
mainland. The British Army, especially those units on the
Peloponnese, had gathered for evacuation from Kalamata to
Crete and Egypt and had been obliged to abandon large quantities
of supplies and materiel, including individual weapons and
ammunition. These were quickly in Greek hands and hidden for
future use.

But when the army evacuated from Crete, it was a different
story. It was not a case of a gathering of the retreating army for
the exodus as it had been at Kalamata. On Crete it had been
anything but an orderly retreat, with a rear-guard action holding
off the pursuing Germans. The retreat had been more of an
every-man-for-himself withdrawal, or, at best, small groups of
soldiers tortuously climbing a barricade of mountains to land's
end to the south. It had been a trek down the other side to find
tiny beach enclaves, hewn out by nature in the stony face that
plunged to the water's edge. It was on those last spits of land
that the Commonwealth soldiers hoped the British Navy would
again be able to pluck them off in the nick of time. Those soldiers
had not left an arsenal of weapons behind.

Twenty-five-year old Patrick Leigh Fermor was one of
the British SOE officers selected for insertion into this eager
population of Cretan resisters to encourage, coordinate and lead
an effective fight against the German occupiers. During the
terrible winter of 1940, Fermor had served as a British liaison
officer to the Greek Army fighting the Italians in Albania, and he
later fought in Crete. He was no stranger to this battlefield.

But his unique qualifications that made him a natural for
SOE intelligence was his knowledge of the Greek language

that he had acquired during his teenage years when, in 1933, as a young wanderlust, anxious to see the world, he had walked across Europe, from the Hook of Holland to Constantinople. This gregarious, charming young man met, talked with, and shared life with peasants and notables alike, always taking notes, always listening to eager storytellers. He rubbed elbows with everyone, slept in caves and on the ground with shepherds, on barges on the rivers, as well as in the fine surroundings of country estates. A final trek brought him to Greece where he continued his romantic, fantasy life until the outbreak of war.[20]

"I had walked from Rotterdam to Constantinople just looking at things and writing books," he said, "... and I had learned pretty fluent Greek. So people like me were rather in demand, and so I was whisked off into intelligence. The Cretans were passionate resisters, and in on everything, and full of ideas; and were longing to get to grips with the Germans, to get rid of them, and that was what we were all hoping for, that there would be some, great triumphant day when we would attack them and turn them out.

"There were only half a dozen [SOE] officers, at the most, with their wireless sets and their operators. In a way it was a terrific hardship. There wasn't much to eat, and they [Cretans] never let us go short."

The British commitment to Greece and Crete during their darkest days of invasion now paid dividends in trust and confidence. The Greeks had seen the British send elements of their finest army to try to defend against the German onslaught even though their own nation was hard pressed with bombing at home, war at sea, and on land in North Africa. They had seen the British troops hold until the bitter end and endure evacuation, twice, for a Balkan effort that much of the world deemed an exercise in futility.

Pragmatism had defied Churchill's logic to defend the indefensible and many had scoffed at his idea of "succour to Greece." In the short run, Germany prevailed and the pragmatists raised arrogant eyebrows, but an examination of the long run revealed that Germany had bitten off more than it could chew and now, proverbially, had a tiger by the tail. Nowhere on either the Greek mainland or on the island of Crete did Germany have control of anything but a small percentage of the land, and except for patrolling activity, ceded control of the larger portions to the guerrillas who had developed the capability to conduct unrelenting attacks that threatened the entire German war effort. Hitler's Commando Order of October 1942 provided ample proof of The Führer mindset concerning this unanticipated threat.

Perhaps because of increased guerrilla activity, General Andrea was relieved of command and General Friedrich Mueller arrived to command the 22nd Bremen Panzer Grenadier Division that garrisoned the island. If Andrea had been ruthless, Mueller actually made him look saintly.

"He killed many, many people all over Crete, burned a lot of villages, and created a fear during 1943," said George Tizikas.

Mueller conducted systematic attacks against villages as reprisals for guerrilla activities. His brutality included torching houses with gasoline and burning them in roaring infernos, including the people within. He mined village squares and blew up unsuspecting pedestrians. On one occasion he executed six boys between ages twelve and eighteen, before machine gunning a hundred more. General Mueller's crackdown began to slow down the guerrilla activity since the British could not meet the demands for weapons, food and ammunition.

But just when it seemed that he would get the upper hand, the United States jumped into the fray and their equivalent to the SOE, the OSS, began making the supply runs, allowing the guerrillas to rearm to a level where they were able to conduct meaningful attacks against the German enemy. Suddenly many of the resistance fighters were seen and photographed with the distinctive Eisenhower jackets that were the OSS's trademark uniform.

But overenthusiasm had reaped disastrous results before. A few Germans ambushed had often led to hundreds of innocent civilians slaughtered by the German reprisal machine. But the fall of Italy, and the rearming of the Resistance by the United States, was intoxicating to the guerrilla leader Manoli Bandouvas. Always a scourge to the Germans, he now became a man possessed.

On September 11, 1943, Bandouvas executed a spectacular ambush on a two-company force of 200 Germans patrolling toward a village in the Viannos district whose garrison he had previously attacked. His ambush destroyed the responding patrol. The official casualty count was 71 Germans killed and 113 wounded.

General Mueller was quick to respond, and the reprisals were ghastly. On September 15 and 16, Mueller attacked with a force of 2,000 Germans through the Viannos region and killed over 300 people and burned seven villages to the ground, scattering Bandouvas's band to the south.[21]

"The whole place was a pillar of smoke in that part of Crete," said Patrick Leigh Fermor. "It was a horrifying holocaust. We wondered what to do. I'd had the idea, that we might take the German general; waylay the German general and take him prisoner. That would be a terrific smack in the eye for the Germans and their morale. And it should be an Anglo-Cretan thing, not something entirely English, organized from the outside, and as a symbol of the very, very close and loving relationship which had grown up between the English and the Cretans ..."[22]

The idea of kidnapping General Mueller would be just as Fermor had described, "a terrific smack in the eye." It would not be an ambush, or detonation of a fuel dump, or an aircraft sabotaged. It would be "something which would hit the enemy hard on a different level, and one which would offer no presentable pretext for reprisals,"[23] said Fermor. "So we made our plans."

Fermor formed his team upon his return to Cairo and selected Captain W. Stanley (Billy) Moss as his second in command, and then selected two experienced veterans of the conflict: Manoli Paterakis, who had been a Cretan policeman, and George Tyrakis, an abandoned soldier who had fought in the Greek Army in Albania.

AS THE BRITISH SOE planned their kidnapping venture, the Americans were not idle. In 1943 the OSS* had been operational for one year, and had planned its upcoming operation for just about that long. On Christmas Day, the Liberty Ship, *Pierre L'Enfant*, departed from Hampton Roads, Virginia to join a convoy destined for Cairo. On board were eighteen officers and 182 enlisted men of an outfit called the Greek Battalion, more technically, the 122nd Infantry Battalion of the United States Army. They were all Greek-American volunteers, having trained in the mountainous terrain of Colorado to replicate the terrain they would face in Greece, and they had been recruited as clandestine saboteurs.

"We were going in to help liberate Greece," said Lt. John (Yannis) Giannaris, the commander of Group II of the seven-group OSS force that now bore the name 2671st Special Reconnaissance Battalion. "We were going to blow up trains, blow up bridges, mine roads, harass the enemy, and kill as many of them as we could."[24]

Pierre L'Enfant docked in Egypt on January 23, 1944, and the Greek Battalion further embarked for the Italian Port of Taranto, arriving on February 8, and then proceeded on to Bari.

"Our plan was to parachute into Greece just southwest of the island of Corfu," said Giannaris, "But each and every time, something would come up to delay our mission. Either the weather would be too bad to jump, or there would be too much German troop activity in the area to go in."[25]

The German Army was being pushed back in the east, and the Anglo-American Army, quartered in the United Kingdom, was poised for invasion onto the European Continent, and it was evident that as German fortunes waned, they would soon be forced to withdraw their occupying army stationed in Greece to participate in the hard fighting against the Allied advances on the eastern and western fronts. That army, in Greece, was the 12th German Army, plus SS troops, a force totaling over 70,000 men.

---

* Office of Strategic Services, forerunner to the CIA (Central Intelligence Agency).

"And the way out of Greece," said Giannaris, "was the railroad and the main road that ran from Athens on up north to Salonica (Thessaloniki,) and from there, up into Yugoslavia and on into Germany. Our mission was to sabotage this withdrawal ... our code name was *Smash 'Em*"[26]

Giannaris's target, once he should finally get into Greece, was going to be that vital rail and road line traversing through the Valley of Lamia, but in the meantime, he was forced to while away the hours and days in Italy, waiting for action. While he waited, the Anglo-American Army struck. Eisenhower's forces smashed ashore at Normandy on D-Day, June 6, 1944, and Giannaris was now more anxious than ever because the Germans would certainly begin that anticipated withdrawal out of Greece.

Finally, orders came, not to board aircraft to parachute into Greece, but to report for embarkation to Monopoli, Italy for further transportation across the Adriatic Sea aboard a British LCI (Landing Craft Infantry). He departed on the evening of June 16 and landed after midnight on the eighteenth on the western Greek coastline. It took fourteen more days on foot, accompanied by local guerrilla fighters and a train of mules for their equipment, for the twenty-two men of Group II to reach their base of operations at the small, 20-house village of Papas, high on a mountaintop. Papas was 100 miles northwest of Athens but was just north of their target area, the Valley of Lamia, and the road and rail lines.[27]

"We began to make reconnaissances of the whole area in and around the Valley of Lamia," said Giannaris, "to familiarize ourselves with mountain paths, the valleys, the German strongholds, the roads and the railroad tracks ..."[28]

It was during their reconnaissance, while crossing a dried-out lake, that the men of Group II saw the evidence of what they were fighting for. They discovered a mass grave northwest of Lamia.

"The dried-out lake was called Xinias," said Giannaris. "The German's machine gunned a hundred and three Greek civilians. When I saw this mass grave, my heart went out to all enslaved people under the Nazis. When I saw that mass grave, I couldn't wait to go on missions against these Huns."[29]

Group II wasted no time going into action. The target area was called the Five Mile Area and was a strip of railroad track that ran between high hills instead of the mostly open ground in the valley. Beginning on July 1, they began operations by blowing up sections of railroad track. But it was at the end of July that they set about on an ambitious attack.

Giannaris formed a team of eight Greek ELAS guerrillas and twelve of his own men to attack and destroy a German troop train in the area of the Gorgopotamos Viaduct that had been so famously attacked in November 1942. British intelligence had provided the information and Giannaris's team began the forty-mile hike to the target area on July 31. They were armed with two bazookas, one Browning Automatic Rifle (BAR,) Thompson submachine guns, rifles, and enough explosives to attack the train.[30]

"All trains stopped in Lianokladion, a switching junction and freight yard just west of Lamia," said Giannaris. "We decided to attack where the train slowed down at a level place, about seventy-five yards long in the southeast end of the valley. The spot we picked was 3,000 yards north of the Gorgopotamos bridge, which was heavily fortified by German troops.

"We covered thirty miles in fourteen hours. We reached the target area, this short stretch of tracks where the ground leveled off. The bridge was to the south of us. The whole area was heavily patrolled [and] we had to determine at what intervals the German patrols would be passing through.

"We moved into position and placed plastic explosives on the tracks, enough to stop the train."[31]

The attack force moved to the side of the tracks and spread out, five yards between positions, and formed a killing zone of seventy-five yards. The Andartes covered the north and south ends of the track to engage anyone who might arrive from either end. The waiting began.

The time for the train's arrival came and went and still the night was silent. Could the intelligence have been wrong? Had the train already passed or was it coming on another day? The waiting was frustrating as the minutes ticked by. Finally the faint sound of an approaching train drifted toward them. The ambushers could hear it long before they could see it as it wound its way through the mountainous area toward them. It made its last turn past the last hill and came into full view of Giannaris. It was quite a surprise to him.

"It was lit up like a Christmas tree!" he exclaimed. "I had to make an immediate decision. I figured it couldn't be a German troop train, all lit up like that at night, exposing itself. So I quickly gave the order to remove our demolitions ...

"The train approached and passed, full of civilians. A minute or two later I thought I heard something else. I pressed my ear to the ground and heard the sound of another train ... I gave an order to a bazooka team to get into position within fifteen yards of the tracks."[32]

The team crept into position as the second train approached very slowly. Unlike the first train clipping along with blazing lights, this new train was as black as the night, and made little noise other than the slow, rhythm of the huff of its steam engine. It was a black specter moving through the dark, probably following in close trace of the passenger train for safety against ambushes.

The engine entered the killing field, and rolled past the prone bodies of the men of Group II and toward the bazooka team, whose gunner was already on one knee with the shoulder weapon aimed at the boiler. When the entire train was in the killing field, Giannaris gave the order to fire and the bazooka flamed its telltale back blast. The rocket round impacted on target with a deep *crump*, the night turned orange and lit the geyser of steam that jetted skyward. Five other rounds quickly found their mark on the locomotive and the second car.

"One round was all that was needed," Giannaris said, "It hit the boiler and the boiler became a sieve. The locomotive lost its steam and all its power. Then I gave the command to open fire. My men began firing away with the Browning Automatic Rifle and Thompson submachine guns. The engineers jumped out, hollering, in Greek, '*Paidia!* We're Greeks! Boys! Don't shoot! We're Greeks!'"

But the rest of the train was not Greek, and the Germans

returned fire, feebly, since the shock of the attack had overwhelmed them. The train and all of its supplies were now ablaze and illuminated the ambush site. The constant chatter of automatic weapons' fire and explosions lasted for seven minutes and then the attackers began to withdraw. There was no more fire from the destroyed train.

The withdrawal was through enemy territory and lasted through the next morning. The four-day operation from July 31 to August 3 ended after the forced march back to Papas and home base.

During the 134 days of operations from July 1 until the group departed Greece on October 30, 1944, Group II waged unrelenting war against the Germans, participating in fourteen separate operations. They were the most prolific of the seven United States OSS teams formed from the old Greek Battalion. When it came to blowing up rail track, Group II was in a class by itself, accounting for 7,400 yards of the 9,900 total.

"We attacked three trains, destroyed three locomotives, thirty-one railroad cars, six trucks, blew up a bridge and attacked a truck convoy," reported a proud Giannaris. During that period, Group II suffered one man killed and seven wounded, only one severely—Giannaris himself.* They also inflicted 675 casualties on the German Army.[33]

ON FEBRUARY 5, 1944, in the night skies above the mountains of Crete, during the same week that the American OSS teams arrived in Taranto, Italy, a British aircraft began its final run to insert a four-man team onto the rugged mountain terrain. The aircraft had taken off from Brindisi, in Italy, and carried the SOE team of Patrick Leigh Fermor, William Stanley Moss, Manoli Paterakis, and George Tyrakis. Cairo had approved the daring

---

* On September 8, John Giannaris managed to crawl from his battlefield and was first helped by two Greek shepherd girls and then by many Greeks to a safe village. Ten days later, he was rescued by air and flown out of Greece by a daring British pilot, Lt. Norman Attenborrow, who flew in and out alone. It took two years for Giannaris to recover from his wounds.

plan to kidnap General Mueller, and the team was on a final approach to insert into Crete to accomplish that mission.

The first man out into the black skies over the rugged island was Major Fermor himself, and the pilot banked to retrace his path for a second run since the drop zone was so tiny only one man could be dropped at a time.

"We had reached our target and spotted the ground signals, but the landing ground had been so small that the pilot resolved to drop only one of us at each circuit," said second-in-command Bill Moss. "But then the plane 'had got lost in a cloud.' For over an hour the pilot had tried to rediscover the signals, but without success, and we had been forced to return disconsolate to Brindisi."[34]

Twelve subsequent runs by the plane failed to parachute the other three members of the team into Crete, so, like Giannaris and his men, the rest of the SOE team found itself, much later, on board a small boat, in the dark of night, silently approaching the rocky southern coast of the island. It had been two months since Fermor had disappeared out the small black hole in the floor of the aircraft and departed the rest of the team.

But upon the boat's arrival, the two-month's interval evaporated as if it were yesterday. Fermor still had his jump suit on and greeted the landing party as if they had all just gathered on the drop zone.

"Crete appeared to me to be one huge conglomeration of rocks," observed Bill Moss. "We reached the top of each peak only to see a fresh skyline towering over us."[35]

Because of the two-month delay, the mission would have to slightly change. On March 1, a new commander of the 22nd Division, General Heinrich Kreipe, had replaced the original target of the operation, the Butcher of Crete, General Friedrich Mueller. But to the SOE, a German general was a German general and the mission would go forward.

A long trek from the landing beach found the team moving into the village of Kastamonitsa not far from Heraklion, a major city on the northern coast. Fermor had arranged for a clandestine meeting with the SOE's chief contact in Heraklion, Micky Akoumianakis.

"Micky, whose father was murdered by the Germans, is ready and anxious to help us in every possible way," said Moss. "... He owns a house in Knossos, which is next door to General Kreipe's sleeping quarters, the Villa Ariadne. From his house he will be able to make a first-rate reconnaissance and closely to watch the comings and goings of the General."[36]

With those plans in place, Fermor departed with Micky Akoumianakis toward Heraklion to begin the surveillance while Moss accompanied the Andartes whom had met him on the beach. It took hours to climb the steep sides of a mountain and Moss thought it would never end as he followed the locals ever higher. Even the mules balked and slipped along an invisible path of pure stone, and finally the group reached a lofty surface to make a headquarters inside a cave. The long climb had been worth it. In their new hideout, they were safe from any German patrols. Far below them was the town of Knossos and Villa Ariadne, and General Kreipe's quarters.

"Micky and another boy, Elias Athanassakis, spied out the land," said Fermor, "and noticed how [General Kreipe] would spend the day at Arkhanais, and then stay and play bridge there, and then drive back about nightfall to his living quarters. We thought the best way to do it was to dress up as Germans ... and, after dark, wait in the road and stop him, dressed up like traffic police corporals."[37]

That plan had been greatly enhanced by details provided by the prying eyes of Micky and Elias. They had determined that General Kreipe made twice daily trips from his quarters at Villa Ariadne to German Headquarters in Ano Arkhanais, once for his 0900 to 1300 stint, and again for his 1600 to 2030 regimen. Sometimes he remained later to engage fellow officers in bridge, which was his favorite pastime. That occasional late dinner and bridge habit offered the kidnappers a window of opportunity.

"The best and most obvious moment at which to attempt an abduction was during his last journey home," Moss observed, "because by that time it was fairly dark ... [and] the guard at the Villa Ariadne, imagining that the general had stayed at his headquarters for dinner or a game of cards, would not become immediately suspicious of his absence."[38]

Micky had somehow procured two German corporal uniforms, and Elias had memorized everything about the car and stated that "he could pick it out in the dark among a thousand." Additionally, Elias had devised an electric powered bell to be used as a signal to alert the kidnappers when the general's car was approaching the site. One ring would signal that the general's car was alone, two rings meant that it had an escort. A team member named Mitso Zatzas was assigned to listen for the rings and relay that signal to Major Fermor and Captain Moss by a flash from his signal light. The snatch was set for April 24.[39]

Fermor and Moss prepared a letter to be left in the general's car announcing who had done the kidnapping and to emphasize that the Cretans had nothing to do with it and should not have reprisals launched against them. #

TO THE GERMAN AUTHORITIES IN CRETE

April 23, 1944
GENTLEMEN,
Your Divisional Commander, General KREIPE, was captured a short time ago by a BRITISH raiding force under our command. By the time you read this both he and we will be on our way to CAIRO.
We would like to point our most emphatically that this operation has been carried out without the help of CRETANS or CRETAN partisans, and the only guides used were serving soldiers of HIS HELLENIC MAJESTY'S FORCES in the Middle East, who came with us.
Your General is an hounourable prisoner of war, and will be treated with all the consideration owing to his rank.
 Any reprisals against the local population will be wholly unwarranted and unjust.
Auf baldiges Weidersehen.˙

The Cretans, of course, were very much involved in the planned kidnapping.
˙ "See you soon."

The letter was signed by Fermor and Moss and attached with wax seals impressed with the two officers' rings. They added a postscript: "We are very sorry to leave this beautiful car behind."[40]

The site of the attack was at a T-junction between the headquarters and the general's living quarters. The car would have to slow down there and the embankments along the side of the road and the ditches offered spots for concealment. Micky and Elias took positions three hundred meters south of the ambush site toward Arkhanais to give the appropriate signal, and Fermor and Moss prepared to step out onto the road in their corporal's uniforms. Other members of the team took positions in the ditches in case anything went wrong. Once the headlights had passed those hiding in the ditches, they would jump out when Fermor would open the doors and tackle any other passengers in the back seat.

But the April 24 attack was scrapped when General Kreipe returned to Villa Ariadne early before sunset. Because of the delay and the danger of the plan's exposure, all the Andartes were sent away, leaving a much smaller team to handle the abduction. On the twenty-fifth the General stayed at his quarters all day and did not go to the headquarters.

On April 26, at 1800, Elias informed Fermor and Moss that General Kreipe had gone to his office in the afternoon, and should be on schedule in the evening.

"It was eight o'clock when we reached the T-junction," said Bill Moss. "When we reached the road we went straight to our respective posts and took cover. There were five false alarms during the first hour of our watch ... It was a strange feeling to be crouching so close to them, almost within arms reach of them, while they drove past with no idea that nine pairs of eyes were so fixedly watching them."

But the general's car had not appeared by 2115. That nagging doubt that rises when a time schedule is frustrated rose in the consciousness of Moss. Maybe the general was in one of those vehicles that had passed earlier and was not in his regular car. Maybe he had gone elsewhere for the evening. How much longer could the operation be postponed without information about it leaking out to the Germans?

"Paddy asked me the time. I looked at my watch and saw the hands were pointing close to half-past nine. And just at that moment Mitso's torch blinked. We scrambled out of the ditch on to the road. Paddy switched on his red lamp and I held up a traffic signal, and together we stood in the center of the T-junction."

General Kreipe's car approached and its powerful headlights spotlighted the two "*Feldpolizei* corporals" on the road. As the chauffeur slowed down, Fermor gave the order to halt and the car stopped. He and Moss slowly walked on opposite sides of the vehicle to the doors. When they had passed the reflections of the headlights, they drew their pistols and gripped their signal lights.

Fermor asked in his best German, "Ist dies das General's Wagen?" And when the answer came back, "Ja, ja," everything happened in a flash. Fermor and Moss ripped open the doors and, in one sweep of their flashlights, saw that the car was otherwise unoccupied. The chauffeur reached for his weapon and Moss immobilized him with a blow to the head from his heavy flashlight. The bewildered general stumbled out of the vehicle following a violent pull by Fermor.

"I seized him around the body, pulled him out, Manoli and another chap got hold of him and meantime Billy Moss struck the driver with a life-preserver* on the head and he was pulled out. And then the general was put in the back, laid out behind the front seat, and then three chaps got in, Manoli and George and another chap named Savio Stratis, all heavily armed. I put his general's cap on and we were off, and it took under one minute to do."

The car sped off with the general and the five members of the kidnapping team, while the other team members vanished into the night. Paddy Fermor did not forget his manners and introduced General Kreipe to his abductors.

"I told the General 'you are an honorable prisoner of war. I am a British Major, this is a British Captain, sergeant, and

---

* Crook-necked heavy flashlight.

these are all very trusted, splendid Cretan resistance figures, they are all friends of ours.'"[41]

Billy Moss drove and Paddy Fermor sat erect in the passenger's seat wearing the general's cap while the general lay prone on the floor in the back with a knife to his throat. The other three abductors readied their weapons should they be needed, and the car sped on toward Heraklion and the coastal road and a series of perhaps twenty roadblocks that were known to be along their route. They passed the Villa Ariadne and the sentries, recognizing the approaching car, had already swung open the large gates, bristling with barbed wire. But Moss honked the horn, waved, and sped down the road. Those sentries would now conclude that Kreipe must have had other business. They would not miss him at a later hour, and they would be even less likely to report his absence.

A flashing red light in the center of the road signaled the first of the dangerous checkpoints. Moss slowed the car to just a crawl, to allow the German sentries to recognize Kreipe's pennants flying on two staffs on either side of the hood, and then accelerated. He observed in the rear view mirror, the silhouettes of the sentries now at attention and rendering salutes.

The anticipated twenty control points turned out to be twenty-two, five that did not allow the car to simply roll through because they were equipped with swinging wooden arms that lowered across the road. All vehicles were forced to stop. As the car approached these barricades, the three rear-seat occupants slipped their fingers into the trigger guards of their weapons and slid down out of view, but ready to go into action. But the general's pennants worked like magic and resulted in a rush to swing the blocking arms upward, with the sentries coming to rigid attention as the car moved forward.[42]

Only once did the flying pennants not work. That sentry stood in the middle of the road as an immovable obstacle, with several other Germans on the road behind him. As the car was almost stopped, he approached Fermor's side where the general would have been sitting. Three rifles in the back seat raised to the ready, and Moss and Fermor gripped pistols in their laps, but at the last second, following the plan for just such a situation,

Fermor shouted out, "General's Wagen!" just as the approaching German soldier cleared the headlights. On queue, Billy Moss pressed down on the accelerator and rolled forward, and chimed-in in a loud voice, "Gute Nacht!" In seconds they were past the control point and their only dangerously close call.[43]

The entire journey took almost two hours and, at the end the car had left the populated areas behind and had ascended high into the mountains. General Kreipe and three of the team left the vehicle to proceed on foot for the long journey to the southern coast and, hopefully, to evacuation. Paddy Fermor and one man drove the car, and then abandoned it in a most northerly location to deceive the Germans that the escape had been in that direction rather than to the south.

"I drove on with the car," said Fermor, "about three miles, to a place within about a mile of the sea, and pinned [the] note, addressed to the German High Staff and High Command, on the front seat, so they couldn't miss it."[44]

Now the problem was to escape, and without the aid of the local Cretans, that would have been impossible. The abduction team melted into the hills with the general, and came under the care and responsibility of the legendary guerrilla leader Georgis Petrakoyiorgis.

"They guided us from cave to cave, one deep cave after another," said Fermor, "right over the crest of the whole watershed of Crete ... We went on and changed guides at nearly every village, and in the end hundreds of people knew where we were. One felt that the whole of the island was on our side."

The only people who didn't know where they were were the pursuing Germans frantically searching for them. The Germans however had not been thrown off track by the note and positioning of the car. They mounted a furious search for the kidnapped general and set up an enormous cordon leading to the south that was only bypassed through the efforts of the Cretan guerrillas.

It was a high-tension game of cat and mouse for two and a half weeks. From the night of the abduction on April 26 until the night of May 14, the SOE team, with the help of Greek and Cretan patriots, evaded capture. In the end they were rescued from a tiny beach enclave on the Cretan southern shore by dinghy, and ferried to Cairo where they presented General Kreipe to a delighted British Command. They had pulled off one of the most daring and successful clandestine exploits of WWII.*

LESS THAN FOUR MONTHS later, with the Allied Armies pinching them in from both east and west, the Germans began their withdrawal from Crete and Greece.

On August 26, Adolph Hitler authorized the evacuation of Army Group E from the Greek Islands and the Peloponnese, to begin on September 2, 1944. Athens and the Port of Piraeus would be held to facilitate the island evacuations. On September 10, the British landed unopposed on the island of Kythera, just off the Peloponnese, and two days later, the Germans left Rhodes and other Greek islands in the Eastern Mediterranean.

On October 4, the British launched Operation Manna to bring relief to Greece and the British 2nd Airborne Brigade jumped into Patras to take control of that port. They also initiated simultaneous landings at Crete and other islands in the Aegean, and six days later, in a reversal of roles from three years earlier, it was the British turn to take the Corinthian Canal with the Germans in full retreat to the north.

On October 15, almost four years from that fateful day when Prime Minister Metaxas uttered his famous "OXI" to the Italian Foreign Minister seeking to invade Greece, the British Army's III Corps, with Greek units attached, landed at the Port of Piraeus and liberated Athens. They were under direct orders from Winston Churchill to be prepared to eliminate the armed wing of the Greek Communist Party, "with bloodshed if necessary."[45]

---

* Assisting the SOE team of Fermor, Moss, Manoli Peterakis, and Georgos Tyrakis in the kidnapping were: Micky Akoumianakis, Elias Athanassakis, Stratis Saviolis, Grigoris Chnaiakis, Leonidas Papalionidas, Nikos Komis, Andoni Zoidakis, and Dimitri "Mitso" Zatzas.

In Messini, young Kitini Kakkava heard shouts in the streets.

"I heard people shouting, 'The Germans are leaving! The Germans are leaving!' The Germans really were leaving, but there was a river separating us—there's a river a little way outside the city, the Pamisos—so ... we crossed the river, and our boys started up right away and raised the flag on the clock tower. The Germans were on the opposite bank firing at them, and they wrecked both bridges, because a train crossed there ... they destroyed both the railway tracks and the bridge for cars and pedestrians ... they blew them both up and they fell into the river."[46]

On November 5, the British occupied Thessaloniki to help the new government and to ensure Communism did not become part of the new political leadership. On November 23, the Allies were finally able to report that the last Germans had been evicted from Macedonia on the Greek-Yugoslav border. Greece was German-free for the first time since April 6, 1941.

EPILOGUE

THE WAR IN EUROPE LASTED almost six years, from Hitler's invasion of Poland on September 1, 1939 until the final destruction of his Third Reich on May 8, 1945. Greece was involved from October 28, 1941 until the end and suffered terrible casualties. The war against Italy had caused almost 100,000 casualties, and the starvation in the winter of 1941 under Fascist occupation killed over a quarter million more. Thousands more died in fighting the German invasion, and in the Resistance, and in Nazi reprisals, and over 60,000 Greek Jews were exterminated in the Final Solution.

Some of the perpetrators of atrocities and war crimes in Greece were brought to justice. Many were not.

Benito Mussolini, who brought the war to Greece, did not survive the war. He was captured and executed by Italian Partisans on April 27, 1945. His body was hung by its heels in the Piazzale Loreto in Milan along with seven others, including Clara Petacci, his mistress. Adolph Hitler committed suicide several days later in his bunker in Berlin.

Mussolini's son-in-law, Count Galeazzo Ciano, the Italian Foreign Minister, had been executed by a firing squad on January 11, 1944 with the blessings of Mussolini himself despite the pleadings of his own daughter to spare her husband's life. Ciano's last writings described his plight: "Within a few days a sham tribunal will make public a sentence which has already been decided by Mussolini under the influence of that circle of whores and pimps which for some years have plagued Italian political life and brought our country to the brink of the abyss. I accept calmly what is to be my infamous destiny."[1]

General Gastone Gambara, who led Italy's army successfully

in Spain and snatched victory from the jaws of defeat, and who hurled his army against the Greek defenses on Hill 731 in Albania, lived until 1962 and died in Italy. General Ugo Cavallero, the patronizing Commander in Chief of the defeated Army in Albania, who Count Ciano claimed "would go so far as to bow to the public lavatories if this would be helpful to him," committed suicide in 1943.

Higher SS and Police Leader General Jurgen Stroop, who had overseen the destruction of the Warsaw Ghetto in Poland and the transportation of Jews to extermination camps, served in a similar capacity in Greece from August through October 1943. He had met his match in the defiance by Archbishop Damaskinos who stood him down in his attempts to round up Greek Jews, leading to his ineffectiveness in Greece. He was arrested at war's end and tried in two separate courts for war crimes. In 1947 he was tried at Dachau for summarily executing captured Allied soldiers and sentenced to death. That sentence was postponed and he was extradited to Poland and tried for his crimes, especially the atrocities at the Warsaw Ghetto. He was found guilty again and executed in March 1952.

SS General Walter Schimana, who succeeded Jurgen and continued the persecution of Greek Jews and offensives against the Resistance and murderous reprisals against the Greek population, committed suicide before the Allies could try him.

Dieter Wisliceny, the SS head of the Rosenberg Commando, whose mission in Greece was to confiscate Jewish treasure and property as well as expedite movement to extermination camps, was tried in 1948 in Czechoslovakia for his crimes, found guilty, and hanged.

General Friedrich Wilhelm Mueller, the Commander of Crete, nicknamed the Butcher of Crete, was tried in Athens, convicted and executed by firing squad on May 20, 1947, the sixth anniversary of the invasion. Executed with him was his predecessor, General Bruno Brauer. General Andrae was sentenced to life in prison.

Kidnapped General Heinrich Kreipe was imprisoned in Canada until 1947. He died in Northeim Germany in 1976.

A Special Collaborator's Court tried the leaders of the three collaborationist, quisling governments during the occupation. Georgios Tsolakoglou was sentenced to death, but commuted to life in prison where he died, unrepentant, in 1948. Konstantinos Logothetopoulos was sentenced to life in prison but released in 1951. He died in 1961, scorned by his countrymen. Ioannis Rallis was sentenced to life in prison and died there in 1946.

Archbishop Damaskinos served for a while as Prime Minister of Greece after the German withdrawal and when Communist guerrillas and Nationalist forces fought each other. He futilely called for peace on both sides and relinquished his position when King George II was recalled in 1946. He died May 20, 1949, the eighth anniversary of the Invasion of Crete.

General Alexander Papagos, who had led the Greek Army in its successful war against Italy only to see the German Army overwhelm his country, rose to the rank of Field Marshal in 1950. In 1949 he led the Army in its final victorious attacks against the Communists and became Prime Minister in 1952 where he died in office in 1955.

Patrick Leigh Fermor, the SOE saboteur who planned and executed the kidnapping of General Kreipe on the island of Crete, continued his love of travel after the war. The British awarded him the Distinguished Service Order [DSO] for his heroism. He became a noted author, and in 2004 was knighted by Queen Elizabeth. In 2007 the Greek Government made him Commander of the Order of the Phoenix.

William Stanley Moss who pulled off the kidnapping with Fermor, was awarded the Military Cross. He too continued a career of travel after the war and became a best-selling author in the 1950s, especially with his book *Ill Met by Moonlight* chronicling the Kreipe kidnapping. He died in 1965 at the age of forty-four in Jamaica.

Captain Geoffery Gordon-Creed who led the SOE attack on the Asopos Viaduct was awarded the DSO for his heroism. He was a native South African and returned to Kenya in 1947, engaging in wine trade and seafish farming. In 1976 he moved to the United States to South Carolina and twenty years later published his exploits in wartime Greece in a book titled *A Fool Rushed In.* He died in 2002.

Lt. John Giannaris received the Silver Star for his heroism and was released from the Army in 1947 because of his wounds received in action with the OSS operations against the Germans in Greece. He pursued a career in business and state and federal services. He lives in Elk Grove Village, Illinois.

Dennis Georges (Georgountzos) continued to serve in the Greek Air Force after the war and fought in Korea. He was later sent to the United States to learn about radar, and after his service became a businessman operating a successful trading company in New Orleans. He died in 2003. His younger brother Konstantinos still lives on the family farm in Arfara on the Peloponnese in Greece. His younger cousin Konstantine became a doctor of Obstetric Medicine and practiced in Athens where he still lives. The young five-year-old boy in Arfara who almost gave away Dennis's secret hiding place in the well, was forever teased about the incident and always called "Uncle German." Dennis George's future son, John, would run for Governor of the State of Louisiana in 2007.

AT WAR'S END, the Allies celebrated the great victory, but the Anglo-American Alliance looked warily at its Russian Ally who displayed all the signs of a country bent on land and power aggrandizement.

Despite having signed the United Nations Declaration stating that there would be no such aggrandizement, the understanding of this agreement was in the interpretation of Joseph Stalin, and he contended that none of this applied to lands he had aggrandized in the early years when he and Germany were friendly, and neither side had had second thoughts about partitioning the lands and boundaries of strategic countries. Ironically, the world had gone to war over Poland and at war's end Poland was not free.

While the liberated countries in Western Europe had been truly liberated by the Anglo-American forces, the painful truth in Central and Eastern Europe was that the Red Army occupied their liberated countries, and the slavery of the defeated evil, totalitarian Germans was now replaced with the slavery of the victorious, evil, totalitarian Russians. The occupied countries

fell behind what Winston Churchill called "the Iron Curtain,"*
and those countries included Eastern Germany, Poland, Hungary,
Rumania, Bulgaria, Yugoslavia and Albania.

The only exceptions to the Soviet Union's total occupation
of East-Central Europe were Finland in the north, Turkey in the
East and Greece in the south. For over four years the Greeks
had fought against Fascist totalitarianism. They had fought
for three and a half years against the Germans and had died
by the thousands and tens of thousands rather than submit to
enslavement and had seen the results of their resistance pay off
in the dust of the retreating German Army.

They had formed their own Pact of Steel with their British
Ally who had become their blood brothers. The British had
risked all to first try to save them from the enemy assault, and
then stood with them to form, encourage and supply a resistance
effort, and finally, had landed forces to ensure freedom as the
German Army withdrew and before the Russian Red Army could
enter. Prime Minister Winston Churchill had been emphatic in
his order to his generals be prepared to eliminate the armed wing
of the Greek Communist forces.

So, with the end of World War II, instead of the free world
breathing a collective sigh of relief, it now witnessed new battle
lines drawn for a war that would last for the next forty-four years
and would be called the Cold War. The first hot battle in that
Cold War was to be fought in Greece.

That war had begun with the formation of the resistance against
the Germans when EAM, and its ELAS military arm, sought
to engage the occupying Fascists and at the same time lay the
groundwork for a return to power that had been thwarted during
the reign of Prime Minister Ioannis Metaxas. By early 1944,
ELAS had attack and destroyed all rival guerrilla organizations
except EDES, and set up their own political government in the
mountains and staked their claim to future legitimacy.

---

* Churchill delivered his "Iron Curtain" speech in Fulton, Missouri in early 1946.

The viciousness of the ELAS attacks against their Greek rivals was never more evident than in September 1944 in the tiny town of Meligalas, just to the north of Kalamata on the Peloponnese. This was some of the same ground where the teen-aged guerrilla leader Dennis Georges had led his forces successfully against the Fascists.

Between September 2 and 16, ELAS forces waged a pitched battle with a Security Battalion force of the Greek puppet government of quisling leader Ioannis Rallis. The Security Battalions had been formed in 1943 to combat the ever-increasing influence of ELAS forces, and were composed of a mixed breed of soldiers and officers. In their ranks were pro Nazi Greeks, but also contained volunteers who were fearful of the Communists. Ex-Army officers found a home there as well as those who thought Germany would prevail and wanted to be on the right side at war's end.

At Meligalas ELAS got the upper hand and the leader of the Security Battalion force sought a cease-fire and negotiated surrender, accepted by the ELAS commander. But after laying down their arms, the Security Battalion soldiers were marched to their execution as well a 1,500 innocent civilians, children included. They were brought to the site of the Pigada (the Big Well) and, with hands bound, were thrown into the huge well to become a writhing, screaming mass of humanity crushed by the weight of those thrown in later. The savagery continued for two days until there was no one left to kill.[2]

The Communist guerrillas under Aris Velouchiotis ignored any customs or rules of war, especially when it came to prisoners, civilians or non-combatants, such as medical personnel at hospitals or aid stations or ambulances. Those were often targeted for their medical supplies, but, after the attack, few adversaries were left alive, including patients killed while confined to beds. The Communist penchant for barbarism, including mutilation, brought the thunder of retaliation from the Germans upon the heads of the Greek population, rarely affecting the guerrilla perpetrators themselves, but their lust for power disregarded the lives of the innocent.[3]

They had disavowed the legitimate Greek monarchy and

government in exile in London, and when Churchill brought that government back to Athens from exile, and even included EAM in the new coalition government, the Communist ELAS Army balked. Churchill demanded that they be disarmed. They refused and instead, on December 3, mounted a banned demonstration in Athens that disintegrated into a firefight between them and Greek and British forces. The Greek-British forces finally put the rebellion down and, on February 9, 1945, the Communists signed the Varzika Agreement and agreed to disarm ELAS.

But Velouchiotis would have nothing to do with it and fled with some of his loyalists into the mountains of Central Greece where he continued his war against the new Greek government. Elements of the Greek Army ambushed him in June of 1945, severed his head from his corpse and hung it in the square in Lamia, his birthplace.

But Velouchiotis's death did not end the war. In May 1946 Greek Communists resumed their war, supported by the Soviet satellite nations of Albania, Yugoslavia and Bulgaria. Britain responded by committing 40,000 troops to the battle but when the military and economic drain became too great, the United States stepped in and began its national policy of "Containment," outlined by President Harry Truman, to stop the spread of Communism.

Congress enacted the Greece-Turkey Aid Act of 1947 and ELAS formed a Communist government, which they called the Free Greek Government. They attacked with a 25,000-man army from their mountain hideout and pushed south to the outskirts of Athens where they finally stalled. But the Truman Doctrine and financial aid provided by the new Marshall Plan brought stability to the Greek Government, and a new U.S. military mission provided assistance to stop the Communist forces. The Greeks then mounted their own offensive and drove the Communists back to the Yugoslav border. On October 16, 1949, the defeated ELAS forces surrendered. Greece had delivered the first victory in the Cold War.

WHEN NORTH KOREA invaded South Korea in a surprise attack on June 25, 1950, the United Nations reacted, authorizing armed forces led by the United States to combat this unprovoked aggression. Thirteen other nations sent forces to join with the United States to fight the Communists. Greece sent 1,263 men mostly of the Greek Battalion that arrived in December 1950 and was attached to the U.S. 1st Cavalry Division. They fought with courage and bravery and on June 17-18, 1953, Company P of the Greek Battalion,* outnumbered ten to one, earned the Distinguished Unit Citation for its successful defense of Outpost Harry against a regimental attack by Chinese Communist Forces.

Greece also sent an air transport battalion to the United Nations Command. Serving in that battalion with its nine C-47 aircraft was former teen-age resistance leader from WWII, now Master Sergeant, Dennis Georges.

Few people are aware of the Greek involvement in World War II. Perhaps that is because in the aftermath of the war, Greece was involved in a bloody civil war and more in the news because of that long struggle against Communism than because of the valuable ally that they were. There was also a certain amount of intellectual snobbery on the part of historians and educators to ignore Greece because of the stigma attached to the word fascist. They had indeed been a Fascist government under the leadership of Ioannis Metaxas, but not linked in any way with the murderous mindset of Hitler or Mussolini.

In most commemorations and memorials about WWII, the flags of the Allies are generally flown in honor of their participation. They usually include Great Britain, the United States, Canada, Norway, The Netherlands, Russia, Poland and Belgium, even though King Leopold had decided to back the Nazis. But the Greek flag is rarely presented even though Greece delivered the first defeat against the Fascist powers in World War II, and was the only ally fighting with Great Britain before American or Russian involvement.

---

* Part of the U.S. Army's 15th Infantry Regiment.

Finally, to understand the depth of Greek involvement in World War II, it was necessary to tell the complete story from Mussolini's initial paranoia concerning his prestige and relationship with Germany's Adolph Hitler, to the end of the war and the beginning of the Cold War. It was tempting to isolate certain heroic feats and concentrate only on them as a testimony to Greece's struggle, but that would have given short shrift to the heroism of Greece as a nation. The free world owes Greece a belated thank you and a hearty "job well done," and her story celebrated in the history and heritage of the free world today.

ACKNOWLEDGMENTS

The idea for this book began a few days after Christmas 2006 with my receiving a phone call from Mr. George Tobia, noted entertainment and media attorney in Boston, Massachusetts. As I listened, George laid out a proposal for a new book that would finally tell the untold story of the Greek nation in the course of WWII.

My good friend and colleague, Dr. Douglas Brinkley, was also interested in such a project, and I had often written on the subject of WWII. Brinkley and I had a long history at the Eisenhower Center at the University of New Orleans. I had joined the renowned historian and author, Dr. Stephen Ambrose, as his Assistant Director at the Center in 1987, and had worked with him during those early years when we researched and wrote about the WWII generation: especially the Normandy invaders and the Band of Brothers.

In the early 1990s Ambrose had selected Doug to be his successor at the Eisenhower Center, and when Ambrose retired in 1995, I continued with Doug at the helm. It was an instant friendship and we continued on our paths of historical research and writing. Doug was more into presidential and social events while I continued to track down and write about the events of war, heroism and military themes. We made the perfect fit, and he and his wife Anne and the Drezes have enjoyed a wonderful friendship.

In 2005 Doug had envisioned the beginnings of a new Theodore Roosevelt Center at Tulane University. He asked if I would join him, and I accepted, but just weeks before that undertaking became a reality Hurricane Katrina changed lots of plans.

One year after the great storm, about which Doug produced a best-selling book, *The Great Deluge*, the thought of a book about the Greek Army and Resistance moved past the dreaming stage. We made the acquaintance of Mr. John Georges, a local businessman, whose father had been in the Greek Resistance during WWII.

I was immediately interested in the project, but realized it would be a daunting task. Unlike most of the events of WWII, of which I had collected thousands of testimonies, the war in Greece had few documents, few researchers, few memoirs and even less historiography. It was truly the overlooked theatre. My first research visit to the archives of the Imperial War Museum in London revealed a paltry six memoirs, several with pitifully few pages.

The official history of the Greek Army produced by the Hellenic Army General Staff turned out to be a very rare book, even the volume written in Greek; and the English version is almost nonexistent. Visits to the Military Museum in Athens provided no book, and no archive of memoirs or oral histories. All searches for the book were futile. The library of University of New Orleans, a depository for federal documents, listed a volume but a thorough search of its shelves could not turn it up.

Finally, after a three-month day and night search on the internet, a single copy suddenly popped up, listed at an obscure bookseller in London for a premium price. But it was mine as fast as I could hit the "buy" button, and it became a treasure trove. Military maps and chronological daily entries spilled out of the volume, detailing the movements and events of the Greek Army in its war with the Italians and the Germans. What many would consider dull reading—half sentences intermingled with mind-numbing map coordinates and unit designations—was, to me, the Rosetta Stone.

Greece was the next stop to walk the land and to talk with locals. I had with me the name and address of members of the Georgountzos (Georges) family, and it was indeed special to visit the small village of Arfara on the Peloponnese, where George's father, Dennis, had led Resistance fighters when he was nineteen during WWII.

On my final day in Arfara, Konstantinos Georgountzos, Dennis's brother, invited my wife and I to take a ride with him. He took us to ambush sites where the Resistance had targeted German patrols, and to a terrible site of execution during the later Civil War. But most memorable was a wild, high-speed ride up the face of the mountain that my wife describes as "death-defying, careening, and terrifying on hairpin turns."

The lofty perch at the top towered 1,000 feet above Arfara and it was there that the Resistance had their hideouts. It was amid the old ruins of the ancient Greek village, built during the time of the Turkish occupation, that the Resistance fighters of Dennis Georges had found safety. The Turks had relegated the Greeks to the high mountain while they had occupied the fertile low ground.

But those ancient, lofty, tumbledown, stone ruins provided the Resistance with the perfect home base from which to launch raids and attacks on the Germans. It also provided a safe haven from those Germans who were not at all anxious to ascend the heights, bristling with Greek fighters and ambush sites lurking behind every rocky outcropping. It was a heady thing to stand upon the ground that had been the heartbeat of this Resistance. I am thankful for that unique opportunity.

The Jewish Museum of Greece in Athens provided a collection of memoirs of the hidden Jewish children in occupied Greece. It was a unique collection for which I am grateful. And I owe special thanks to any and all who gave testimonies, wherever they were recorded. Some I interviewed, some were on far-flung websites, and some were snippets in unlikely collections and in the Greek Army museum. Many were the equivalent to finding needles in haystacks.

Photos were exceedingly hard to find, and the few grainy photos presented here are rare indeed and to be treasured. Unlike many battlefields that had photographers and newsmen in the ranks of the soldiers, the Greek Army in its offensive against the Italians in the hostile environs of the Pindus Mountains and Albania were mostly alone. The world could get only mental pictures of what was happening through the words of a few war correspondents. The origin of the pictures of the Women of Pindus, with shovels in the snow, keeping the lifeline road open, is unknown to me, as is the snapshot of Greek soldiers and their mules on the road to battle. But they are treasures and speak to the valiant effort of all Greeks in their war against all odds.

The story of the participation of the British SOE and the American OSS in the struggle with the Resistance against the enemy occupiers could not have been told had it not been for the testimonies and writings of Patrick Leigh Fermor, W. Stanley Moss, George Psychoundakis and John Giannaris. John Giannaris also provided a delightful interview and a copy of his memoir, *Yannis*, for which I am grateful.

Doug Brinkley and George Tobia provided great friendship and valuable guidance in reading every word of the manuscript, and in eventually getting the story into the hands of Ghost Road Press and the capable hands of Matthew and Gail Davis and Evan Lee, who make a fabulous team. Their enthusiasm is contagious and their layout and editing skills have added immensely to this manuscript.

Although I have never named one of my books in the past —the publishers always came up with much better titles—this is an exception, and there was no argument about *Heroes Fight Like Greeks*. Could there possibly have been a more appropriate name?

Special thanks to my dear friends Gerry and Virginia McCavera who accompanied Judy and I to Greece for a research trip and who helped with insight and suggestions for the telling of the story.

Finally I thank my wife Judy and my children and grandchildren for being so enthusiastic about storytelling, history, and uncovering lost stories and heroes. This is one of the best.

Ronald J. Drez

SOURCE NOTES

1. THE ROAD TO WAR

[1] Galeazzo Ciano, *Diary 1937-1943* (New York: Doubleday 1946/Enigma Books, 2002), p. 206.

[2] Cesare Salmaggi and Alfredo Pallavisini, *2194 Days of War* (Milano: Gallery Books, 1979), p. 10.

[3] Ciano, *Diary 1937-1943*, p. 2.

[4] Ibid, p. 41.

[5] Ibid.

[6] Ibid, p. 52.

[7] Ibid.

[8] Ibid, p. 62.

[9] Ibid.

[10] Ibid, p. 73.

[11] Ibid, p. 108.

[12] Ibid, p. 119.

[13] Ibid, p. 165.

[14] Ibid, p. 170.

[15] Ibid, p. 178.

[16] Ibid, p. 181.

[17] Ibid, p. 209.

[18] Salmaggi & Pallavisini, *2194 Days of War*, p. 62.

[19] Ciano, *Diary 1937-1943*, p. 234.

[20] Ibid, p. 258.

[21] Chester Wilmot, *The Struggle for Europe* (New York: Harper & Brothers, 1952) p. 63.

[22] Ciano, *Diary 1937-1943*, p. 265.

[23] Ibid, p. 268-9.

[24] Ibid, p, 282.

[25] Ibid, p. 284.

[26] Ibid, p. 286.

[27] Ibid, p. 295.

[28] Ibid, p. 301.

[29] Ibid, p. 322.

[30] Ibid, p. 341.

[31] Ibid. p. 363.

[32] Ibid, p. 364.

[33] Ibid, p. 366.

[34] Ibid, p. 368.

[35] Ibid, p. 276.

[36] Ibid, p. 388.

[37] Ibid.

[38] P. J. Vatikiotis, "Praises to Metaxas," (The Metaxas Project: Inside Fascist Greece, 1936-1941) www.metaxas-project.com.

[39] "John Metaxas: Bone and Gristle," *Time* magazine, February 10, 1941.

[40] P. J. Vatikiotis, "How Others Saw the Metaxas Regime." (The Metaxas Project: Inside Fascist Greece, 1936-1941) www.metaxas-project.com.

[41] Quoted in (The Metaxas Project: Inside Fascist Greece, 1936-1941).

[42] Ibid, p. 376. The 1923 incident involved the murder of an Italian delegate and four members of his staff while on Greek soil determining the boundaries between Greece and Albania. Mussolini demanded 50 million lire and an apology. Greece refused, and the Italian navy shelled Corfu and occupied it. The League of Nations forced Italy to withdraw and Greece paid the 50 million lire without the apology.

[43] Ibid, p. 390.

[44] Ibid. p. 389.

[45] Italian Minister to Greece

[46] Ciano, *Diary 1937-1943,* p. 390.

2. PREPARATION AND PROVOCATION

[1] Virgil, *Aeneid,* Book 2, 19 BC. This line is always misquoted as: "Beware of Greeks bearing gifts." This incorrect translation and misquote blunts the true impact of Virgil's warning, and that is to always "beware of Greeks, EVEN when they are bearing gifts!"

[2] Hellenic Army General Staff, *An abridged History of the Greek-Italian an Greek-German War 1940-1941 (Land Operations),* (The Army History Directorate: Athens, 1996), p. 6.

[3] Galeazzo Ciano, *Diary 1937-1943* (New York: Doubleday 1946/Enigma Books, 2002), p. 2.

[4] Ibid, p. 212.

[5] Ibid, p. 218.

[6] Ibid, p. 213

[7] *An Abridged History,* p. 11.

[8] Ibid, p. 21.

[9] The Greek island of Tinos had itself been occupied by an Italian state (Venice) for 500 years until it returned to Greek possession in 1715.

[10] The falling asleep - the passing of the Virgin Mary to be assumed into heaven. The Roman Catholic Church celebrates this date as the Feast of the Assumption.

[11] Melas, Spyros "Burning Seas", published by "Embros" Athens, 1940. The Hellenic Maritime Museum.

[12] Ibid.

[13] http://regiamarina.net

[14] Ibid.

[15] Melas, "Burning Seas."

[16] *An Abridged History,* p. 22.

[17] G. Mezeviris Vice-Admiral R.H.N., "The torpedoing of light cruiser "Elli" August 15, 1940: The RHN on War Footing", *Four Decades in the Service of the RHN* (Athens, 1971).

[18] It is not believable that De Vecchi could have acted independently to order the attack on *Elli* without Mussolini's approval, and The Duce's stated desire to settle things peacefully does not make sense for the man who had ordered the act of war as a provocation. A diary entry by Ciano on August 17 clears things up. Hitler had clipped Mussolini's wings. It noted that "an eventual action against Greece is not at all welcome by Berlin." Ciano, *Diary 1937-1943,* p. 377. A 1945 article by Grazzi, the Italian Minister to Athens, states that, "The torpedoing of "Elli" was a direct result of orders from Rome [Mussolini]." *An Abridged History,* p. 22.

[19] http://reginamarina.net.

[20] Willingham, Matthew, *Perilous Commitments: Britain's involvement in Greece and Crete 1940-41* (Great Britain: Spellmount, 2005) p. 20.

[21] *An Abridged History,* p. 26.

[22] Quoted in Willingham, p. 21.

[23] Cervi, Mario, *The Hollow Legions: Mussolini's Blunder in Greece 1940-1941* (London: Chatto & Windus, 1972), p. 12.

[24] Willingham, *Perilous Commitments,* p. 21.

[25] Ibid, p. 20.

[26] Ibid, p. 22.

[27] Ibid, p. 22.

[28] Quoted in, L. S. Stavrianos, *GREECE: American Dilemma and Opportunity* (Chicago: Henry Regnery Company, 1952) p. 45.

[29] Ciano, *Diary 1937-1943.* p. 388.

[30] Quoted in MacGregor Knox, "*Mussolini Unleashed 1939-1941: Politics and Strategy in Fascist Italy's Last War.* (Cambridge University Press: London, 1982) p. 211.

[31] Ibid, p. 213.

[32] Ibid, p. 214.

[33] Quoted in *Perilous Commitments*, p. 24.

[34] Ciano, *Diary 1937-1943.* p. 389.

[35] U.S. Army, *The Military- Political Situation in the Balkans, (October 1940- March 1941)* p. 12.

[36] Quoted in *Perilous Commitments*, p. 23.

[37] The bombing should hardly have been a tactic since surprise was the stated goal, but Italy had indiscriminately bombed Greek targets at other times. On January 12, 1940, three planes bombed the Greek ships, *Irion* and *Hydra* at Crete, and six months later on July 30, a single plane bombed the destroyers *Vasileus Georgios* and *Vasilissa Olga* and two additional submarines in port at Lepanto. Metaxas downplayed all of these events: a further testament to his commitment to neutrality.

[38] Stavrianos, *GREECE*, p. 44.

[39] New York Times, "*Text of Italian Note to Greece.*" October 29, 1940.

[40] Stavrianos, *GREECE*, p. 45.

[41] Ibid.

[42] G. C. Kiriakopoulos, *Ten Days to Destiny: The Battle for Crete,* (New York, Franklin Watts Ltd., 1985) p. 13.

[43] Stavrianos, *GREECE*, p. 45.

[44] Cervi, *The Hollow Legions*, p. 54.

[45] The Greek word is "*Polemos!*"

[46] Quoted in MacGregor Knox, "*Mussolini Unleashed 1939-1941,*" p. 211.

[47] Stavrianos, *GREECE,* p. 45-46.

3. INVASION

[1]Testimony of Chrysoula Korotzi, "MEMORY 2000: Memoriali del XX Secolo," (www.padovanet.it)

[2] Testimony of Vasilsi Rosas, Ibid.

[3] Katherine Mezinis, "The History of 'OXI' Day: October 28," *Ta Nea*, American Hellenic Progressive Association, vol. 151, October 2000.

[4] Pronounced "O-hee," meaning "No."

[5] Katherine Mezinis, "The History of 'OXI' Day.

[6] Testimony of Ptolemaios Kaliafas, MEMORY 2000.

[7] Ibid.

[8] Testimony of Elfetherios Sklavos, "MEMORY 2000: Memoriali del XX Secolo," (www.padovanet.it)

[9] Quoted on www.macedoniaontheweb.com-WWII & Greece, p. 1.

[10] Minutes of 30 October 1940 Metaxas meeting with newsmen, (The Metaxas Project: Inside Fascist Greece, 1936-1941) www.metaxas-project.com.

[11] Ibid.

[12] Ibid.

[13] Ibid.

[14] Ronald Drez, interview with Konstantin Georgountzos, April 2007, Athens.

[15] Ibid.

[16] Ronald Drez interview with Dimitri Tsaras, February 28, 2007.

[17] Ibid.

[18] Ibid.

[19] Royal Hellenic Order of Battle, Greek War Museum, Athens.

[20] From Official Greek Army History, Greek War Museum, Athens.

[21] "Blunder in the Mountains: The Italian Invasion of Greece 1940," Balkan Military History, www.balkanhistory.com.

[22] Hellenic Army General Staff, *An Index of Events in the Military History of the Greek Nation.* (Hellenic Army General Staff; Army History Directorate, 1998) p. 125.

[23] Alekos Raptis, "The Participation of Yanniote Jews in the War: The Epirote Struggle," October 2005, (Kehila Kedosha Janina Synagogue and Museum).

[24] Quoted in W. W. Turnbow, "The Italian Army in WWII," (www.jma.dk)

[25] The Italian XXV Corps, commanded by General Carlo Rossi fielded 61 artillery batteries of which 18 had heavy guns. The Greeks could bring only sixteen batteries (2 heavy) to bear. "OXI No Day: The Opponents Forces at

the Start of the War." Hellenic Electronic Center (www.greece.org)

[26] Quoted in "Murk," *Time* magazine, Monday Nov. 18, 1940.

[27] Willingham, Matthew, *Perilous Commitments: Britain's involvement in Greece and Crete 1940-41* (Great Britain: Spellmount, 2005) p. 26-27.

[28] Katherine Mezinis, "The History of 'OXI' Day: October 28,"

[29] Hellenic Army General Staff, *An Abridged History of the Greek-Italian an Greek-German War 1940-1941 (Land Operations),* (The Army History Directorate: Athens, 1996), p. 58.

[30] Ibid, p. 59.

[31] Knox, *Mussolini Unleashed,* p.232.

[32] Greek Army Museum, Athens Greece; Alexander Papagos, *The Battle of Greece 1940-1941,* (J.M. Scazikis "Alpha": Athens, 1949). npn.

[33] Leland Stowe, *No Other Road to Freedom* (New York: Knopf, 1941), p. 224-25.

[34] MacGregor Knox, "*Mussolini Unleashed 1939-1941: Politics and Strategy in Fascist Italy's Last War.* (Cambridge University Press: London, 1982) p. 232.

[35] Ibid; W. W. Turnbow, "The Italian Army in WWII," (www.jma.dk)

[36] Ibid.

[37] Ibid, p. 127.

[38] Hellenic Army, *An Index of Events,* p. 125-26.

[39] *An Abridged History,* p. 64.

[40] Ibid, p. 64-65.

[41] "Kalpaki Battle Chronology," Kalpaki Military Museum, Kalpaki Greece; Greek Military Museum, Athens.

[42] "First Round: Helles."

[43] L. S. Stavrianos, *GREECE: American Dilemma and Opportunity* (Chicago: Henry Regnery Company, 1952) p. 46.

[44] "Those Greek Women," *St. Louis Post Dispatch,* n.d. 1940.

[45] "Murk," *Time* magazine, Monday, Nov. 18, 1940.

[46] Mezinis, "The History of 'OXI' Day: October 28," p. 5.

[47] "Kalpaki Battle Chronology," Kalpaki Military Museum, Kalpaki Greece.

[48] Hellenic Army, *An Index of Events,* p. 127.

[49] "First Round: Helles," *Time* magazine, Monday, Nov. 25, 1940.

[50] Quoted in Knox, *Mussolini Unleashed,* p. 234.

[51] Ciano, Galeazzo, *Diary 1937-1943* (New York: Doubleday 1946/Enigma Books, 2002), p. 393.

[52] Ibid.

[53] Ibid.

[54] Quoted in Knox, *Mussolini Unleashed,* p.235.

[55] Ibid, 236.

[56] Supreme Command and Royal Army.

[57] Quoted in Knox, *Mussolini Unleashed,* p.236.

4. INTO ALBANIA

[1] MacGregor Knox, *"Mussolini Unleashed 1939-1941: Politics and Strategy in Fascist Italy's Last War.* (Cambridge University Press: London, 1982) p. 237.

[2] Galeazzo Ciano, *Diary 1937-1943* (New York: Doubleday 1946/Enigma Books, 2002), p. 394.

[3] Ibid, p. 390.

[4] Ibid, p. 395.

[5] Cristiano Adamo, "Operation Judgment, Taranto's Night: November 11-12, 1940," www.regiamarina.net.

[6] "R. N. at Taranto," *Time* magazine, Nov. 25, 1940.

[7] Cristiano D'Adamo and Sebastiano Tringali, "Fairey Swordfish," www. regiamarina.net.

[8] Quoted in "Taranto 1940," Royal Navy website, www.royalnavy.mod.uk.

[9] Cristiano Adamo, "Operation Judgment."

[10] Galeazzo Ciano, *Diary 1937-1943,* p. 395.

[11] Hellenic Army General Staff, *An Abridged History of the Greek-Italian an Greek-German War 1940-1941 (Land Operations),* (The Army History Directorate: Athens, 1996), p. 124.

[12] "Blunder in the Balkans: The Italian Invasion of Greece," www. balkanhistory.com.

[13] Quoted in *"Mussolini Unleashed 1939-1941,* p. 238.

[14] Ibid.

[15] Galeazzo Ciano, *Diary 1937-1943,* p. 400.

[16].Ibid, p. 396.

[17] "Zeto Hellas," *Time* magazine, Monday, Dec. 02, 1940.

[18] Mario Cervi, *The Hollow Legions,* (New York: Doubleday and Company, 1971) p. 245-46.

[19] *An Abridged History,* p. 72.

[20] Ibid, p. 75.

[21] L. S. Stavrianos, *GREECE: American Dilemma and Opportunity* (Chicago: Henry Regnery Company, 1952) p. 48.

[22] Testimony of Elftherios Sklavos, "MEMORY 2000: Memoriali del XX Secolo," (www.padovanet.it)

[23] Ibid.

[24] Ibid.

[25] Ibid.

[26] "Battle of Pogradec," www.wikiphantis.com.

[27] Hellenic Army General Staff, *An Index of Events in the Military History of the Greek Nation.* (Hellenic Army General Staff; Army History Directorate, 1998) p. 127.

[28] "OXI No Day," Hellenic Electronic Center (www.greece.org)

[29] Vasilis Katsikis, "MEMORY 2000: Memoriali del XX Secolo," (www. padovanet.it)

[30] "Children of Socrates," *Time* magazine, Monday, Dec. 09, 1940.

[31] Hellenic Army, *An Index of Events,* p. 128.

[32] Ibid, 129.

[33] Galeazzo Ciano, *Diary 1937-1943,* p. 398-99.

[34] Ibid, p. 400.

[35] Ibid, p. 401.

[36] Quoted in L. S. Stavrianos, *GREECE,* p. 49.

[37] Ibid. p. 50.

[38] Ibid; Lt. Gen. D. Katheniotes, *The Main Strategic Phases of the War 1940-41* (Athens, 1946), p. 55.

[39] Galeazzo Ciano, *Diary 1937-1943,* p. 401.

[40] Quoted in Mikia Pezas, *The Price of Liberty,* (New York: Ives Washburn, 1945) p. 76.

[41] L. S. Stavrianos, *GREECE,* p. 49.

[42] Ibid, p. 406.

[43] December 16, 1940.

[44] "Surprise No. 6," *Time* magazine, Monday Dec. 16, 1940.

[45] Quoted in *Manchester Guardian,* April 19, 1941.

[46] L. S. Stavrianos, *GREECE,* p. 48-51.

[47] Ibid, p. 49.

[48] Quoted in, Cesare Salmaggi and Alfredo Pallavisini, *2194 Days of War* (Milano: Gallery Books, 1979), p. 71.

[49] Ibid, p. 77.

[50] Ibid.

[51] Winston S. Churchill, *The Second World War,* (London: Cassell, 1948-50), v. II, p. 307.

[52] Ibid, v. III, p. 5.

[53] Quoted in John Connell, *Wavell:Scholar and Soldier,* (New York: Harcourt, Brace & World, 1964), p. 310.

[54] Churchill, *The Second World War,* p. 16.

[55] Ibid , v. III, p. 16-17.

5. BETWEEN THE APSOS AND THE AOOS:
THE BALKAN FRONT

[1] Winston S. Churchill, *The Second World War,* (London: Cassell, 1948-50), v. III, p. 17.

[2] John Connell, *Wavell:Scholar and Soldier,* (New York: Harcourt, Brace & World, 1964), p. 313.

[3] Ibid, p. 314.

[4] Ibid.

[5] Quoted in Galeazzo Ciano, *Diary 1937-1943* (New York: Doubleday 1946/Enigma Books, 2002), p. 405.

[6] "Toward the Capital," *Time* magazine, Monday, Mar. 24, 1941.

[7] MacGregor Knox, *"Mussolini Unleashed 1939-1941: Politics and Strategy in Fascist Italy's Last War.* (Cambridge University Press: London, 1982) p. 247.

[8] Ibid, p. 408.

[9] Ibid, p. 201.

[10] Quoted in, "First Round: Hellas," *Time* magazine, Monday, Nov. 25, 1940.

[11] "Children of Socrates," *Time* magazine, Monday, Dec. 09, 1940.

[12] Galeazzo Ciano, *Diary 1937-1943,* p. 401.

[13] Ibid, p. 400.

[14] Ibid, p. 408.

[15] Ibid, p. 489.

[16] Ibid, p. 412.

[17] Ibid, p. 413.

[18] "Children of Socrates."

[19, 20] Hellenic Army General Staff, *An Index of Events in the Military History of the Greek Nation.* (Hellenic Army General Staff; Army History Directorate, 1998) p. 129..

[21] Ibid, p. 414.

[22] Ibid, p. 416.

[23] Galeazzo Ciano, *Diary 1937-1943,* p. 415.

[24] Department of the Army Pamphlet 20-260, *The German Campaigns in the Balkans (Spring 1941),* (Washington: U.S. Army, 1953) p. 15.

[25] Ibid.

[26] The Metaxas Project: Inside Fascist Greece (1936-1941), "Selected Quotes by Ioannis Metaxas," collected by Andreas Markessinis, www.metaxas - project.com

[27] "Wanted: Bone and Gristle," *Time* magazine, Monday, Feb. 10, 1941.

[28] "Death of Metaxas," P. J. Vatikiotis, (The Metaxas Project: Inside Fascist Greece, 1936-1941) www.metaxas-project.com.

[29] "Wanted: Bone and Gristle."

[30] *Ibid.*

[31] "Selected Quotes by Ioannis Metaxas,"

[32] John Connell, *Wavell: Scholar and Soldier,* (New York: Harcourt, Brace & World, 1964), p. 331.

[33] Ibid, p. 332.

[34] Ibid, p. 334.

[35] Ibid, p. 333.

[36] Ibid, p. 334.

[37] Cesare Salmaggi and Alfredo Pallavisini, *2194 Days of War* (Milano: Gallery Books, 1979), p. 106.

[38] *Wavell: Scholar and Soldier,* p. 334.

[39] "An Open Letter to Hitler," Georgios Vlachos, *Kathimerini,* March 8, 1941, translated and published on www.wiki.phantis.com

[40] G. Mezeviris Vice-Admiral R.H.N., "Saving the Gold of the Bank of Greece - March 1941" *Four Decades in the Service of the RHN* (Athens, 1971).

[41] Later the gold reserves were transferred first to South Africa and then to London. www.bankofgreece.gr

[42] *Scholar and Soldier,* p. 347.

[43] Ibid. p. 348.

[44] Ibid, p. 349.

[45] Ibid, p. 352.

[46] Ibid, p. 353.

[47] "Il Duce Talks of Tanks," *Time* magazine, Monday, Mar. 03, 1941.

6. OPERAZIONE PRIMAVERA

[1] *Scholar and Soldier,* p. 353.

[2] Hellenic Army General Staff, *An Abridged History of the Greek-Italian*

and Greek-German War 1940-1941 (Land Operations), (The Army History Directorate: Athens, 1996), p. 145.

[3] Ibid, p. 151.

[4] Ibid.

[5] N. G. L. Hammond, "The Opening Campaigns and the Battle of the Aoi Stena in the Second Macedonian War," *The Journal of Roman Studies*, Vol. 56, Parts 1 and 2 (1966), pp. 39-54.

[6] *An Abridged History*, p. 147-48.

[7] Ibid, p. 148-49.

[8] Ibid, p. 152.

[9] Greek Military Museum, Athens.

[10] *An Abridged History,* p. 152.

[11] Quoted in Greek Military Museum, Athens, "The Greco-Italian War," (Winter Operations, Operation Primavera), Army General Staff/History Directorate Edition.

[12] Greek Military Museum, Athens

[13] *An Abridged History,* p. 152.

[14] Ibid, 153.

[15] "Battle of Hill 731," www.militaryphotos.net/forums

[16] Ibid.

[17] *An Abridged History,* p. 154.

[18] Ibid, p. 155.

[19] *An Abridged History,* p. 156.

[20] G. Mezeviris Vice-Admiral R.H.N., "The Naval Operations of March 1941" *Four Decades in the Service of the RHN* (Athens, 1971).

[21] Ibid.

[22] Ibid.

[23] Ibid.

[24] Ibid.

[25] Ibid.

[26] Michael Smith, *Station X: The Codebreakers of Bletchley Park*, Channel 4 Books (London: 1998)
    p.14.

[27] Ibid, p. 15.

[28] Ibid, p. 37.

[29] Ibid, p. 38.

[30] Ibid, p. 31.

[31] Ibid, p. 61-63.

[32] Ibid, p. 69.

[33] Ibid.

[34] Mark De Angelis, "Operation Gaudo' And The Battle Of Matapan, Part III, March 27-29, 1941, www.regiamarina.net

[35] Smith, *Station X,* p. 70.

[36] "Operation Gaudo."

[37] "Memorial Roll to All Commanding Officers Killed or Missing, 1939-1945, www.fleetairarmarchive.net

[38] "Operation Gaudo.'

7. OPERATION MARITA

[1] Smith, *Station X,* p. 69.

[2] "Il Duce Talks Tanks," *Time* magazine, Monday, Mar. 03, 1941.

[3] Hellenic Army General Staff, *An Abridged History of the Greek-Italian and Greek-German War 1940-1941 (Land Operations),* (The Army History Directorate: Athens, 1996), p. 157-58.

[4] Ibid.

[5] Ibid, p. 159.

[6] Ibid, p. 160.

[7] Ibid. p. 161.

[8] Ibid, p. 162.

[9] Ibid, p. 163.

[10] Cesare Salmaggi and Alfredo Pallavisini, *2194 Days of War* (Milano: Gallery Books, 1979), p. 110.

[11] Ibid.

[12] "Toward the Unwelcome," *Time* magazine, Monday, Mar. 24, 1941.

[13] *An Abridged History,* p. 168.

[14] Ibid.

[15] Ibid, p. 169.

[16] Ibid. p. 169-70.

[17] Ibid, p. 169.

[18] H. P. Weiner, "They Lost Their Freedom Fighting for Yours," (unpublished manuscript: 1991) Imperial War Museum, London, p. 25.

[19] Ibid, p. 26.

[20] Ibid. p. 3.

[21] Ibid, p. 174.

[22] Ibid, p. 175-77.

[23] Ibid, p. 180.

[24] Ibid, p. 186.

[25] "Soul v. Steel," *Time* magazine, Monday, Apr. 14, 1941.

[26] Ibid.

[27] *An Abridged History,* p. 187-88.

[28] Ibid, p. 187.

[29] Ibid. p. 188.

[30] Ibid. p. 190.

[31] Ibid, p. 194.

[32] Ibid, p. 196.

[33] Ibid, p/ 199-200.

[34] Ibid, p. 206-07.

[35] Ibid, p. 213.

[36] Ibid, p. 215.

[37] Ibid, p. 216.

[38] Ibid, p. 222.

[39] Ibid, p. 224.

[40] L. S. Stavrianos, *GREECE:American Dilemma and Opportunity,* (Henry Regnery Company: Chicago, 1952) p. 59.

[41] John Connell, *Wavell:Scholar and Soldier,* (New York: Harcourt, Brace & World, 1964), p. 418-19.

[42] H. P. Weiner, "They Lost Their Freedom Fighting for Yours," p. 27.

[43] Ibid, p. 28.

[44] Testimony of Elftherios Sklavos, "MEMORY 2000: Memoriali del XX Secolo," (www.padovanet.it)

[45] Ibid.

[46] Ibid.

[47] Testimony of Vasilis Katsikis, "MEMORY 2000: Memoriali del XX Secolo," (www.padovanet.it)

[48] Testimony of Ptolemaios Kaliafas, "MEMORY 2000: Memoriali del XX Secolo," (www.padovanet.it)

[49] Ibid.

[50] Ibid.

[51] *An Abridged History,* p. 229.

[52] *2194 Days of War,* p. 124.

[53] Ibid, p. 238.

[54] Ronald Drez interview with Konstantin Georgountzos, April 2007, Athens.

[55] H. P. Weiner, "Freedom." P. 28-29.

[56] Ibid, p. 29.

[57] Ibid, p. 30.

[58] Ibid, p. 32.

[59] *An Abridged History,* p. 244.

[60] *Wavell:Scholar and Soldier,* p.419-20.

8. OPERATIONS MERCURY AND SCORCHER: LAST STAND IN CRETE

[1] *2194 Days of War,* p. 124.

[2] Ronald Drez interview with Dimitri Tsaras Feb. 26-28, 2007.

[3] Ibid.

[4] Testimony of Ptolemaios Kaliafas, "MEMORY 2000: Memoriali del XX Secolo," (www.padovanet.it)

[5] Dawn DeDeaux interview with Dennis Georges, 2002,

[6] Ronald Drez interview with Konstantin Georgountzos, April 2007, Athens.

[7] Cesare Salmaggi and Alfredo Pallavisini, *2194 Days of War* (Milano: Gallery Books, 1979), p. 124.

[8] G. Mezeviris Vice-Admiral R.H.N., "The Chronicle of the sinking of Hydra, April 22, 1941";"Four decades in the service of the R.H.N", Athens 1971.

[9] Ibid.

[10] John Connell, *Wavell:Scholar and Soldier,* (New York: Harcourt, Brace & World, 1964), p. 423.

[11] Hellenic Army General Staff, *An Abridged History of the Greek-Italian and Greek-German War 1940-1941 (Land Operations),* (The Army History Directorate: Athens, 1996), p. 258.

[12] *Wavell,* p. 448.

[13] Ibid, p. 453.

[14] Ibid, p. 451-51.

[15] Ibid, p. 452.

[16] Ibid, p. 454.

[17] Ibid, p. 454.

[18] Ibid, p. 455.

[19] Arthur Douglas, quoted in *The 11th Day,* An Archangel Films Production, 2005.

[20] *2194 Days of War*, p. 129.

[21] Kaliopi Kapetanakis, *The 11th Day.*

[22] Chrissa Ninolakis, *The 11th Day.*

[23] Peter D. Antill, *Crete 1941: Germany's lightning airborne assault,* (Osprey Publishing: Oxford, New York, 2005) p. 40.

[24] Ibid, p. 48-49.

25 George Psychoundakis, *The Cretan Runner,* (Penguin Books: London, 1998) p. 41.
26 *Wavell,* p. 465.
27 Battle of Crete: The German invasion of Crete 1941, www.crete-1941.org.uk/
28 Ibid.
29 Ibid.
30 Ibid.
31 Ibid.
32 Ibid.
33 *Wavell,* p. 465.
34 Ibid, p. 471-72.
35 *2194 Days of War*, p. 134.
36 *Wavell,* p. 473-74.
37 Arthur Douglas, *The 11th Day.*.
38 *An Abridged History*, p. 292.
39 *Wavell,* p. 472.
40 Ibid. p. 475.
41 "Battle of Crete," Wikipedia.
42 *An Abridged History,* p. 280.
43 Ibid, p. 296.

9. OCCUPATION, STARVATION, AND RESISTANCE

1 Compton Mackenzie, *Wind of Freedom: The history of the invasion of Greece by the axis powers, 1940-1941,* (Chatto & Windus: London, 1944) p. 243.
2 *The 11th Day,* An Archangel Film Production, 2005.
3 George Psychoundakis, *The Cretan Runner,* (Penguin Books: London, 1998) p. 45.
4 Ibid, p. 45-46.
5 Ronald Drez interview with Dimitri Tsaras, Feb. 28,2007.
6 Tsolakoglou, G.K.S., *Memoirs,* (Akropolis Editions, Athens, 1959); http://www.answers.com/topic/georgiostsolakoglou
7 Hellenic Army General Staff, *An Abridged History of the Greek-Italian and Greek-German War 1940-1941 (Land Operations),* (The Army History Directorate: Athens, 1996), p. 230.
8 Rigas Rigopoulos, *The Secret War,* (Turner Publishing Company: Paducah, KY, 2003) p. 23.

[9] Pictorial History of the Second World War, Vol. 1,(Wm. H. Wise and Co., Inc., New York, 1944) p. 438-39.

[10] http://www.mlahanas.de/Greece/History/GreekResistance.html

[11] *The Secret War,* p. 24.

[12] Ibid.

[13] U.S. Army Center of Military History, *German Antiguerrilla Operations in the Balkans (1941-1944),* (CMH Publication 104-18) Chap. 4-I.

[14] George Kotsonis, "World War II, 1940."http://www.memoryarchive.org/

[15] Ronald Drez interview with Konstantin Georgountzos, Athens, April, 2007.

[16] Testimony of Philippos Mavrogenis, "MEMORY 2000: Memoriali del XX Secolo," (www.padovanet.it)

[17] Ibid.

[18] Testimony of Chrysoula Korotzi, "MEMORY 2000: Memoriali del XX Secolo," (www.padovanet.it)

[19] Testimony of Tasos Zografos, "MEMORY 2000: Memoriali del XX Secolo," (www.padovanet.it)

[20] *The Secret War,* p. 36.

[21] Ibid.

[22] Ronald Drez interview with Dimitri Tsaras, Feb. 28, 2007.

[23] Galeazzo Ciano, *Diary 1937-1943* (New York: Doubleday 1946/Enigma Books, 2002), p. 435.

[24] Ibid, p. 434.

[25] Ibid, p. 435.

[26] "Plunderpraxis," *Time* magazine, Monday, Aug. 25, 1941

[27] "The New Disorder," *Time* magazine, Monday, Aug. 25, 1941.

[28] Ibid.

[29] "Executioner's Week," *Time* magazine, Monday, Sep. 29, 1941.

[30] Ciano, *Diary 1937-1943,* p. 451.

[31] Ibid.

[32] Ibid, p. 453.

[33] Ibid.

[34] Ibid, p. 464.

[35] Ibid, p. 487.

[36] Ibid, p. 463.

[37] Ibid.

[38] Ibid.

[39] "Executioner's Week."

[40] Ibid.

[41] Ciano, *Diary 1937-1943,* p. 552.

[42] Stefanidis, Yiannis D., "Macedonia in the 1940s", I. Hassiotis & I. Koliopoulos (eds), *Modern and Contemporary Macedonia* (Paratiritis & Papazisis: Thessaloniki, 1992) vol. II, 104-137.   http://www.macedonian-heritage.gr/downloads/index.htmltesy

[43] Ibid.

10. TERROR AND REBELLION

[1] *The Secret War,* p. 30-31.

[2] Stefanidis, Yiannis D., "Macedonia in the 1940s", I. Hassiotis & I. Koliopoulos (eds), *Modern and Contemporary Macedonia* (Paratiritis & Papazisis: Thessaloniki, 1992) vol. II, 104-137.   http://www.macedonian-heritage.gr/downloads/index.htmltesy

[3] Rigas Rigopoulos, *The Secret War,* (Turner Publishing Company: Paducah, KY, 2003) p. 41.

[4] Ibid, p. 26.

[5] Ibid. p. 41.

[6] Testimony of Alkicee Georgountzos, April 2007.

[7] Dawn DeDeaux interview with Dennis Georges, 2002.

[8] Ronald Drez interview with Konstantinos Georgountzos in Arfara, April, 2007.

[9] Dawn DeDeaux interview with Dennis Georges, 2002.

[10] Ronald Drez interview with Konstantin Georgountzos in Athens, April, 2007.

[11] *Ibid.*

[12] Ronald Drez interview with Konstantinos Georgountzos, in Arfara, April 2007.

[13] "SHORT HISTORY OF THE JEWISH COMMUNITIES IN GREECE,", p. 6; http://www.afjmg.org/resources/jewingreece.pdf

[14] "SHORT HISTORY," p. 3.

[15] *The Secret War,* p. 30-31.

[16] Ronald Drez interview with Dimitri Tsaras, February, 2007.

[17] Testimony of Kitina Kakkave, "MEMORY 2000: Memoriali del XX Secolo," (www.padovanet.it)

[18] Testimony of Yiorgos Zervulakos, "MEMORY 2000: Memoriali del XX Secolo," (www.padovanet.it)

[19] Ibid.

[20] Stephen Ambrose/Ronald Drez interview with Anthony Brooks, London, 1986.

[21] "The Special Operations Executive and its Records." Foreign & Commonwealth Office, http://www.fco.gov/uk

[22] Testimony of Philippos Mavrogenis, "MEMORY 2000: Memoriali del XX Secolo," (www.padovanet.it)

[23] *The Secret War,* p. 42.

[24] Ibid, p. 50.

[25] Ibid, p. 67.

[26] Ibid, p. 72.

[27] Ibid, p. 183.

[28] Ibid, 87.

[29] Ibid, 88.

[30] M. B. McGlynn, *Special Service in Greece,* part of *The Official History of New Zealand in the Second World War 1939-1945* (Historical Publications Branch: Wellington NZ, 1950) p. 3-12.

[31] Ibid, p.9.

[32] Ibid, p. 13.

[33] Ibid, p. 22.

[34] *The Trial of Major German War Criminals,* Sitting at Nuremberg, Germany January 7 to January 19, 1946, Vol. 4, Session 28, January 7, 1946, p. 1-6. http://www.nizkor.org/hweb/imt/tgmwc/tgmwc-04/

[35] Dawn DeDeaux interview with Dennis Georges, 2002.

[36] Ronald Drez interview with Konstantinos Georgountzos, in Arfara, April 2007.

[37] McGlynn, *Special Service in Greece,* p. 23.

[38] Ibid, p. 24-25.

[39] Ibid, p. 23.

[40] Ibid, p. 25.

[41] Ibid.

[42] Ibid, p. 26.

[43] Ibid, p. 26-27.

[44] Ibid.

[45] Ibid, p. 28.

11. DARKNESS AND LIGHT

[1] Ibid, p. 29.

[2] *Hidden Children in Occupied Greece,* (Jewish Museum of Greece: Athens, 2003) p. 18-19.

[3] Ibid, p. 62-63.

[4] Cesare Salmaggi and Alfredo Pallavisini, *2194 Days of War* (Milano: Gallery Books, 1979), p. 419.

[5] Stavrolakis, Nikos, "A Short History of the Jews in Greece: Athens During the Occupation," *http://www.greecetravel.com/jewishhistory/index.html*

[6] Quoted in Trunk, Isaiah, *Judenrat: the Jewish Councils in Eastern Europe under Nazi Occupation*, (New York: Macmillan, 1972).

[7] Stavrolakis, Nikos, "A Short History."

[8] Burns, Margie, "Archbishop Damaskinos," The International Raoul Wallenberg Foundation. *http://www.raoulwallenberg.net/?en/news/2953/archbishop-damaskinos.2992.htm*

[9] Ibid.

[10] Ibid.

[11] "The Holocaust in Greece," United States Holocaust Memorial Museum; http://www.ushmm.org p.17.

[12] *Hidden Children,* p. 62-63

[13] Ibid.

[14] George Tzitzikas, quoted in *The 11th Day,* An Archangel Films Production, 2005.

[15] Leslie Newton, quoted in *11th Day.*

[16] Stelios Anezakis, quoted in *11th Day.*

[17] Quoted in *11th Day.*

[18] George Tzitzikas, quoted in *The 11th Day.*

[19] Eleftherios Skoulas, quoted in *The 11th Day.*

[20] Quoted in *The 11th Day.*

[21] Fermor, Patrick Leigh, *Words of Mercury,* (John Murray: London, 2003) p. 2-3.

[22] Ibid, p. 86.

[23] Fermor, quoted in *The 11th Day.*

[24] *Words of Mercury*, p. 86.

[25] Giannaris, John, *Yannis,* (Pilgrimage Publishing Inc: Tarrytown, New York, 1988) p. 1.

[26] Ibid, p. 4.

[27] Ibid, p. 5,98.

[28] Ibid, p. 82-84.

[29] Ibid, p. 92.

[30] Ibid, p. 93.

[31] Ibid, p. 203.

[32] Ibid, p. 122-23.

[33] Ibid.

[34] Ibid, p. 99, 200.

[35] Moss, W. Stanley, *Ill Met By Moonlight,* (Harrap: London, 1950) p. 22.

[36] Ibid, p. 33.

[37] Ibid, p.47.

[38] Fermor, quoted in *The 11th Day.*

[39] Stanley, *Moonlight,* p. 78.

[40] Ibid, p. 75.

[41] Ibid, p. 76.

[42] Fermor, quoted in *The 11th Day.*

[43] Stanley, *Moonlight,* p. 97-98.

[44] Ibid, p. 101.

[45] Fermor, quoted in *The 11th Day*

[46] *2194 Days of War,* p. 598.

EPILOGUE

[1] Galeazzo Ciano, *Diary 1937-1943* (New York: Doubleday 1946/Enigma Books, 2002), p. 591.

[2] Interview with Konstantinos Georgountzos at Meligalas, April 2007.

[3] U.S. Army Center of Military History, *German Antiguerrilla Operations in the Balkans (1941-1944)* CMH Publication 104-18 (GPO: Washington D.C., 1953) Chapter 9 III, p. 6.

INDEX

NUMERALS

A

LaVergne, TN USA
18 November 2009
164553LV00005B/35/P